Espresso
Quick
Reference
Guide

by
Phillip
Janssen

published by

eightball

entertainments
publishers of eightball books

Seattle, Washington
1998

ISBN # 0- 9643547-3-X
Printed in the United States of America

310.0113

Cover design by Shaun Wolden
Interior design by Marci Jordan
Desktop composition by Chris Roth

Cover photograph of the Brasilia espresso machine
is courtesy of Mario Rosito.

First printing, August of 1993.
Second printing, November of 1993.
Third printing (rev. ed.), October 1994.
Fifth Printing, October of 1997.
Sixth Printing (initial rev. Eightball ed.) July 1998.

10   9   8   7

Published by

eightball

entertainments
publishers of eightball books

Seattle, Washington

All of the beverage recipes contained within can be prepared using a minimum number of ingredients and appliances. There are no blender drinks, no raw eggs, ice cream, vegetable juices, teas, or alcoholic beverages, as required ingredients.

Thus the home or professional user can prepare and enjoy these delicious beverages while adhering to the utmost in sober simplicity.

The word *espresso* first appeared in American print in 1945.

The word *cappuccino* first appeared
in American print in 1948.

Acknowledgments

Special thanks to the hundreds of people without whose support and input this project would not have been possible.

To my sons Scott and Greg and my daughter Bunny for your valuable assistance and support in this project.

Special thanks to Rich Abker, for without his numerous contributions and dedicated support, this work could not have been completed.

I'm especially grateful to Paul and Elsa Rodriguez for providing so many of the marvelous new recipes that expand this collection. Many thanks to Kirsten Atik, as well, for her careful work in testing the new additions.

To Dennis Simon, Tim Matelich, Robin Krause, Kristin Connors, Frank Shrontz, Jerry Long, Paul Blauert, and Gary Laidler, for handling the production and business end of this project.

Chris Roth's meticulous attention to page layout and design have made Espresso Quick Reference Guide much more attractive and accessible for our many readers. Thanks, Chris, for bringing so much to the party.

To Cherie Crowley and Thom Head for the illustrations and graphics.

To Jennifer Johnson, Mary Whittington and Linda Packard for your editing services.

To Ian Bersten, Ph.D., author of *Coffee Floats— Tea Sinks,* and to Dr. Ernesto Illy, two of the world's foremost espresso and coffee experts, who have answered many of my questions.

To Jim Glang, owner of Crossroads Espresso, one of my first and most knowledgeable teachers.

To Mauro Cipolla, owner of Caffé D'arté, one of Seattle's top gourmet roasters. I've lost count of the number of Coffee Academy sessions I have attended. Thank you, Mauro. You have been a great teacher. "Taste the difference."

To Bill Stearns, president of Stearns & Lehman Inc., makers of Dolce "Italian Style" syrups, for his help and encouragement of this work.

To Neal Cowan, author of *Sip of Seattle*, the first espresso coupon book ever.

To Craig Walters and Bob Perna, producers of *Gourmet Coffee*, great video for home espresso.

To Bruce Milletto and Ed Ardvison, producers of *Espresso 101*, winner of *Fresh Cup* magazine's 'Spressy award for the best overall espresso "how to" video, September 1994.

To Dana Rafferty, Vice President of Saeco® USA Inc., for your expert advice on home espresso equipment.

To: Barbara Hausner of Melitta® North America Inc., and Phil Campbell and Susie Cover of RSVP International, wholesale distributors, for your advice and continued support.

To Craig Kiggens of Espresso Gears, commercial espresso equipment repair service, for the knowledge you've imparted on troubleshooting espresso equipment.

To David Schomer, gourmet roaster, coffee trade writer, and retail operator. I've learned so much from you.

To the staff and publishers of the outstanding national espresso trade publication *Fresh Cup*—Portland, OR. Your encouragement and assistance were invaluable.

To William "Fergy" Ferguson, writer of *How to Open Your Espresso Cart*, and Keri Goodman, cowriter of *Java "U" Business Basics*, both great manuals.

To Bob Burgess and Vic Belonis of Burgess Enterprises, pioneers of the Northwest espresso movement, for your valuable input.

To my friends Debi and Ken McAlpine, owners of Le Bistro Coffeehouse in Gig Harbor, WA, for your assistance.

To Craig Bunney, owner of Northstar, for your suggestions and advice.

To David Latimer and Kathleen McGee of "Coffee Works," *The Cafe Business Journal,* San Francisco, CA, for your network support.

To Ted Lingle, executive director of the Specialty Coffee Association of America, and to your wonderful organization, for all of the invaluable statistical data.

Special thanks for your recipes and other contributions: Bill Mohrweis, Dan Pietela, Todd Wilson, Cheryl and Larry Appel, Cindy Tripp, Dan Lundenberg, Matt Brandenburger of Torani Syrups, Dane Poulton of Stasero Syrups, Dale Nelson of Vitali Syrups, Doug Gerber of DaVinci™ Syrups, Alan Johnson and Lars-Erik Persson of Monin Syrups, Ali Vincent of Caravali Coffees, Joseph Stafficri of San Marino Syrups, Earl Greiner, Rick Swanson of Oscar's Syrups, Marvin Allain, Steve, Sandy and Betty Peterson, Bruce Ewen, Steve and Sandy Hosch, Doug and Wendy Koehly, Barbara Abker, Jeff Whitehead, Ron Smick, Bernie Dorsey, Gary Smith, David Baron, Leonard Rivero, and Josh and Robyn, baristas at Caffé D'arté.

To Sue Bowden, for your assistance and your mixology and equipment presentation skills.

And to all the many others, THANK YOU!

About the Author

Phil Janssen draws from over 35 years experience to create *Espresso Quick Reference Guide.* As top producing representative for a leading commercial espresso equipment manufacturer, Janssen has sold, installed, and performed training on over one hundred commercial espresso operations in the Seattle area. He is a professional mixologist experienced in trend analysis and has published widely in beverage industry trade journals.

As a working professional in America's premier espresso marketplace, Janssen recognized the absence of an essential reference guide. Responding to repeated requests from his customers and professional colleagues, he devoted over 6,000 hours to creating a text intended primarily to serve that trade audience.

His first book, *Espresso Seattle Style Quick Reference Guide,* appeared in September 1993. In it Janssen prominently featured instruction on the preparation of Seattle-style beverages, and he included technical suggestions on the use and maintenance of professional espresso equipment. Trade response was immediate and profound: The first printing sold out in under two months, and as this new edition goes to press some 70,000 copies have been sold.

Heartened by the acceptance of the professional marketplace, Janssen has turned to the home espresso maker in this new and much expanded edition of his reference guide. Included are new recipes, new techniques, a survey of emerging trends, and thousands of snippets of trivia—all intended to make it easy and fun to practice the "inexact science" of espresso and Italian syrup beverages at home.

Contents

Introduction

Espresso and the gourmet coffee craze are sweeping the U.S. and spreading worldwide.

This specialty coffee renaissance was pioneered in Seattle, where gourmet coffee sales have reached a 40% market share, almost twice the current national average. This anomaly is largely explained by two factors: First, strong regional brands have emerged among custom coffee roasters. Second, a unique retail phenomenon has evolved in the Northwest, the espresso street vending cart. The first such cart appeared in 1978 beneath the Seattle monorail, and by 1994 over 450 carts were in operation in the metropolitan area alone.

Such is the current popularity of espresso in Seattle that businesses featuring it include hardware stores, car washes, salons, department stores, nurseries, hospitals, bike shops, and even one dentist whose marquee advertises "Espresso Dental."

A recent national survey showed that in the past decade there has been an increase in the U.S. by 28% of those abstaining from alcohol. The moderation trend of the '80s has opened the door for the booming gourmet coffee industry.

The soda fountains of the '50s have become the espresso bars of the '90s, complete with a wide array of hot and cold espresso based beverages and Italian style sodas.

Espresso quite literally means *fast coffee:* Water heated to 195°F is forced at 130 pounds of pressure through finely ground roasted coffee beans. Within 18 to 23 seconds, the process is complete. Highly concentrated flavor and aroma characterize the finished beverage and distinguish it from coffee produced by the common drip method.

In Italy where coffee and espresso are synonymous, over 90% of espresso is consumed straight. The inverse proportion is true in the U.S. where over 90% of all espresso beverages are diluted with milk in the form of lattes, mochas and cappuccinos.

The art of preparing espresso beverages is both fun and easy. We generally use only a limited number of ingredients: ground coffee, milk, and Italian style syrups. Quality home espresso machines and coffee grinders now make it possible for the homemaker to enjoy these same espresso creations that were only previously available at retail espresso bars.

In this reference guide we have attempted to remove much of the Italian terminology and to simplify the preparation technique so that the home user can master espresso, the social beverage of the '90s.

Chapter 1

Preface to the Recipes

Anyone can make coffee or espresso. In order to learn the art of making great coffee and great espresso, a serious understanding of coffee and extraction is necessary. This understanding is learned through education and training from those who have the knowledge.

Espresso means fast coffee: 130 pounds of pressurization allows the beverage to be extracted in 18-23 seconds compared to the 4- to 6-minute brewing cycle of drip ground coffee.

Other distinctions between espresso and coffee are:
1. Espresso is brewed from a more flavorful gourmet bean than the commercial Robusta bean.
2. The Arabica bean contains approximately half the caffeine of the Robusta bean.
3. The espresso bean is generally roasted slightly longer for a darker roast.
4. Beans used for espresso are ground to a finer consistency just prior to brewing.
5. Espresso is brewed one cup at a time as opposed to batch brewing.
6. In the U.S. most espresso drinks are combined with steamed milk; in Europe sugar is generally added to straight espresso.

Worldwide, 11 billion pounds of coffee change hands each year. Of that imported each year into the United States, gourmet specialty coffee sales have increased fivefold in the past ten years.

Over 60% of gourmet coffee purchasers in the U.S. are women.

The SCAA's first annual convention was held in New Orleans in 1988. Its first "formal" meeting in 1982 was attended by 42 coffee professionals. The most recent SCAA annual conventions have been attended by 7,000+ per annual gathering, and the attendance is accelerating as America's love of specialty coffee continues unabated.

Why have gourmet coffee and espresso become the social beverages of the 90s? Is it because in the past 10 years, the teetotaler count is up by 28% in the U.S.? We're drinking mochas, not martinis. . . .

The Specialty Coffee Association of America projects that by the year 1999, some 10,000 coffee cafes, espresso bars, and carts will be in operation in the U.S.

About Mochas: Caffeine content per ounce: Dark Chocolate, 20 mg/Milk Chocolate, 6 mg.

To stop carbonated beverages from fizzing over, try rinsing the ice cubes with water first.

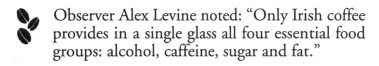 Observer Alex Levine noted: "Only Irish coffee provides in a single glass all four essential food groups: alcohol, caffeine, sugar and fat."

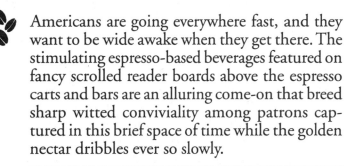 Americans are going everywhere fast, and they want to be wide awake when they get there. The stimulating espresso-based beverages featured on fancy scrolled reader boards above the espresso carts and bars are an alluring come-on that breed sharp witted conviviality among patrons captured in this brief space of time while the golden nectar dribbles ever so slowly.

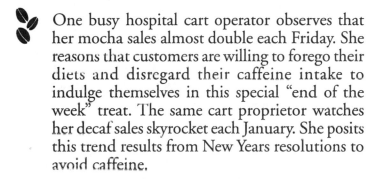 One busy hospital cart operator observes that her mocha sales almost double each Friday. She reasons that customers are willing to forego their diets and disregard their caffeine intake to indulge themselves in this special "end of the week" treat. The same cart proprietor watches her decaf sales skyrocket each January. She posits this trend results from New Years resolutions to avoid caffeine.

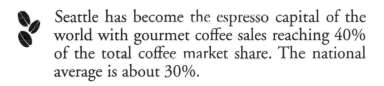 Seattle has become the espresso capital of the world with gourmet coffee sales reaching 40% of the total coffee market share. The national average is about 30%.

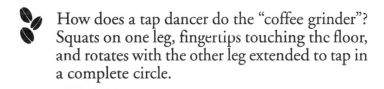 How does a tap dancer do the "coffee grinder"? Squats on one leg, fingertips touching the floor, and rotates with the other leg extended to tap in a complete circle.

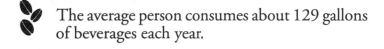 The average person consumes about 129 gallons of beverages each year.

Hazelnut syrup was not used to flavor anything in the U.S. until the year 1985.

Syrups take away the "snob" appeal of gourmet coffee.

Ninety percent of espresso in Italy is consumed straight, the other 10% is taken cappuccino style with foamed and steamed milk. The name *cappuccino* is said to have derived from either the chocolate color of Capuchin monks' robes or from the curl of their hoods, which is duplicated in foamed milk on the top of a perfect cappuccino.

A barista is a title given to one who has mastered the art of making espresso beverages.

In the U.S., 90% of espresso beverages are served with steamed and/or foamed milk.

Milk contains lactose (milk sugar) and casein which diminish the bitterness in coffee. The popularity of milk based espresso beverages can be attributed to this marriage.

The latte made with foamed/steamed milk is the most called-for espresso beverage in the U.S. The actual word is derived from the Italian *Caffè Latte*.

Latte is the Italian word for milk. If you request a latte in Italy, you will be served a glass of milk.

In Italy the most common coffee beverages are straight espresso with sugar, espresso with a dollop of milk foam called an espresso macchiato, and cappuccino. Cappuccinos are commonly served in a small bowl at breakfast.

A taste romance ensues when hot milk is married with gourmet coffee. Heating by steaming actually alters the proteins and sugars of milk. The process creates a pleasantly different taste that blends well with espresso.

In the Puget Sound area of Washington, the popularity of whole bean coffee is such that a local dairy has begun delivering coffee beans to home route customers along with fresh milk.

The espresso machine was invented in France but was perfected and first manufactured in Italy at the turn of the 20th century.

Gourmet coffee roasters in the U.S. use the high grade Arabica beans almost exclusively.

An espresso blend is made by mixing two or more straight Arabica bean varieties to improve its flavor, aroma, or taste attributes.

Approximately 2,000 coffee cherries yield about one pound of coffee beans.

Each cherry contains two coffee beans. Approximately 60 of these beans produce a shot of espresso made with seven grams of ground coffee.

The art of espresso mixology is fun and creative. Chances are if you ordered a mocha at ten separate retail locations, the mocha would be prepared at least four separate ways.

A mocha is a chocolate latte, usually topped with whipped cream and chocolate garnish.

A mocha can be made with any type of chocolate: thick chocolate syrup, thin chocolate syrup, sweet powdered chocolate, or chocolate milk.

In 1905 Milton Hershey began mass-producing chocolate bars. Hershey, Pennsylvania, was named after him. Today his syrup in the plastic squeeze bottles is popular for flavoring our mochas.

Seattle has become the espresso and gourmet coffee hub of the world. This is due largely to the consumer awareness created by the city's major coffee roasters.

Heavy-bodied roasts are generally better for coffee beverages made with milk, such as lattes or cappuccinos.

Cheap truck stop style coffee in the Midwest I sometimes referred to as "Swedish gasoline."

The order for pouring ingredients into a serving cup for hot espresso specialty beverages is:

(1) Flavoring (optional)
(2) Espresso
(3) Steamed and foamed milk.

To prevent curdling of certain flavored syrups in espresso beverages, always add the syrups first, and don't steam the milk too hot. High acid content flavors are the worst culprits.

Syrups and sugar sweeteners are best dissolved if poured into the cup before the espresso or at least before the steamed milk.

Heat intensifies the sweetness of sugar. Thus, ¾ to 1 ounce of Italian flavored syrup is recommended to sweeten and flavor a 12-ounce hot espresso based beverage, and for a 16-ounce cold beverage filled Å with ice, a 2-ounce portion of syrup would be recommended.

For flavored whipped cream, add four ounces of flavored syrup to one pint of whipping cream and beat in a chilled container.

One Northwest caterer, whose clients are among the well-to-do, serves flaming lattes at the end of meals. He ignites fruit flavored extracts containing 80% alcohol and dusts this flame with ground cinnamon, creating sparks. Use caution when trying this technique.

Major Contributor

Rich Abker, operations manager for Caffé D'arté in Seattle, Washington, has developed and perfected many techniques for making flavored espresso beverages, as well as Italian soda beverages. Rich's unique method of separately flavoring the espresso and the milk for his Double Funn Cappuccinos, along with his other flavoring and mixology techniques, have truly captured the "Seattle Style" theme.

The following are some of his useful methods for creating signature drinks from basic espresso beverages.

Rich's Espresso Royales

Americano Royale
—Pour flavored syrup into serving cup.
—Fill ¾ way with hot water.
—Pour double shot of espresso into hot water.
—Top with whipped cream.
—Use flavored syrup to decorate whipped cream or garnish with toasted almonds, shredded coconut, grated maraschino cherries, etc.

Latte Royale
—Prepare a latte with no foam.
—Use flavor if desired.
—Add flavored whipped cream.

Latte Royales are two-flavored lattes that use only one syrup in the milk. The flavored whipped cream adds an enjoyable and interesting contrast.

Rich's Fun Cappuccinos

—Use the same preparation technique applied in Rich's favorite cappuccino, except use flavored syrups of your choice.

—Pour one ounce of flavored syrup into milk to be steamed and frothed with dense foam cappuccino style (ex. vanilla).

—Garnish dense foam with a thick, flavored syrup or a mix of syrup and honey.

—Use pinched cup and pour thin strings of syrup over dense foam. (See illustration of pinched cup technique on page 22.)

Rich's Double Funn Cappuccinos

The "Double Funn" is a two-flavor, two-color cappuccino that is enjoyable beyond expectations. The techniques used in making these creative espresso drinks are simple and easy.

—Pour ¼ oz of the dominant of the two syrup flavors into the serving cup (ex. chocolate).

—Pour about 1 oz of the mildest flavored syrup directly into the milk to be steamed and frothed (ex. vanilla).

—Pour ristretto espresso into the cup with flavored syrup; stir espresso when any *thick* syrup is used.

—Fill serving cup ¾ full with steamed flavored milk.

—Top with flavored dense foam two to three inches high until it forms a pointed cap.

—Garnish with a heavy flavored syrup. Use a pinched paper cup to apply thin strings of syrup in a decorative fashion. (See Rich's Funn Cappuccino examples.)

Examples of flavored syrups to be used in Rich's Double Funn Cappuccinos:

1. Strongest flavors into cup.
2. Mild flavored syrups into milk become dense foam and steamed milk.

Popular syrup flavors and examples of how they can be used. (Use your own creativity and other flavors.)

1. **Flavors into cup:**

Blackberry	Cranberry
Blueberry	Grape
Boysenberry	Irish Cream
Butterscotch	Kahlua
Cherry	Lemon
Chocolate	Lime
Chocolate Mint	Orange
Coffee	Pineapple
Creme de Cacao	Raspberry
Creme de Menthe	Strawberry

2. **Flavors into milk:**

Almond	Hazelnut
Amaretto	Honey
Apricot	Peach
Apple	Praline
Banana	Rum
Cinnamon	Vanilla
Coconut	

HOW TO PREPARE RICH'S DOUBLE FUNN CAPPUCCINOS

2. Pour ½ ounce of dominant flavor—example: Chocolate—into serving cup.

3. Add espresso to flavor and stir.

1. Add ½ ounce flavored syrup—example: Vanilla—to cold milk, then foam and steam.

4. Pour flavored foamed/steamed milk over flavored espresso.

RICH'S DOUBLE FUNN CAPPUCCINOS & LATTE ROYALES

Milk is flavored before it is foamed and steamed.

Flavored whipped cream topping

Crushed nuts

Flavored foamed milk

Chocolate syrup

Flavored steamed milk

Espresso

LATTE ROYALE

One flavor goes in the milk. The second goes into the serving cup.

DOUBLE FUNN CAPPUCCINOS

Examples of Rich's Double Funn Cappuccino Recipes
(Use your imagination and pinched cup technique for designs.)

1) Toasted Marshmallow
   —Irish cream into cup
   —Caramel (thin) into milk
   —Prepare cappuccino (See page 9)
   —Garnish with thick caramel syrup

2) Candy Apple Red
   —Cherry syrup into cup
   —Apple syrup into milk
   —Prepare cappuccino
   —Garnish with mixture of honey and cherry
     flavored syrup

3) Chocolate Wafer
   —Chocolate syrup into cup
   —Vanilla syrup into milk
   —Prepare cappuccino
   —Garnish with heavy chocolate syrup

4) Rum Runn
   —Use either butterscotch or praline in cup
   —Rum syrup into milk
   —Prepare cappuccino
   —Garnish with honey/rum syrup mixture

5) Coffee Nudge
   —Kahlua or coffee syrup into cup
   —Creme de cacao syrup into milk
   —Prepare cappuccino
   —Garnish dense foam with honey mixed with
     coffee syrup

6) Chocolate Covered Cherry
   —Chocolate syrup into cup
   —Cherry syrup into milk
   —Prepare cappuccino
   —Garnish dense foam with thick chocolate
     syrup

Rich's Re-Macchiatos

—Pour ¼ ounce of your favorite syrup or
  combination of syrups into small serving cup.
—Pour double shot of ristretto espresso into cup
  and stir. (See ristretto on page 239.)
—Top with approximately two tablespoons dense
  foamed milk or whipped cream. Stir and serve.

Any single flavor syrup of your choice may be used.
However, there are many two-flavored combinations that
are excitingly good.

Examples of Suggested Combinations of Flavored Syrups

Almond/Honey
Cherry/Almond
Cherry/Coconut
Cherry/Vanilla
Chocolate/Almond
Chocolate/Banana
Chocolate/Cherry
Chocolate/Coconut
Chocolate/Praline
Chocolate/Rum
Cinnamon/Honey
Irish Cream/Almond
Irish Cream/Kahlua
Lemon/Honey
Orange/Chocolate
Orange/Vanilla

Rich's Favorite Espresso Techniques

A. Straight Espresso
1. Ristretto: short pour (1 ounce single, 2 ounce double)
2. Lungo: long pour (1½ ounce single, 3 ounce double)

B. Americano
—Fill either 8 ounce or 12 ounce double cup ⅔ full with hot water. (Use a double cup to protect hands.)
—Pull a double shot of ristretto espresso and pour into hot water. (Dense crema should float on top.)
—Leave room for cream or sweetener if desired. Serve.

C. The Perfect Latte
—See description on page 236.

D. The Perfect Cappuccino
—See description on page 238.

E. The Perfect Mocha
—Pour thick chocolate syrup into serving cup. (Add a few drops of caramel if you like.)
—Pull a double shot of ristretto.
—Begin steaming and frothing fresh cold milk while the espresso is pouring.
—Prepare milk as you would for *The Perfect Latte,* page 236.
—Pour espresso over chocolate and stir.
—Pour in steamed/frothed milk.
—Whipped cream is optional, so leave room if you choose to use it.
—Garnish with thick chocolate syrup. (Use pinched cup method.)

F. Brevé

A brevé is any milk based espresso drink where half-and-half is substituted for milk. Brevés can be flavored or not.

—If flavored, pour flavored syrup into cup.
—Pull a double shot of ristretto.
—Steam and froth half-and-half as for a latte.
—Pour espresso into serving cup.
—Pour steamed and frothed milk into espresso. Serve. Garnish may be used.
—Brevé lattes and brevé mochas are popular.

G. Iced Americano

—Fill 16 ounce clear cup with crushed or small cubed ice ¾ full.
—Fill with cold water ¾ full.
—Pull a double shot of ristretto espresso and pour into cup. Add cream, sweetener, or flavored syrup. Stir and serve.

H. Iced Latte/Brevé

—Fill 16 ounce clear cup with crushed or small cubed ice ¾ full.
—Fill cup with cold milk or half-and-half ¾ full.
—Pull a double shot of ristretto espresso and pour into cup.
—Garnish with golf ball-sized whipped cream and large colored straw. Serve.

I. Iced Mocha

—Fill 16 ounce clear cup ¾ full with crushed or small cubed ice.
—Fill cup with fresh cold milk.
—Pour 2 ounces chocolate in pouring glass.
—Pull espresso directly over chocolate. Stir.
—Pour chocolate espresso into milk.
—Garnish with golf ball-sized whipped cream. Add a few drops of chocolate onto whipped cream. Use large colored straw. Serve.

Rich's Favorite Italian Soda Techniques

A. Iced Italian Soda (single flavor)

—Fill 16 ounce clear cup ¾ full with crushed or small cubed ice.

—Fill cup ¾ full with either soda, seltzer, or mineral water.

—Pour in 2 ounces of your favorite flavored syrup. To make this an Italian Cream Soda, sometimes called a Cremosa, simply float in two tablespoons of half-and-half.

—Garnish with a golf ball-sized whipped cream with a few drops of flavored syrup on the whipped cream. Use a large colored straw. Serve.

B. Rich's Italian Dream Sodas (two flavored syrups)

—Fill 16 ounce clear cup ¾ full with crushed or small cubed ice.

—Pour in one ounce of the lightest of the two flavored syrups (vanilla, lemon, coconut).

—Fill cup ¾ full with either soda, seltzer, or mineral water.

—Pour in one ounce of the most colorful syrup (orange, cherry).

—Float 2 tablespoons of half-and-half.

—Garnish as usual for Italian Sodas.

—Serve and enjoy.

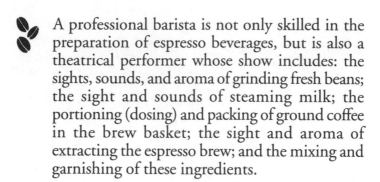

A professional barista is not only skilled in the preparation of espresso beverages, but is also a theatrical performer whose show includes: the sights, sounds, and aroma of grinding fresh beans; the sight and sounds of steaming milk; the portioning (dosing) and packing of ground coffee in the brew basket; the sight and aroma of extracting the espresso brew; and the mixing and garnishing of these ingredients.

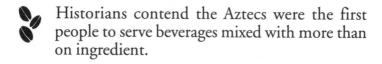

Historians contend the Aztecs were the first people to serve beverages mixed with more than on ingredient.

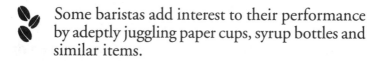

Some baristas add interest to their performance by adeptly juggling paper cups, syrup bottles and similar items.

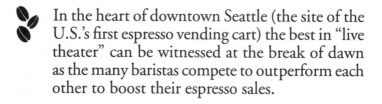

In the heart of downtown Seattle (the site of the U.S.'s first espresso vending cart) the best in "live theater" can be witnessed at the break of dawn as the many baristas compete to outperform each other to boost their espresso sales.

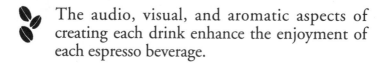

The audio, visual, and aromatic aspects of creating each drink enhance the enjoyment of each espresso beverage.

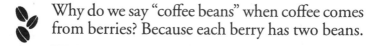

Why do we say "coffee beans" when coffee comes from berries? Because each berry has two beans.

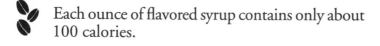

Each ounce of flavored syrup contains only about 100 calories.

One pound of ground espresso beans will yield approximately 50 single shot servings, while the same amount of ground commercial coffee beans yields roughly 45 8-ounce servings.

A tall latte (12 ounce cup) made with whole milk contains approximately 133 calories; with nonfat milk, 77 calories.

A teaspoon of cane sugar contains about 18 calories.

Club soda has zero calories per ounce. Colas have 12 calories per ounce, and natural fruit juices have between 10 and 20 calories per ounce.

The popularity of iced coffee drinks has been attributed to the French colonial troops in North Africa, who took up drinking the chilled beverages to "beat the heat."

Phyllis Jordan, whose retail coffee stores are located in New Orleans, sells far more iced coffee than hot coffee. She has developed a cold water steeping method to reduce the acids in the chilled product.

For their iced coffee, the Japanese prefer darker roasted beans. Most iced coffee served in Japan is served with sugar syrup and cream.

Pioneer Square in Seattle, Washington is reputed to have been the first location to serve iced lattes. The year—1978.

A "juice drink" may contain up to 50 percent juice. An "aid drink" may contain up to 25 percent juice, and a "drink" can have as little as as 10 percent juice.

Just as tart lemonade is a better thirst quencher than sweet lemonade, diet drinks are better than sugary ones. Alcohol dehydrates you as well, increasing your thirst. Nonalcoholic Italian sodas and coffee beverages are better thirst quenchers.

The word *granita* is derived from the Italian words *gran* which means granular ice, and *ita* from the Italian *bibita*, which means soft drink, therefore, a granular ice drink.

Granita was introduced in Paris in 1660.

Such is the popularity of espresso in Seattle that businesses featuring it include hardware stores, car washes, salons, department stores, nurseries, hospitals, bike shops, and even one dentist whose marquee advertises "Espresso Dental."

Lemon or orangeade ice cubes add zest to any Italian soda beverage and will not dilute the drink as they melt.

For iced coffee recipes, brewing fresh coffee and then pouring it into ice cube trays will provide you with ice cubes that won't water down as they melt. Make the cubes of frozen milk or of real fruit juices for a variation on this theme.

Simple syrup (water and sugar) is much better for sweetening cold drinks than granulated sugar alone, which doesn't dissolve easily.

One Washington State espresso cart operator, due to limited refrigerator storage, handles only two milks—2% and half-and-half. When customers request that their lattes be made with whole milk, he mixes the two.

If you stir sweetened, condensed milk into your steeping black coffee, you are following Vietnamese tradition that goes back to colonial times.

One homemade ice cube, when melted, makes about one ounce of water.

For crystal clear ice cubes pour hot rather than cold water into the trays.

A swizzle was a rum-based beverage served in the Caribbean and the West Indies. The stir sticks were named after the drink.

One soda fountain in Dallas is reportedly doing a brisk business selling "Jr. Rum and Cokes" with nonalcoholic Italian style rum-flavored syrup.

Remember: do not stir soda or carbonated based beverages vigorously, or they lose their sparkle.

The key word is *passion*; all successful industry people share this passion for coffee.

DECORATIONS

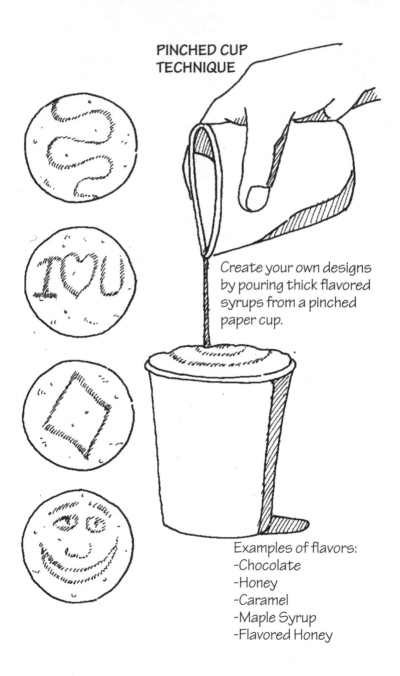

PINCHED CUP TECHNIQUE

Create your own designs by pouring thick flavored syrups from a pinched paper cup.

Examples of flavors:
-Chocolate
-Honey
-Caramel
-Maple Syrup
-Flavored Honey

Cherry-flavored and colored toothpicks with a fruit garnish add a special touch to iced Italian beverages.

 In ancient Sicily, disputes over water rights to the olive groves often left some growing regions dry. Drinking vessels were sanitized by wiping the inside with lemon rind.

 The very first coffee cart? The year was 1672: an Armenian served coffee from a kiosk at the St. Germane Fair in Paris. Business was good. Soon he sent young men door-to-door with coffee in urns heated by charcoal braziers or lamps.

 Provide a candy cane as a stir stick for your vanilla lattes during the Christmas season.

 A frosty and very classy sugar rim on your cold drink glass can be achieved by having two saucers—one with a dampened towel and the other with ¼ inch of sugar. Dampen the rim of the glass on the towel, then dip it in the sugar.

 Real whipped cream topping will hold its surface much better than canned, which is too light and will rapidly wilt at room temperature.

 For cappuccinos, decorate the white head of foam with garnishes of powdered chocolate, nutmeg, cinnamon, or colored sprinkles.

 Only the unique interaction of certain flavors creates the symphonies of taste in multi-flavored syrup recipes.

FIVE BASIC ESPRESSO DRINKS

ESPRESSO

Whipped cream

Crema

MOCHA

CAPPUCCINO

AMERICANO
Shot of espresso poured on top of hot water

Brown and white marble swirl

Marbleized with espresso and dense foamed and steamed milk.

Espresso

Foamed milk
Steamed milk

LATTE

*Heavy-bodied roasts are generally better for coffee beverages made with milk, such as lattes or cappuccinos.

Chapter 2

Recipes

BASIC ESPRESSO AND ICED ITALIAN STYLE BEVERAGES

Americano

A gourmet cup of coffee, made by pouring one or two shots of espresso over a 6 oz cup of hot water. The crema from the espresso will float on top.

Brevé

Any milk based espresso beverage where half-and-half is substituted for milk. Brevés can be flavored.

Cappuccino

An espresso based beverage, topped with equal parts of steamed and foamed milk (wet cappuccino). A dry cappuccino is topped with all foamed milk. The milk is foamed/steamed prior to the espresso extraction, allowing the foam to set, or jell. The foam topping is shaped to form a peak (cap) on the cappuccino. Cappuccinos are usually dusted with nutmeg, cinnamon, or chocolate powder.

Doppio

Double shot of espresso with one shot of water.

Espresso

Properly done, espresso is made from a special blend of Arabica coffees, chosen for intense aromatic flavors and quality of performance during extraction. Espresso uses freshly roasted beans that are finely ground in the correct amount, firmly packed and then extracted under pressure. The end result will be a rich concentration of coffee taste and aroma, topped with a dense golden-brown foam called crema.

Espresso Con Panna

An espresso serving topped with a dollop of whipped cream.

Espresso Romano

A serving of straight espresso, with a twist of lemon added.

Iced Espresso based Beverages

Are served in clear plastic or clear glassware. If flavored, the flavoring is added first, then the espresso. Stirred if thick syrup is used. Ice is then added. Cup is filled with *cold milk.* Can be topped with whipped cream.

Italian Soda

An iced beverage usually served in a 14-16 oz clear plastic cup, flavored by 2 oz of Italian style syrup or syrups (usually fruit-based) and filled to the top with soda water. The recommended mix ratio is one part syrup to four parts soda water. Italian sodas can be topped with whipped cream.

Italian Cream Soda (Cremosa)

Same as the Italian soda, but the soda water pour is stopped ½" from the top of the cup, and the beverage is filled with approximately 2 oz of half-and-half. Italian cream sodas can be topped with whipped cream.

A variation in the order of ingredients for Italian cream sodas: after pouring the flavors first, add the half-and-half second and the soda water last. A successful cart operator claims this approach is his key to increased sales.

Latte

An espresso based beverage, where a very dense mixture of foamed/steamed milk at 140°F is poured down the side of a cup containing a serving of espresso. The pour allows the milk and espresso to marbleize, forming a very dense mixture. The taste of the espresso can be experienced with the first sip.

For a flavored latte in:

8 oz cup	add ½ oz flavoring
12 oz cup	add ¾ oz flavoring
16 oz cup	add 1 oz flavoring

Latteccino

An espresso based beverage with two parts steamed milk and one part foamed milk (a cross between a cappuccino and a latte).

Lungo

This is the Italian word for *long* and refers to a long pour of espresso. This extraction usually takes about 25 to 30 seconds and is primarily for straight shots, using 1½ to 2 ounces of hot water for extracting the correct amount of coffee in a single portion.

Macchiato

The Italian word for *marked.* There are two types of macchiatos: 1) straight espresso marked with a dollop of warm milk froth and 2) a steamed milk macchiato (latte or cappuccino) where the steamed milk is marked with an espresso poured slowly over the milk foam at the side of a clear glass. This will display a layered effect and is used in restaurants.

Mocha

A chocolate flavored latte with an option of whipped cream for garnish and enjoyment.

Ristretto

Ristretto means *restricted* in Italian. It is a short pour of espresso (highly concentrated) using ¾ to 1 ounce of hot water for extracting the correct amount of coffee in a double or single portion.

Steamer

A serving of foamed/steamed milk, which has been flavored with 1 oz of Italian style syrup. Usually topped with whipped cream. *No espresso.* (Same as hot chocolate, but using Italian style syrup to flavor the milk).

Cup sizes used for the following recipes unless otherwise noted are:

 Hot drinks
12 oz

 Cold drinks
16 oz

Simple rule for order of the ingredients in both hot and cold drinks:

First—Flavor
Second—Espresso
Third—Milk or beverage used
Fourth—Garnish

Cup Sizes:

8 oz—Short
12 oz—Tall
16 oz—Grandé

Thin Italian style syrups will mix with the espresso without stirring.

Thick syrups such as Hershey's chocolate should be stirred *after* adding the espresso.

Purists generally agree to a 1 oz to 1¼ oz single shot portion of espresso. Some commercial operations even pour a double shot standard in all their drinks. In the majority of the following recipes, the espresso shot size will not be specified. We will just say "Pour Espresso," and let you determine your own shot size portion.

A

 ACE OF CLUBS SODA

Over Ice, Pour ⅔ oz each Syrup: Creme de Cassis, Lemon, Peppermint. Fill with Soda Water.

 AFTER DINNER DELIGHT

Pour 1 oz Crème de Cacao Syrup, 1 oz Tiramisu Syrup. Fill with Foamed/Steamed Milk.

 AFRI-COLA

Over Ice, Pour 1 oz Irish Cream Syrup. Add 2 shots, Espresso, 3 oz Half-and-Half. Stir.

 AFTER SUPPER COOLER

Over Ice, Pour ⅔ oz each Syrup: Apricot, Lemon, Mango. Fill with Soda Water.

 ALABAMA SLAMMER

Over Ice, Pour 1 oz each Syrup: Amaretto, Peach. Fill with Soda Water.

 ALBEMARLE FIZZ

Over Ice, Pour ½ oz Lemon Syrup, 1½ oz Raspberry Syrup. Fill with Soda Water.

 ALEXANDER

Pour 2 oz Creme de Cacao Syrup. Add Espresso. Add Ice. Fill with Half-and-Half. Top with Whipped Cream.

 ALMOND CINNAMON COFFEE

Pour ½ oz Almond Syrup. Add 1 tsp Sugar. Add Espresso and 6 oz Hot Milk. Stir. Finish with Cinnamon Stick.

 ALMOND FUDGE ICED COFFEE

Pour 1 oz each Syrup: Almond, Chocolate Fudge. Add Espresso and Ice. Fill with Cold Water.

A

ALMOND ICED COFFEE

Pour 1½ oz Almond Syrup, ½ oz Vanilla Syrup. Add Espresso. Add Ice. Fill with Cold Milk.

ALMOND JOY

Pour ¼ oz each Syrup: Chocolate, Coconut, Almond. Add Espresso. Fill with Foamed/ Steamed Milk. Top with Whipped Cream.

ALMOND LATTE

Pour ¾ oz Almond Syrup. Add Espresso. Fill with Foamed/ Steamed Milk.

ALMOND MIST STEAMER

Pour 1 oz Almond Syrup. Fill with Foamed/Steamed Milk and top with Whipped Cream.

ALMOND MOCHA

Pour ¾ oz Thick Chocolate Syrup, ½ oz Almond Syrup. Add Espresso. Stir. Fill with Foamed/Steamed Milk. Top with Whipped Cream and Chocolate Sprinkles.

ALMOND MOCHA CREAM SODA

Over Ice, Pour 1 oz each Syrup: Almond, Chocolate. Add 3 oz Soda Water. Fill with Half-and-Half. Top with Whipped Cream. Dust with Chocolate Powder.

ALMOND MOCHA ITALIAN SODA

Over Ice, Pour 1 oz each Syrup: Almond, Creme de Cacao. Fill with Soda Water.

A

ALMOND MOCHA STEAMER

Pour ½ oz each Syrup: Almond, Chocolate. Fill with Foamed/ Steamed Milk. Top with Whipped Cream. Dust with Chocolate Powder.

ALMOND MOO

Pour ¾ oz Almond Syrup. Add Espresso. Fill with Foamed/ Steamed Milk. Top with Whipped Cream and Chocolate Sprinkles.

ALMOND ROCA MOCHA

Pour ½ oz each Thick Syrup: Chocolate, Butterscotch. Add ¼ oz Almond Syrup. Add Espresso. Stir. Fill with Foamed/Steamed Milk. Top with Whipped Cream and Chocolate Sprinkles.

AMALFIS

Over Ice, Pour 2 oz any Flavored Syrup. Fill with Soda Water to ½" from top of cup. Stir. Top with Heavy Cream.

AMARETTO & CREAM SODA

Over Ice, Pour 2 oz Amaretto Syrup. Add Soda Water to ½" from top of cup. Top with Half-and-Half.

AMARETTO COFFEE

Pour ¾ oz Amaretto Syrup and 5 oz Hot Water. Add Espresso.

AMARETTO COFFEE

Pour 1 oz Amaretto Syrup. Add Espresso and 6 oz Hot Water. Top with Whipped Cream.

AMARETTO EGG NOG LATTE

Pour ¾ oz Amaretto Syrup. Add Espresso. Fill with Foamed/ Steamed Egg Nog. Top with Whipped Cream. Dust with Nutmeg.

AMARETTO MIST

Over Ice, Pour 1½ oz Amaretto Syrup, ½ oz Lemon Syrup. Fill with Soda Water.

AMARETTO ORANGE ITALIAN SODA

Over Ice, Pour 1 oz each Syrup: Amaretto, Orange. Fill with Soda Water.

AMARETTO ROSE

Over Ice, Pour 1½ oz Amaretto Syrup, ½ oz Lime Syrup. Fill with Soda Water.

AMARETTO STRAWBERRY LATTE

Pour ½ oz each Syrup: Amaretto, Strawberry. Add Espresso. Fill with foamed/Steamed Milk.

AMARETTO SOUR COOLER

Over Ice, Pour 1⅓ oz Amaretto Syrup, ⅔ oz Lemon Syrup. Fill with Soda Water.

AMARETTO SOUR LATTE

Pour ½ oz Amaretto Syrup, ¼ oz Lemon Syrup. Add Espresso. Fill with Foamed/ Steamed Milk.

AMARETTO STINGER

Over Ice, Pour 1½ oz Amaretto Syrup, ½ oz Creme de Menthe Syrup. Fill with Soda Water.

AMBASSADOR'S MORNING LIFT

Pour ¾ oz Creme de Cacao Syrup. Add Espresso. Fill with Foamed/Steamed Egg Nog.

AMERICANO

Pour 6 oz Hot Water. Top with Espresso.

A

 ANGEL FACE
Over Ice, Pour 1 oz each Syrup: Apricot, Apple. Fill with Soda Water.

 ANGEL'S MIST
Over Ice, Pour 1 oz each Syrup: Orange, Pineapple. Add Soda Water to ½" from top. Fill with Half-and-Half and splash with Lime Syrup.

 ANGEL'S TOUCH
Over Ice, Pour 1 oz each Syrup: Creme de Cacao, Creme de Cassis. Fill with Half-and-Half.

 ANGEL'S TOUCH 2
Over Ice, Pour 1 oz each Syrup: Creme de Cassis, Vanilla. Add 3 oz Soda Water. Fill with Half-and-Half.

 APPLE & SPICE SPRITZER
Over Ice, Pour 1½ oz Apple Syrup, ½ oz Cinnamon Syrup. Fill with Soda Water. Splash with Lime Syrup.

 **APPLE CIDER**
Splash each Syrup in cup: Cinnamon, Lemon. Fill with Steamed Apple Cider. Dust with Nutmeg. Add 2 Cinnamon Sticks.

APPLE COFFEE
Pour ½ oz Apple Syrup, ¼ oz Praline Syrup. Add 4 oz Hot Water and Espresso. Top with Cinnamon Stick.

 APPLE COLADA
Over Ice, Pour ⅔ oz each Syrup: Apple, Coconut. Add Soda Water to ½" from top of cup. Top with 2 oz Half-and-Half.

 APPLE PIE
Over Ice, Pour ¼ oz each Syrup: Cinnamon, Amaretto. Add 1½ oz Apple Syrup. Fill with Soda Water to ¼" from top of cup. Top with Whipped Cream.

A

APPLE RUM DUM COOLER

Over Ice, Pour ¾ oz each Syrup: Apple, Rum. Add ¼ oz each Syrup: Almond, Lime. Fill with Soda Water.

APPLE SOUR COOLER

Over Ice, Pour 1½ oz Apple Syrup. Add ½ oz Lemon Syrup. Fill with Soda Water. Splash with Lemon Syrup.

APPLE SPARKLE

Over Ice, Pour 1¾ oz Apple Syrup, ¼ oz Lemon Syrup. Fill with Soda Water.

APPLE TODDY

Steam 8 oz Apple Juice. Pour into cup. Add ½ teaspoon Brown Sugar. Stir. Sprinkle with Cinnamon.

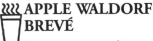**APPLE WALDORF BREVÉ**

Pour ½ oz Apple Syrup, ¼ oz each Syrup: Cinnamon, Hazelnut. Add Espresso. Fill with Foamed/Steamed Half-and-Half and top with Whipped Cream. Dust with Cinnamon Powder or Nutmeg Powder.

APPLEJACK

Over Ice, Pour 1½ oz Apple Syrup, ½ oz Lemon Syrup. Fill with Soda Water.

APPLEJACK PUNCH

Over Ice, Pour 1½ oz Apple Syrup, ½ oz Orange Syrup. Fill with Soda Water. Splash with Grenadine Syrup.

APRICOT-MANGO CREAM SODA

Over Ice, Pour 1 oz each Syrup: Apricot, Mango. Add Soda Water to ½" from top of cup. Fill with Half-and Half.

A

 APPLESAUCE LATTE

Pour ½ oz Apple Syrup, splash of Cinnamon Syrup. Add ½ teaspoon Brown Sugar. Add Espresso. Stir. Fill with Foamed/ Steamed Milk. Dust with Cinnamon Powder.

 APRES TENNIS BRACER

Over Ice, Pour ½ oz Orange Syrup. Fill with Ginger Ale.

 APRICOT ALMOND SPICED SODA

Over Ice, Pour ⅔ oz each Syrup: Apricot, Almond. Add ¼ oz each Syrup: Lemon, Cinnamon. Fill with Soda Water.

 APRICOT COOLER

Over Ice, Pour 2 oz Apricot Syrup. Fill with Soda Water.

 APRICOT FIZZ

Over Ice, Pour 1¾ oz Apricot Syrup, ¼ oz Lemon Syrup. Fill with Soda Water.

 APRICOT LADY

Over Ice, Pour 1¾ oz Apricot Syrup, ¼ oz Lime Syrup. Fill with Soda Water to ¼" from top of cup. Top with Half-and-Half.

 APRICOT PIE SODA

Over Ice, Pour 1½ oz Apricot Syrup. Add ¼ oz each Syrup: Cinnamon, Rum. Fill with Soda Water. Splash with Lemon Syrup.

ARIZONA SUNSHINE

Pour a double shot Espresso. Add Ice. Add ¾ oz each Syrup: Rum, Vanilla. Fill with Cold Water. Stir.

B

 ASIAN ICED COFFEE

Pour 1 oz Pineapple Syrup. Add Espresso. Add Ice. Fill with Cold Water.

 AZTEC GOLD SODA

Over Ice, Pour ⅔ oz each Syrup: Passion Fruit, Mandarino, Almond. Fill with Soda Water.

 B-52

Pour ½ oz Kahlua Syrup, ½ oz Irish Cream Syrup, ¼ oz Brandy Syrup. Add Espresso and 6 oz Hot Water or Foamed/Steamed Milk.

B-52 LATTE

Pour ½ oz Irish Cream Syrup, ½ oz Coffee Syrup, ¼ oz Orange Syrup. Add Espresso. Fill with Foamed/Steamed Milk.

 BAHAMA MAMA 1

Over Ice, Pour ⅔ oz each Syrup: Creme de Cacao, Coconut, Pineapple. Fill with Soda Water. Splash with Grenadine Syrup.

 BAHAMA MAMA 2

Over Ice, Pour ½ oz each Syrup: Coconut, Coffee, Pineapple, Rum. Fill with Soda Water. Top with a splash of Grenadine Syrup.

BAHAMIAN COFFEE

Pour ¾ oz Praline Syrup. Add Espresso. Fill with Steamed Milk. Add Cinnamon Stick.

BAKLAVA SWOON

Pour ½ oz Almond Rocca® Syrup, ¼ oz Praline Syrup, ¼ oz Toasted Walnut Syrup, 1 tbs Honey. Combine and steam together with 6 oz Milk. Add Espresso. Drizzle 1 tbs Honey over finished drink and garnish with Powdered Cinnamon and Cinnamon Stick.

B

 BALI HAI SODA
Over Ice, Pour ½ oz
each Syrup: Rum,
Lime, Almond, and
Apple. Fill with Soda
Water.

 **BALTIMORE
BRACER**
Over Ice, Pour 1 oz
each Syrup: Orange,
Anisette. Fill with Soda
Water.

 BANANA BOGIE
Pour ½ oz Kahlua
Syrup, ½ oz Banana
Syrup. Add Espresso.
Fill with Foamed/
Steamed Milk.

 **BANANA BREAD
LATTE**
Pour ⅜ oz each Syrup:
Banana, Creme de
Cacao. Add a splash of
Cinnamon Syrup. Add
Espresso. Fill with
Foamed/Steamed Milk.
Splash with Banana
Syrup.

 **BANANA CHERRY
CREAM SODA**
Over Ice, Pour 1 oz
each Syrup: Banana,
Cherry. Add 3 oz Soda
Water. Fill with Half-
and-Half.

 **BANANA
COCONUT LATTE**
Pour ½ oz each Syrup:
Banana, Coconut. Add
Espresso. Fill with
Foamed/Steamed Milk.

 **BANANA COFFEE
CREAM SODA**
Over Ice, Pour 1 oz
each Syrup: Banana,
Coffee. Add Soda Water
to ½" from top of cup.
Fill with Half-and-
Half.

 BANANA COW
Over Ice, Pour ½ oz
Creme de Cacao Syrup,
1½ oz Banana Syrup.
Fill with Milk. Splash
with Banana Syrup.

B

BANANA CREAM BREVÉ

Pour ¾ oz Banana Syrup. Add Espresso. Fill with Foamed/Steamed Half-and-Half. Top with Whipped Cream. Dust with Nutmeg.

BANANA EGG NOG LATTE

Pour ¾ oz Banana Syrup. Add Espresso. Fill with Foamed/Steamed Egg Nog. Dust with Nutmeg.

BANANA GORILLA

Pour ¾ oz Thick Chocolate Syrup. Add ½ oz Banana Syrup. Add Espresso. Stir. Fill with Foamed/Steamed Milk. Top with Whipped Cream and Chocolate Sprinkles.

BANANA MANGO CREAM SODA

Over Ice, Pour 1 oz each Syrup: Banana, Mango. Add Soda Water to ½" from top of cup. Top with Half-and-Half.

BANANA MANGO FIZZ

Over Ice, Pour 1 oz each Syrup: Banana, Mango. Splash with Lime Syrup. Fill with Soda Water.

BANANA MOO

Pour ¾ oz Banana Syrup. Add Espresso. Fill with Foamed/Steamed Milk.

BANANA NUT CREAM

Over Ice, Pour 1 oz each Syrup: Banana, Hazelnut. Add 3 oz Soda Water. Fill with Half-and-Half. Top with Whipped Cream.

BANANA NUT LATTE

Pour ⅔ oz Banana Syrup, ¼ oz Hazelnut Syrup. Add Espresso. Fill with Foamed/Steamed Milk.

B

 BANANA NUT TOFFEE LATTE

Pour ¼ oz each Syrup: Banana, Hazelnut, Caramel, Coffee. Add Espresso. Fill with Foamed/Steamed Milk.

 BANANA ORANGE CREAM SODA

Over Ice, Pour 1 oz each Syrup: Banana, Orange. Add Soda Water to ½" from top of cup. Top with Half-and-Half.

 BANANA RUM CREAM SODA

Over Ice, Pour 1 oz each Syrup: Banana, Rum. Add Soda Water to ½" from top of cup. Top with Half-and-Half.

 BANANA SPLIT

Pour ⅓ oz each Syrup: Thick Chocolate, Banana, Strawberry. Add Espresso. Stir. Fill with Foamed/Steamed Milk. Top with Whipped Cream and Chocolate Sprinkles.

 BANANA SPLIT II

Pour ¼ oz Banana Syrup, ¼ oz Raspberry Syrup, ½ oz Chocolate Syrup. Add Espresso. Fill with Foamed/Steamed Milk. Top with Whipped Cream and Banana Slices. Dribble with Cherry Syrup.

 BANGER

Over Ice, Pour 1 oz Orange Syrup, ¾ oz Almond Syrup, ½ oz Vanilla Syrup. Fill with Soda Water.

 BANSHEE

Over Ice, Pour 1½ oz Banana Syrup, ½ oz Creme de Cacao Syrup. Fill with Half-and-Half.

BAPTIST WINE

Over Ice, Pour 1 oz Creme de Cassis Syrup. Add Soda Water to ½" from top of cup. Fill with Ginger Ale.

B

 BARBERRY COAST CREAM COOLER

Over Ice, Pour 1 oz each Syrup: Rum, Creme de Cacao. Add Soda Water to ½" from top of cup. Top with Half-and-Half.

 BATIDA CARNIVAL

Over Ice, Pour ⅓ oz each Syrup: Mango, Orange, Rum. Fill with Soda Water. Splash with Grenadine Syrup.

 BAVARIAN MINT LATTE

Pour ½ oz each Syrup: Chocolate Mint, Coffee. Add Espresso. Fill with Foamed/ Steamed Milk.

 BEACH BLANKET BINGO

Over Ice, Pour 1 oz each Syrup: Cranberry, Grape. Fill with Soda Water. Splash with Lime Syrup.

 BEACHCOMBER

Over Ice, Pour 1 oz Coconut Syrup, ½ oz Orange Syrup, ½ oz Lime Syrup. Fill with Soda Water. Splash with Grenadine Syrup.

 BELGIAN BREVÉ

Pour ½ oz Vanilla Syrup. Add Steamed Half-and-Half to ¾" from top and Foamed Half-and-Half to ¼" from top. Pour Espresso through the Half-and-Half, and top with Whipped Cream.

 BELGIAN ORANGE COFFEE

Pour ½ oz Orange Syrup. Add ¼ oz each Syrup: Cinnamon, Vanilla. Fill with Hot Water to ½" from top of cup. Top with Espresso. Dust with Cinnamon Powder.

B

 BELIZ CREAM SODA

Over Ice, Pour ⅔ oz each Syrup: Coconut, Coffee, Pineapple. Add Soda Water to ½" from top of cup. Fill with Half-and-Half. Splash with Cherry Syrup.

 BELLEVUE SODA

Over Ice, Pour ¾ oz Pineapple Syrup, ½ oz each Syrup: Coconut, Orange, Lime. Fill with Soda Water. Splash with Lime Syrup.

 BELLINI

Over Ice, Pour 1½ oz Peach Syrup, ½ oz Apple Syrup. Fill with Soda Water. Splash with Creme de Cassis Syrup.

 BELLINI SODA

Over Ice, Pour 1⅓ oz Peach Syrup. Add ⅓ oz each Syrup: Apple, Grape. Fill with Soda Water. Splash with Lime Syrup.

 BERMUDA BANQUET

Over Ice, Pour 1 oz Apricot Syrup. Add ½ oz each Syrup: Lemon, Orange. Fill with Soda Water.

 BERMUDA ROSE

Over Ice, Pour 1½ oz Apricot Syrup, ½ oz Grenadine Syrup. Fill with Soda Water.

 BIRD OF PARADISE

Over Ice, Pour ½ oz each Syrup: Pineapple, Passion Fruit, Orange, Lemon. Fill with Soda Water. Splash with Grenadine Syrup.

 BLACK & TAN

Over Ice, Pour 5 oz Cola. Fill with Milk.

 BLACK BELT SODA

Over Ice, Pour 1½ oz Creme de Cassis Syrup, ½ oz Pineapple Syrup. Fill with Soda Water.

B

BLACKBERRY DEMITASSE

Pour ½ oz Blackberry Syrup, ½ oz Brandy Syrup. Add 2 shots Espresso and 6 oz Hot Water.

BLACK CARAMEL LATTE

Pour ½ oz Caramel Syrup, ¼ oz Blackberry Syrup. Add Espresso. Fill with Foamed/ Steamed Milk.

BLACK CHERRY ITALIAN SODA

Over Ice, Pour 1 oz each Syrup: Blackberry, Cherry. Add splash of Anisette Syrup. Fill with Soda Water.

BLACK CURRANT CREAM SODA

Over Ice, Pour 2 oz Creme de Cassis Syrup. Add Soda Water to ½" from top of cup. Fill with Half-and-Half.

BLACK FOREST MOCHA

Pour 1 oz Thick Chocolate Syrup. Add ⅓ oz Cherry Syrup and Espresso. Stir. Fill with Foamed/Steamed Milk. Top with Whipped Cream. Dust with Chocolate Powder.

BLACK GRAPE COLA

Over Ice, Pour Cola to ¼" from top of cup. Top with ½ oz Creme de Cassis Syrup.

BLACK LICORICE SODA

Over Ice, Pour 1 oz each Syrup: Creme de Cacao, Licorice. Fill with Soda Water.

BLACK MAGIC

Pour ¾ oz Coffee Syrup. Add Espresso. Fill with Foamed/ Steamed Milk. Splash with Lemon Syrup.

B

 BLACK MARIA
Pour ¾ oz Cherry
Syrup. Add Espresso.
Top with Foamed Milk
and Chocolate Powder.

 **BLACK
MARSHMALLOW
SODA**

Over Ice, Pour ¾ oz
Vanilla Syrup. Fill with
Cola.

 BLACK ORCHID

Over Ice, Pour 1 oz
Creme de Cassis Syrup.
Add ½ oz each Syrup:
Peach, Lemon. Fill with
Soda Water.

 BLACK PRINCE

Over Ice, Pour 1¼ oz
Blackberry Syrup, ¾ oz
Chocolate Syrup. Fill
with Soda Water.

**BLACK RUSSIAN
COLA**

Over Ice, Pour 1 oz
Coffee Syrup, ½ oz
Lime Syrup. Fill with
equal parts Soda Water
and Cola.

BLACK WIDOW
Pour 1 oz Black
Currant Syrup. Add
Espresso. Fill with
Foamed/Steamed Milk.
Top with Whipped
Cream and dust with
Powdered Chocolate
and Maraschino Cherry.

 **BLACKBERRY
COCONUT LATTE**

Pour ½ oz each Syrup:
Blackberry, Coconut.
Add Espresso. Fill with
Foamed/Steamed Milk.

 **BLACKBERRY RUM
CREAM SODA**

Over Ice, Pour 1 oz
each Syrup: Blackberry,
Rum. Add Soda Water
to ½" from top of cup.
Top with Half-and-
Half.

 **BLACKBERRY
SUPREME COOLER 1**

Over Ice, Pour 1 oz
Blackberry Syrup, ½ oz
Lemon Syrup. Add
Soda Water to ½" from
top of cup. Fill with
Ginger Ale. Splash with
Blackberry Syrup.

B

 BLACKBERRY SUPREME COOLER 2

Over Ice, Pour 1½ oz Blackberry Syrup, ½ oz Coconut Syrup. Fill with Soda Water. Splash with Lemon Syrup.

 BLUE COYOTE

Over Ice, Pour 1¼ oz Blue Curacao Syrup, ¾ oz Coconut Syrup. Fill with Soda Water.

 BLUE MILK SPECIAL

A latte made with Nonfat Milk.

 BLUEBERRY CREAM BREVÉ

Pour ½ oz each Syrup: Blueberry, Vanilla. Add Espresso. Fill with Foamed/Steamed Half-and-Half.

 BLUEBERRY LEMON FIZZ

Over Ice, Pour 1⅓ oz Blueberry Syrup, ⅔ oz Lemon Syrup. Fill with Soda Water.

 BLUEBERRY RUM FIZZ

Over Ice, Pour 1 oz Blueberry Syrup, ¾ oz Rum Syrup, ¼ oz Lemon Syrup. Fill with Soda Water.

 BOCA CHICA COFFEE

Pour a double shot Espresso. Add Ice. Add 1 oz Rum Syrup, ½ oz Vanilla Syrup. Fill with Cold Water. Stir.

 BOCCIE BALL

Over Ice, Pour 1¼ oz of Amaretto Syrup, ¾ oz Orange Syrup. Fill with Soda Water.

 BOLERO COOLER

Over Ice, Pour 1 oz Rum Syrup, ½ oz each Syrup: Apple, Lemon. Fill with Soda Water.

 BOONOONOONOOS

Pour ½ oz Rum Syrup, ½ oz Coffee Syrup. Add Espresso and 6 oz Hot Water. Garnish with Powdered Allspice and Lime Wedge.

B

 BORA-BORA

Over Ice, Pour ¾ oz
Pineapple Syrup, ½ oz
each Syrup: Passion
Fruit, Lemon, ¼ oz
Grenadine. Fill with
Soda Water. Splash
with Grenadine Syrup.

 BORGIA

Pour ¾ oz Creme de
Cacao Syrup. Add
Espresso. Top with
Whipped Cream. Dust
with Nutmeg.

 BOSTON BANGER

Over Ice, Pour 1 oz
Orange Syrup, ¾ oz
Almond Syrup, ½ oz
Vanilla Syrup. Fill with
Soda Water.

 BOSTON COOLER

Over Ice, Pour ½ oz each
Syrup: Lemon,
Grenadine. Add Soda
Water to ½" from top of
cup. Fill with Ginger Ale.

 BOSTON GOLD

Over Ice, Pour 1½ oz
Orange Syrup, ½ oz
Banana Syrup. Fill with
Soda Water.

 **BOYSENBERRY
NUT LATTE**

Pour ½ oz each Syrup:
Boysenberry, Almond.
Add Espresso. Fill with
Foamed/Steamed Milk.

 **BRANDIED
ALMOND COFFEE**

Pour ½ oz Amaretto
Syrup, ½ oz Brandy
Syrup. Add Espresso
and 6 oz Hot Water.

 **BRANDIED
ALMOND COFFEE
II**

Pour ⅔ oz Amaretto
Syrup, ⅓ oz Almond
Syrup. Add 8 oz Hot
Water and Espresso.
Top with dollop of
Whipped Cream.

 **BRANDIED
CHERRY COLADA**

Over Ice, Pour ¾ oz
each Syrup: Coconut,
Pineapple. Add ¼ oz
each Syrup: Amaretto,
Cherry. Fill with Soda
Water.

B

BRANDIED CHERRY LATTE

Pour ¾ oz Cherry Syrup, ¼ oz Amaretto Syrup. Add Espresso. Fill with Foamed/Steamed Milk. Splash with Amaretto Syrup.

BRANDY ALEXANDER MOCHA

Pour 1 oz Thick Chocolate Syrup, ½ oz Napoleon Brandy Syrup. Add Espresso. Stir. Fill with Foamed/Steamed Milk

BRAVE BULL

Over Ice, Pour 1 oz each Syrup: Coffee, Creme de Cacao. Fill with Soda Water. Splash with Lime Syrup.

BRAZIL COOLER

Over Ice, Pour 1½ oz Apple Syrup, ½ oz Lime Syrup. Fill with Soda Water. Splash with Grenadine Syrup.

BRAZILIAN COFFEE

To 2 shots Espresso, add 4 oz Hot Water and 4 oz Steamed/Foamed Chocolate Milk. Top with Whipped Cream.

BRAZILIAN COFFEE II

Pour 1 oz Coffee Syrup. Add Espresso. Top with Whipped Cream.

BRAZILIAN COFFEE MELANGE

Pour ½ oz Chocolate Syrup, ¼ oz Vanilla Syrup. Add 6 oz Hot Water and Espresso. Fill with 3 oz Half-and-Half. Sprinkle with Cinnamon Powder.

BREAKFAST EGG NOG COOLER

Over Ice, Pour 1¼ oz Apricot Syrup. Add Espresso. Fill with Egg Nog. Sprinkle with Nutmeg or Cinnamon.

B

BREVÉ
Prepare as for latte. Substitute Half-and-Half for Milk.

BREVÉ VANILLA
Pour ¾ oz Vanilla Syrup. Add Espresso. Fill with Foamed/Steamed Half-and-Half.

BROWN CALF BELT
Pour ½ oz Coffee Syrup, ½ oz Peppermint Syrup, ½ oz Irish Cream Syrup. Add 2 shots, Espresso and 6 oz Hot Water.

BROWN COW
Over Ice, Pour ⅔ oz each Syrup: Coffee, Creme de Cacao, Vanilla. Fill with Milk.

BROWN GRASSHOPPER
Pour 1 oz Crème de Menthe Syrup and ½ oz Amaretto Syrup. Add Espresso and Ice and fill with Soda Water. (Special note: Peppermint Syrup may be substituted for White Crème de Menthe in this recipe.)

BROWN VELVET
Pour ½ oz Creme de Cacao Syrup, ¼ oz Orange Syrup. Add Espresso. Fill with Foamed/Steamed Milk.

BULLFROG
Over Ice, Pour 1 oz Lemon Syrup. Add Espresso. Fill with Milk.

BULL'S MILK
Over Ice, Pour 1½ oz Creme de Cacao Syrup, ½ oz Lime Syrup. Fill with Milk. Sprinkle with Cinnamon or Nutmeg.

BUTTER PECAN BREVÉ

Pour ½ oz Thick Butterscotch Syrup, ¼ oz each Syrup: Hazelnut, Almond. Add Espresso. Stir. Fill with Foamed/Steamed Half-and-Half.

BUTTER PECAN LATTE

Pour ½ oz each Syrup: Butterscotch, Pecan. Add Espresso. Fill with Foamed/Steamed Milk. Top with Whipped Cream.

BUTTERSCOTCHED BANANA LATTE

Pour ½ oz each Syrup: Butterscotch, Banana. Add Espresso. Fill with Foamed/Steamed Milk. Top with Whipped Cream.

C. C. CRUSH

Over Ice, Pour 1½ oz Orange Syrup. Fill with Soda Water. Splash with Coconut and Pineapple Syrup.

CABANA CREAM

Pour ¾ oz each Syrup: Orange, Banana. Add 1 oz Honey. Stir. Add Ice. Fill with Cold Milk.

CACAO BANANA CREAM SODA

Over Ice, Pour 1 oz each Syrup: Creme de Cacao, Banana. Add 3 oz Soda Water. Fill with Half-and-Half.

CADIZ

Over Ice, Pour ¼ oz Apple Syrup, ¾ oz Blackberry Syrup, ½ oz Orange Syrup. Fill with Soda Water to ½" from top of cup. Top with Half-and-Half.

CAFE AU LAIT

French version of the latte. 1 or 2 shots of Espresso. Two times as much Foamed Milk.

C

CAFE AU CHOCOLATE

Pour ¾ oz Chocolate Syrup. Fill with Hot Water to ½" from top of cup. Top with Espresso and Whipped Cream. Dust with Chocolate Powder.

CAFE BON BON

Pour ½ oz Chocolate Mint Syrup, ¼ oz Cherry Syrup. Add Espresso. Top with Foamed/Steamed Milk.

CAFE BRULOT

Pour ¼ oz Rum Syrup, ¼ oz Brandy Syrup, ¾ oz Chocolate Syrup. Add 2 shots, Espresso and 6 oz Hot Water. Garnish with Orange Slice, Whole Cloves and a Cinnamon Stick.

CAFE CACAO

Pour 1 oz Crème de Cacao Syrup. Add Espresso and 6 oz Hot Water. Top with Whipped Cream.

CAFE CALYPSO

Pour ½ oz Coffee Syrup, ¼ oz Rum Syrup. Fill with Hot Water to ½" from top of cup. Top with Espresso and Whipped Cream.

CAFE CAPRICE

Pour ¾ oz Simple Syrup. Add Espresso and Ice. Fill with Soda Water.

CAFE CON ESPUMITA

Pour ¼ oz Espresso. Add 1 tsp Sugar. Stir. Add Espresso. Fill with Hot Water.

CAFE CON LECHE

Spanish version of the latte. 1 or 2 shots of Espresso. 3 times as much Foamed Milk.

CAFE CON RUM

Pour ¾ oz Rum Syrup. Add Espresso. Fill with Hot Water. Add a Cinnamon Stick. Top with Whipped Cream.

C

CAFE CONQUISTADOR

Pour ¾ oz Coffee Syrup. Add Espresso. Fill with Foamed/ Steamed Milk. Top with Whipped Cream and Shaved Chocolate.

CAFE CUBANO: MIAMI/ CUBAN VERSION OF ESPRESSO

Pour Espresso in a short cup.

CAFE DE OLLA

Pour ½ oz Cinnamon Syrup. Add a double shot Espresso. Add 3 oz Hot Water. Top with Steamed Evaporated Milk.

CAFE DEN DA

Pour a double shot of Espresso. Add Ice. Fill with Cold Water.

CAFE DI AMARETTO

Pour ¾ oz Amaretto Syrup. Add Espresso. Fill with Foamed/ Steamed Milk. Top with Whipped Cream. Splash with Amaretto Syrup.

CAFE DIABLO

Pour ½ oz Orange Syrup, ¼ oz Licorice Syrup. Add Hot Water to ½" from top of cup. Top with Espresso. Dust with Mexican Chocolate Powder.

CAFE FOSTER

Pour ½ oz Rum Syrup, ¼ oz Banana Syrup. Fill with Hot Water to ½" from top of cup. Top with Espresso and Whipped Cream. Splash with Banana Syrup.

CAFE IBERICO

Pour ½ oz Anisette Syrup, ¼ oz Lemon Syrup. Add Hot Water to 1" from top of cup. Top with a double shot of Espresso.

C

CAFE MARTINIQUE
Pour ½ oz Rum Syrup.
Add Espresso and 6 oz
hot water. Top with
Whipped Cream and
Grated Nutmeg.
Garnish with
Cinnamon Stick.

CAFE MEXICAN
Pour 1 oz Coffee Syrup.
Add dash of Powdered
Cloves. Add Espresso
and 6 oz Hot Water.
Garnish with
Cinnamon Stick.

CAFE MEXICANO
Pour ¾ oz Chocolate
Syrup. Add Espresso
and 6 oz Hot Water.
Top with Whipped
Cream blended with ¼
tsp Ground Cinnamon,
¼ tsp Grated Nutmeg,
and 1 tbs Sugar.

CAFE MILCH
German version of the
Cappuccino.
Simultaneously pour
Espresso and Foamed
Milk into cup.

CAFE MUCK
Pour ½ oz Thick
Chocolate Syrup, ¼ oz
Cherry Syrup. Add a
double shot of
Espresso. Stir. Top with
Whipped Cream. Dust
with Chocolate Powder.

CAFE PUCCI
Pour ½ oz each Syrup:
Amaretto, Rum. Fill
with Hot Water to ½"
from top of cup. Top
with Espresso and
Whipped Cream.

CAFE RIO
Pour ½ oz Orange
Syrup. Add 1 tsp
Brown Sugar and
Espresso. Stir. Fill with
Hot Water. Top with
dollop of Whipped
Cream.

CAFE ROMA
Pour a double shot of
Espresso. Fill with
Foamed/Steamed Milk.

C

CAFE SOIREE
Pour ½ oz Rum Syrup. Add 1 tsp Ground Cinnamon and 1 tsp Ground Cloves to group and pull shot, Espresso. Add 6 oz Hot Water. Top with Whipped Cream.

CAFE SUA DA
Pour a double shot of Espresso. Add Ice. Fill with Sweetened Condensed Milk.

CAFE THEATRE
Pour ½ oz each Syrup: Creme de Cacao, Irish Cream. Fill with Hot Water to ½" from top of cup. Top with Espresso and Whipped Cream.

CAFE YUCATAN
Pour ½ oz Creme de Cacao Syrup. Add Espresso. Top with Whipped Cream. Dust with Nutmeg.

CAFE VIENNESE
Pour 2 oz Thick Chocolate Syrup. Add Espresso. Stir. Add 4 oz Cold Water. Add Ice. Fill with Half-and-Half. Dust with Cinnamon and Nutmeg.

CAFE ZURICH
Pour ⅓ oz each Syrup: Amaretto, Anisette, Orange. Fill with Hot Water to ½" from top of cup. Top with Espresso and Whipped Cream.

CAFFE MEXICANO
Pour ½ oz Kahlua Syrup, ½ oz Chocolate Syrup, 1 oz Half-and-Half. Add Espresso. Fill with Foamed/Steamed Milk.

CAFFE NICO
Pour 1/6 oz Orange Syrup, 1/6 oz Vanilla Syrup. Add 2 shots, Ristretto. Fill with Steamed/Foamed Milk. Garnish with Orange Peel and dust with Grated Nutmeg.

C

 CAFFE NIKKO CREAM SODA

Over Ice, Pour 1 oz each Syrup: Orange, Creme de Cacao. Fill with Soda Water to ½" from top of cup. Top with Half-and-Half.

 CAFFE NIKKO ITALIAN SODA

Over Ice, Pour 1 oz Syrup: Orange, Creme de Cacao. Fill with Soda Water.

 CAFFE NIKKO STEAMER

Pour ½ oz each Syrup: Creme de Cacao, Orange. Fill with Foamed/Steamed Milk and top with Whipped Cream. Dust with Chocolate Powder.

 CAFE OLE!

Pour 1 oz Kahlua Syrup. Add Espresso and 6 oz Hot Water. Garnish with Cinnamon Stick.

CAFE PRALINE ROYALE

Pour ½ oz Praline Syrup, ½ oz Brandy Syrup. Add Espresso and 6 oz Hot Water.

CAFFE SAMBUCA

Pour ½ oz Sambuca Syrup in a short cup. Top with Espresso.

CAFFE SAMBUCA II

Pour ¼ oz Licorice Syrup. Add Espresso.

CAFFE ZINHO

Add 3 heaping tablespoons Brown Sugar. Fill to ½" from top of cup with Hot Water. Stir. Top with a double shot of Espresso.

CAFFEE NATCHEZ

Pour ⅔ oz Brandy Syrup, ⅓ oz Crème de Cacao. Add Espresso and 6 oz Hot Water.

C

 CAJUN COFFEE

Pour ½ oz Molasses.
Add Espresso and 6 oz
Hot Water. Top with
Whipped Cream and
Nutmeg.

 **CALICO JACK**

Over Ice, Pour 1 oz
Rum Syrup, ¾ oz Irish
Cream Syrup, ¼ oz
Lemon Syrup. Fill with
Soda Water.

 **CALIFORNIA
COOLER**

Over Ice, Pour 1 oz
each Syrup: Orange,
Cherry. Fill with Soda
Water.

 **CALIFORNIA
SLAMMER**

Over Ice, Pour 1 oz
each Syrup: Amaretto,
Orange. Fill with Soda
Water.

 CALM VOYAGE

Over Ice, Pour 1 oz
each Syrup: Vanilla,
Passion Fruit. Fill with
Soda Water to ½" from
top of cup. Top with
2 oz Half-and-Half.

 **CALYPSO BREEZE
CREAM SODA**

Over Ice, Pour ⅔ oz
each Syrup: Kiwi,
Passion Fruit, Lemon.
Add Soda Water to ½"
from top of cup. Top
with Half-and-Half.

 **CALYPSO COFFEE**

Pour ¾ oz Rum Syrup.
Add Espresso. Fill with
Steamed Half-and-
Half. Splash with
Creme de Cacao Syrup.

 CALYPSO COOLER

Pour Espresso. Add Ice.
Pour ½ oz each Syrup:
Banana, Creme de
Cacao, Rum. Fill with
Cold Milk. Stir. Dust
with Cinnamon
Powder.

CANDY BAR

Pour ¼ oz Caramel
Syrup, ¾ oz Chocolate
Peanut Butter Syrup.
Add Espresso. Fill with
Steamed/Foamed Milk.
Top with Whipped
Cream.

C

CANADIAN PINEAPPLE

Over Ice, Pour 1½ oz Pineapple Syrup, ½ oz Lemon Syrup. Fill with Soda Water. Splash with Cherry Syrup.

CANADO SALUDO

Over Ice, Pour ¾ oz each Syrup: Orange, Pineapple. Add ½ oz Lemon Syrup. Fill with Soda Water. Splash with Grenadine Syrup.

CANDY APPLE CREAM

Over Ice, Pour ⅔ oz each Syrup: Apple, Cherry, Cinnamon. Fill with Soda Water to ½" from top of cup. Top with Half-and-Half.

CANDY APPLE SODA

Over Ice, Pour ⅔ oz each Syrup: Apple, Cherry, Cinnamon. Fill with Soda Water.

CANDY CANE LATTE

Pour ¾ oz Cherry Syrup, ¼ oz Mint Syrup. Add Espresso. Fill with Foamed/ Steamed Milk and top with Whipped Cream. Place Candy Cane in the cup to stir.

CANEEL BAY CREAM

Over Ice, Pour 1 oz Rum Syrup. Add ½ oz each Syrup: Coffee, Creme de Cacao. Fill with Soda Water to ¾" from top of cup. Top with Half-and-Half.

CANNES-CANNES

Over Ice, Pour ½ oz Rum Syrup, ⅓ oz Orange Syrup. Add 3 oz Grapefruit Juice. Fill with Soda Water.

CAPE CODDER SODA

Over Ice, Pour 2 oz Cranberry Syrup. Fill with Soda Water. Splash with Lime Syrup.

C

~ CAPPUCCINO

First foam and steam Milk. Set pitcher aside. Pour Espresso. Allow Steamed Milk to pour under foam to ½" from top of cup. Top with 2" "cap" of Dense Foam. Dust with Chocolate Powder or Nutmeg.

~ CAPPUCCINO MOCHA

Pour 1 oz Thick Chocolate Syrup. Foam and steam Milk. Set pitcher aside. Pour Espresso. Stir. Allow Steamed Milk to Pour under Foam to ½" from top of cup. Top with 2" "cap" of Dense Foam. Dust with Chocolate Powder.

~ CAPPUCCINO ALMOND

Pour ⅓ oz Almond Syrup. Foam and steam Milk. Set pitcher aside. Pour Espresso. Stir. Allow Steamed Milk to pour under Foam to ½" from top of cup. Top with 2" "cap" of Dense Foam. Dust with Chocolate or Vanilla Powder.

~ CAPRI

Over Ice, Pour 1 oz each Syrup: Creme de Cacao, Banana. Fill with Milk. Sprinkle with Chocolate Powder.

~ CARAMEL ALMOND LATTE

Pour ½ oz each Syrup: Caramel, Almond. Add Espresso. Fill with Foamed/Steamed Milk.

C

 CARAMEL CANDY APPLE CREAM SUPREME

Over Ice, Pour ½ oz each Syrup: Apple, Boysenberry, Caramel, Cinnamon. Add 3 oz Soda Water. Fill with Half-and-Half. Stir.

 CARAMEL CREAM SODA

Over Ice, Pour 1½ oz Caramel Syrup, ½ oz Vanilla Syrup. Fill with Soda Water.

 CARAMEL CREAM STEAMER

Pour 1 oz Caramel Syrup, ½ oz Vanilla Syrup. Fill with Foamed/Steamed Milk. Top with Whipped Cream.

 CARAMEL EGG CREAM

Pour 1½ oz Caramel Syrup, 4 oz Cold Milk. Stir. Add Ice. Fill with Soda Water to ½" from top of cup. Top with ½ oz Vanilla Syrup. Stir again.

 CARAMEL EGG NOG LATTE

Pour ¾ oz Caramel Syrup. Add Espresso. Fill with Foamed/ Steamed Egg Nog.

 CARAMEL NUT LATTE

Pour ¾ oz Thick Caramel Syrup, ¼ oz Hazelnut Syrup. Add Espresso. Stir. Fill with Foamed/Steamed Milk.

 CARAMEL ROYALE

Pour ⅔ oz Caramel Syrup, ⅓ oz Chocolate Syrup. Add Espresso. Fill with Foamed/ Steamed Milk. Top with Whipped Cream. Garnish with threads of Thick Caramel Syrup over Whipped Cream.

 CARAMELED CINNAMON APPLE LATTE

Pour ½ oz Apple Syrup, ¼ oz each Syrup: Caramel, Cinnamon. Add Espresso. Fill with Foamed/Steamed Milk.

C

CARAMELLO

Same as Mocha but substitute Thick Caramel Syrup for Thick Chocolate Syrup.

CARDAMON COFFEE

Add 1 tsp Cardamom to group and pull shot, Espresso. Add 6 oz Hot Water. Top with Whipped Cream.

CARDAMOM COOLER

Over Ice, Pour Espresso pulled with 1 tsp Cardamom. Add 6 oz Water. Garnish with Twist of Lemon or Orange Peel.

CARIBBEAN COOLER

Over Ice, Pour 1½ oz Pineapple Syrup, ½ oz Rum Syrup. Fill with Soda Water. Splash with Grenadine Syrup.

CARIBBEAN DELIGHT

Over Ice, Pour 1 oz each Syrup: Orange, Coconut. Fill with Soda Water. Splash with Cinnamon Syrup.

CARUMBA

Over Ice, Pour 1 oz each Syrup: Caramel, Rum. Add Soda Water to ½" from top of cup. Fill with Half-and-Half.

CASA BLANCA COFFEE

Pour ½ oz Amaretto Syrup, ¼ oz Lime Syrup. Add Espresso. Add Foamed/Steamed Milk. Top with Whipped Cream.

CASINO COOLER

Over Ice, Pour ⅔ oz each Syrup: Lemon, Orange, Cherry. Fill with Soda Water. Top with Whipped Cream.

C

 CENTER COURT
Over Ice, Pour 1½ oz
Strawberry Syrup. Add
2 oz Ginger Ale. Fill to
½" from top of cup
with Soda Water. Top
with Half-and-Half.

 **CHERRY
ALEXANDER**
Over Ice, Pour 1 oz
each Syrup: Creme de
Cacao, Cherry. Fill
with Half-and-Half.
Stir.

 CHARIOTS OF FIRE
Over Ice, Pour 1 oz of
Mandarino Syrup. Fill
to ¾" from top of cup
with Soda Water. Top
with Ginger Ale and
splash with Grenadine
Syrup.

 CHERRY BLOSSOM
Over Ice, Pour 1½ oz
Cherry Syrup. Add
¼ oz each Syrup:
Orange, Lemon. Fill
with Soda Water.
Splash with Grenadine
Syrup.

 CHARLIE CHAPLIN
Over Ice, Pour 1 oz
each Syrup: Cherry,
Apricot. Fill with Soda
Water. Splash with
Lemon Syrup.

 CHERRY BON BON
Pour ½ oz each Syrup:
Chocolate, Cherry. Add
Espresso. Fill with
Foamed Milk and top
with Chocolate
Sprinkles.

 **CHARTREUSE
SUPREME CREAM
SODA**
Over Ice, Pour 1½ oz
Lime Syrup. Add Soda
Water to ½" from top
of cup. Add ½ oz
Pineapple Syrup. Top
with Half-and-Half and
Whipped Cream.

 **CHERRY BRANDY
LATTE**
Pour ½ oz Cherry
Syrup, ¼ oz Amaretto
Syrup. Add Espresso.
Fill with Foamed/
Steamed Milk.

C

 CHERRY CHOCOLATE COFFEE

Pour ½ oz Cherry Syrup, ½ oz Chocolate Syrup. Add 2 shots, Espresso, 6 oz Hot Water, and ½ tsp Dark Brown Sugar. Stir. Top with Whipped Cream.

 CHERRY COBBLER

Over Ice, Pour 1½ oz Cherry Syrup, ½ oz Cinnamon Syrup. Fill with Soda Water.

 CHERRY COKE

Over Ice, Pour ¾ oz Cherry Syrup. Fill with Coke.

 CHERRY COOLER

Over Ice, Pour 2 oz Cherry Syrup. Fill with Soda Water.

 CHERRY CORDIAL

Pour ½ oz Cherry Syrup, ¼ oz each Syrup: Vanilla, Almond. Add Espresso. Fill with Foamed/Steamed Milk.

 CHERRY CREAM TART

Over Ice, Pour 1½ oz Cherry Syrup, ½ oz Lime Syrup. Fill with Soda Water to ½" from top of cup. Top with Half-and-Half.

 CHERRY DAIQUIRI

Over Ice, Pour 1 oz Rum Syrup, ½ oz each Syrup: Cherry, Lime. Fill with Soda Water. Splash with Lime Syrup.

 CHERRY FIZZ

Over Ice, Pour 2 oz Cherry Syrup. Fill with Soda Water. Splash with Lemon Syrup.

 CHERRY JUBILEE LATTE

Pour ½ oz Cherry Syrup, ¼ oz Vanilla Syrup. Add Espresso. Fill with Foamed/Steamed Milk.

C

 CHERRY-LIME RICKEY

Over Ice, fill ¾ full with Soda Water. Add 1 oz each Syrup: Cherry, Lime. Stir gently. Float with ¼ oz Grenadine Syrup.

 CHERRY CHEESECAKE LATTE

Pour ½ oz Irish Cream Syrup, ½ oz Cherry Syrup, ¼ oz Vanilla Syrup, dash Orgeat Syrup. Add Espresso. Fill with Steamed/Foamed Milk.

 CHERRY COCONUT LATTE

Pour ½ oz each Syrup: Cherry, Coconut. Add Espresso. Fill with Foamed/Steamed Milk.

 CHERRY NUT CREAM SODA

Over Ice, Pour 1½ oz Cherry Syrup, ½ oz Almond Syrup. Fill with Soda Water to ½" from top of cup. Top with Half-and-Half.

 CHERRY NUT LATTE

Pour ½ oz each Syrup: Cherry, Almond. Add Espresso. Fill with Foamed/Steamed Milk.

 CHERRY RUM CREAM SODA

Over Ice, Pour 1 oz each Syrup: Cherry, Rum. Fill with Soda Water to ½" from top of cup. Top with Half-and-Half and Whipped Cream.

 CHI CHI

Over Ice, pour ⅔ oz each Syrup: Rum, Pineapple. Add ½ oz Blackberry Syrup. Fill with Soda Water.

 CHICAGO COOLER

Over Ice, Pour ½ oz each Syrup: Grape, Lemon. Add Soda Water to ½" from top of cup. Fill with Ginger Ale.

C

 CHOCA BLOK

Pour ½ oz Chocolate Syrup and ½ oz Honey. Add Espresso and 6 oz Hot Water. Garnish with Whipped Cream and Grated Chocolate.

 CHOCOLATE ALMOND SODA

Over Ice, Pour 1 oz each Syrup: Chocolate, Almond. Fill with Soda Water.

 CHOCOLATE ANGEL WINGS

Over Ice, Pour 2 oz Chocolate Syrup, 3 oz Soda Water. Fill with Half-and-Half. Top with Whipped Cream.

CHOCOLATE CHERRY KISS

Over Ice, Pour 1⅓ oz Cherry Syrup, ⅔ oz Chocolate Syrup, 3 oz Soda Water. Fill with Half-and-Half. Top with Whipped Cream. Dust with Chocolate Powder.

 CHOCOLATE CHERRY MOCHA

Pour ¾ oz Thick Chocolate Syrup, ⅓ oz Cherry Syrup. Add Espresso. Stir. Fill with Foamed/Steamed Milk. Top with Whipped Cream. Splash with Cherry Syrup.

 CHOCOLATE EGG CREAM

Pour 1½ oz Thick Chocolate Syrup, 4 oz Cold Milk. Stir. Add Ice. Fill with Soda Water to ½" from top of cup. Top with ½ oz Vanilla Syrup. Stir again.

 CHOCOLATE ESPRESSO

Pour ⅓ oz Chocolate Syrup. Add a double shot Espresso. Stir. Top with dollop of Whipped Cream.

C

 CHOCOLATE KAHLUA LATTE

Pour ½ oz Thick Chocolate Syrup, ½ oz Creme de Cacao Syrup. Add Espresso. Stir. Fill with Foamed/Steamed Milk.

 CHOCOLATE JAMAICAN

Over Ice, Pour 1 oz Chocolate Syrup, ½ oz each Syrup: Rum, Amaretto; ¼ oz Almond Syrup. Fill to ½" from top with Milk. Top with Half-and-Half. Dust with Chocolate Powder.

CHOCOLATE MARSHMALLOW LATTE

Pour ½ oz each Thick Syrup: Chocolate, Marshmallow. Add Espresso. Stir. Fill with Foamed/Steamed Milk and top with Whipped Cream.

 CHOCOLATE MINT LATTE

Pour ¾ oz Chocolate Mint Syrup. Add Espresso. Fill with Foamed/Steamed Milk.

CHOCOLATE RUM LATTE

Pour ½ oz each Syrup: Creme de Cacao, Rum. Add Espresso. Fill with Foamed/Steamed Milk.

 CHOCOLATE MINT CREAM SODA

Over Ice, Pour 2 oz Chocolate Mint Syrup. Add Soda Water to ½" from top of cup. Fill with Half-and-Half.

 CHOCOLATE MINT ITALIAN SODA

Over Ice, Pour 2 oz Chocolate Mint Syrup. Fill with Soda Water.

C

CHOCOLATE PECAN PIE LATTE

Pour ¾ oz Thick Chocolate Syrup, ⅓ oz Pecan Syrup. Add Espresso. Stir. Fill with Foamed/Steamed Milk. Top with Whipped Cream.

CHOCOLATE RUM COFFEE

Pour ½ oz each Syrup: Chocolate, Rum. Add 6 oz Hot Water and Espresso. Fill with 2 oz Half-and-Half and top with Whipped Cream.

CHOCOLATE RUM SODA

Over Ice, Pour 1 oz each Syrup: Chocolate, Rum. Fill with Soda Water.

CHOCOLATE SHOOTER

Pour ½ oz Chocolate Syrup in a 4 oz cup. Add Espresso. Stir. Fill with steamed Half-and-Half.

CHOCOLATE SPECTACULAR

Over Ice, Pour 1 oz Chocolate Syrup, ½ oz each Syrup: Coffee, Peach. Add Soda Water to ½" from top of cup. Fill with Half-and-Half. Top with Whipped Cream. Dust with Chocolate Powder.

CHOCOLATINO

Add 1 tablespoon Mexican Chocolate Powder. Add Espresso. Stir. Fill with Foamed/Steamed Milk and Whipped Cream. Dust with Mexican Chocolate Powder.

CHOCOLATO

Pour ½ oz Chocolate Syrup. Add Espresso and 2 oz Half-and-Half. Steam together until hot. Garnish with Whipped Cream.

C

CHOCOLATTE
Pour 1 tablespoon Mexican Chocolate Powder. Add Espresso. Stir. Fill with Foamed/Steamed Milk. Dust with Mexican Chocolate Powder.

CHOCONUT EGG NOG LATTE
Pour ¾ oz Thick Chocolate Syrup. Add Espresso. Stir. Fill with Foamed/Steamed Egg Nog. Dust with Chocolate Powder or Nutmeg.

CHRISTMAS CRIMSON COOLER
Over Ice, Pour 1½ oz Cranberry Syrup, ½ oz Creme de Cassis Syrup. Fill with Soda Water. Splash with Lime Syrup.

CINNAMON CAFE CON LECHE
To Espresso, add 1 tsp Sugar. Stir. Fill with Foamed/Steamed Milk. Garnish with Cinnamon Stick.

CINNAMON COFFEE
Over Ice, Pour ½ oz Cinnamon Syrup. Add 2 shots, Espresso. Add 6 oz Cold Water, 1 oz Half-and-Half and 2 tsp sugar. Garnish with Cinnamon Stick.

CINNAMON COLADA
Over Ice, Pour ¾ oz each Syrup: Coconut, Pineapple. Add ½ oz Cinnamon Syrup. Fill with Soda Water.

CINNAMON ESPRESSO
Pour ¼ oz Cinnamon Syrup. Add Espresso. Garnish with Cinnamon Stick.

CINNAMON PEACH LATTE
Pour ½ oz each Syrup: Cinnamon, Peach. Add Espresso. Fill with Foamed/Steamed Milk.

C

 CINNAMON ROLL LATTE

Pour ½ oz Cinnamon Syrup. Add 1 teaspoon of Brown Sugar. Stir. Add Espresso. Fill with Foamed/Steamed Milk. Top with Whipped Cream. Dust with Cinnamon Powder.

 CITRUS COOLER

Over Ice, Pour 1 oz Orange Syrup, ½ oz each Syrup: Lemon, Lime. Fill with Soda Water.

 CITRUS GROVE SPRITZER

Over Ice, Pour 1 oz each Syrup: Orange, Lime. Fill with Soda Water. Splash with Grenadine Syrup.

 CIUDAD COOLER

Pour Espresso. Add Ice. Fill with Cold Milk or Half-and-Half. Dust with Mexican Chocolate Powder. Add a Cinnamon Stick.

CLOVER CLUB CREAM SODA

Over Ice, Pour 1½ oz Irish Cream Syrup, ½ oz Cinnamon Syrup. Fill to ½" from top of cup with Soda Water. Top with Half-and-Half and ¼ oz Mint Syrup.

 COASTAL SPICED COFFEE

Pour 1 oz Brandy Syrup. Add 2 tsp Ground Cloves to group and pull shot, Espresso. Add 6 oz Hot Water. Garnish with Orange Slice.

 COCO CHOCO

Over Ice, Pour 1 oz each Syrup: Coconut, Chocolate. Add Milk to ½" from top of cup. Fill with Half-and-Half.

C

 COCO CUSTARD MOCHA

Pour ½ oz Thick Chocolate Syrup, ¼ oz Vanilla Syrup, splash of Pineapple Syrup. Add Espresso. Stir. Fill with Foamed/Steamed Milk to ¼" from top of cup. Top with Whipped Cream and thin threads of Thick Chocolate Syrup.

 COCO-MINT ITALIAN SODA

Over Ice, Pour 2 oz Chocolate Mint Syrup. Fill with Soda Water.

 COCO-MINT CREAM SODA

Over Ice, Pour 2 oz Chocolate Mint Syrup. Fill with Soda Water to ½" from top of cup. Top with Half-and-Half.

COCO-MOCHO ITALIAN SODA

Over Ice, Pour 1 oz each Syrup: Coconut, Chocolate. Fill with Soda Water.

 COCO-MOCHO STEAMER

Pour ½ oz each Syrup: Coconut, Creme de Cocoa. Fill with Foamed/Steamed Milk. Top with Whipped Cream. Dust with Chocolate Powder.

 COCO-MOCO

Pour 1 oz Thick Chocolate Syrup, ⅓ oz Coconut Syrup. Add Espresso. Stir. Fill with Foamed/Steamed Milk. Top with Whipped Cream and Chocolate Sprinkles.

 COCOA HAZELNUT CREAM COOLER

Over Ice, Pour 1½ oz Creme de Cacao Syrup, ½ oz Hazelnut Syrup. Fill with Milk.

 COCOA-COLADA

Over Ice, Pour ½ oz each Syrup: Creme de Cacao, Rum, Coconut, Pineapple. Add Cold Milk to ½" from top of cup. Top with Half-and-Half.

C

 COCOA MINT COFFEE

Pour ½ oz Coffee Syrup, ½ oz Crème de Menthe. Add Espresso and 6 oz hot water. Top with Whipped Cream.

 COCONUT AND MANGO LATTE

Pour ½ oz each Syrup: Coconut, Mango. Add Espresso. Fill with Foamed/Steamed Milk.

 COCONUT BANANA CREAM

Over Ice, Pour 1 oz each Syrup: Banana, Coconut. Add Milk to ½" from top of cup. Fill with Half-and-Half.

 COCONUT BANG

Over Ice, Pour 1 oz Coconut Syrup. Add ½ oz each Syrup: Orange, Pineapple. Fill with Cold Milk. Splash with Lime Syrup.

 COCONUT CREAM LATTE

Pour ½ oz each Syrup: Coconut, Vanilla. Add Espresso. Fill with Foamed/Steamed Milk.

 COCONUT COFFEE LATTE

Pour ½ oz each Syrup: Coconut, Coffee. Add Espresso. Fill with Foamed/Steamed Milk.

 COCONUT COFFEE SMOOTHIE

Pour Espresso. Add Ice. Add 1 oz Coconut Syrup, ¾ oz Irish Cream Syrup, ¼ oz Coffee Syrup. Fill with Cold Milk.

 COCONUT CUTIE

Over Ice, Pour 1⅓ oz Coconut Syrup, ⅔ oz Orange Syrup. Add Soda Water to ½" from top of cup. Fill with Half-and-Half.

C

 COCONUT GINGER SODA

Over Ice, Pour 1 oz each Syrup: Coconut, Ginger. Fill with Soda Water.

 COCONUT GRAPE LATTE

Pour ½ oz each Syrup: Coconut, Grape. Add Espresso. Fill with Foamed/Steamed Milk.

 COCONUT KISS

Over Ice, Pour 1¼ oz Coconut Syrup, ¾ oz Pineapple Syrup. Add Soda Water to ½" from top of cup. Fill with Half-and-Half. Splash with Grenadine Syrup.

 COCONUT LIPS

Over Ice, Pour 1 oz Coconut Syrup, ½ oz each Syrup: Pineapple, Raspberry. Add Soda Water to ½" from top of cup. Fill with Half-and-Half. Splash with Raspberry Syrup.

 COCONUT MOCHA

Pour ½ oz Coconut Syrup, 1½ oz Thick Chocolate Syrup. Add Espresso. Stir. Fill with Foamed/Steamed Milk. Top with Whipped Cream and Chocolate Powder.

 COFFEE ALEXANDER

Pour Espresso. Add Ice. Add 1¼ oz Creme de Cacao. Top with 2 oz Half-and-Half.

 COFFEE COOLER

Pour Espresso. Add Ice. Add 1 oz Irish Cream Syrup. Fill with Cold Water to ½" from top of cup. Top with Half-and-Half.

 COFFEE CREAM COOLER

Over Ice, Pour 1 oz Rum Syrup, 1 oz Half-and-Half. Add 2 shots, Espresso and 6 oz Cold Water.

C

 COFFEE EGG NOG

Pour Espresso. Add Ice. Add 4 oz Cold Water. Fill with Egg Nog. Stir.

 COFFEE GRASSHOPPER

Over Ice, Pour 1½ oz Creme de Menthe Syrup. Add Espresso. Fill with Milk. Stir.

COFFEE NOGGIN

Pour ¾ oz Creme de Cacao Syrup. Add Espresso. Fill with Steamed Half-and-Half. Sprinkle with Powdered Nutmeg.

COFFEE NUDGE

Pour ½ oz each Syrup: Creme de Cacao, Coffee. Add ⅛ oz Mandarino Syrup. Fill to ¾" from top with Hot Water. Add Espresso. Top with Whipped Cream. Dust with Nutmeg.

COFFEE NUT

Pour ½ oz Hazelnut Syrup, ¼ oz Orange Syrup. Add 6 oz Hot Water. Add Espresso. Top with Whipped Cream.

 COFFEE SCOTCH

Pour 2 oz Thick Butterscotch Syrup. Add Espresso. Stir. Fill with Hot Water.

 COFFEE SOUR

Over Ice, Pour 1½ oz Lemon Syrup. Add Espresso. Fill with Soda Water.

 COLADA BRAZIL

Over Ice, Pour ⅔ oz each Syrup: Chocolate, Pineapple; ⅓ oz each Syrup: Passion Fruit, Rum. Add Soda Water to ½" from top of cup. Fill with Half-and-Half.

 COLUMBIA CLUB SODA

Over Ice, Pour 1 oz each Syrup: Raspberry, Rum. Fill with Soda Water. Splash with Lemon Syrup.

C

 COOLER
Over Ice, Pour 2 oz any Flavored Syrup. Fill with Soda Water.

 COPACABANA CREAM SODA
Over Ice, Pour ⅔ oz each Syrup: Chocolate, Passion Fruit, Rum. Add Soda Water to ½" from top of cup. Fill with Half-and-Half.

 CORTADO
Pour 6 oz Hot Water. Top with Espresso and few drops, Hot Milk.

 COSSACK COFFEE GROG
Pour Espresso. Add Ice. Pour ¾ oz Creme de Cacao Syrup. Add ½ oz each Syrup: Chocolate, Vanilla. Fill with Cold Milk. Dust with Cinnamon Powder.

 COUNTRY CLUB COOLER
Over Ice, Pour 1½ oz Apple Syrup, ½ oz Grenadine Syrup. Fill with Soda Water.

 COZUMEL COFFEE COOLER
Pour double shot of Espresso. Add Ice. Add 1 oz Orange Syrup, ½ oz Rum Syrup. Fill with Cold Water.

 CRANBERRY COOLER
Over Ice, Pour 2 oz Cranberry Syrup. Fill with Soda Water. Splash with Orange Syrup.

 CRANBERRY CREAM SODA
Over Ice, Pour 1½ oz Cranberry Syrup, ½ oz Vanilla Syrup. Add Soda Water to ½" from top of cup. Fill with Half-and-Half.

 CRANBERRY GRAPE COOLER
Over Ice, Pour 1 oz each Syrup: Cranberry, Grape. Fill with Soda Water.

CRANBERRY JUBILEE SODA

Over Ice, Pour 1 oz Cranberry Syrup, ½ oz each Syrup: Lemon, Coconut. Fill with Soda Water.

 CRANBERRY SCENTED SPARKLING CIDER

Over Ice, Pour 6 oz Apple Juice, ½ oz Cranberry Syrup. Splash with Lime Syrup.

 CRANBERRY SPARKLER

Over Ice, Pour 2 oz Cranberry Syrup. Fill with Soda Water. Splash with Lemon Syrup.

 CRANBERRY TANGERINE CREAM SODA

Over Ice, Pour 1 oz each Syrup: Cranberry, Mandarino. Add Soda Water to ½" from top of cup. Fill with Half-and-Half.

 CREAM PUFF SODA

Over Ice, Pour 1 oz each Syrup: Vanilla, Coconut. Fill with Milk to ½" from top of cup. Top with Whipped Cream. Dust with Vanilla Powder.

 CREAM SODA

Over Ice, Pour 2 oz Vanilla Syrup. Fill with Soda Water.

 CREAMCICLE

Over Ice, Pour 1 oz each Syrup: Orange, Vanilla. Fill with Half-and-Half to ½" from top of cup. Top with Soda Water. Stir.

 CREAMY IRISH COFFEE

Pour 1 oz Irish Cream Syrup. Add Espresso and 6 oz Hot Water. Top with Whipped Cream.

C

 CREAMY MALIBU COFFEE

Pour ½ oz Pineapple Syrup, ¼ oz each Syrup: Rum, Coconut. Add Espresso. Fill with Steamed Milk.

 CREME DE CAFE

Over Ice, Pour 1 oz Coffee Syrup. Add ½ oz each Syrup: Amaretto, Anisette. Fill with Milk. Top with Whipped Cream.

 CRÈME DE CAFE II

Pour ¼ oz Coffee Syrup, ¼ oz Brandy Syrup, splash of Rum Syrup, and Anisette Syrup. Add Espresso. Fill with Steamed/Foamed Milk.

 CREME DE MENTHE COOLER

Over Ice, Pour 2 oz Creme de Menthe Syrup. Fill with Soda Water.

 CREOLE LEMONADE

Over Ice, Pour 1½ oz Lemon Syrup, ½ oz Pineapple Syrup. Fill with Soda Water. Splash with Strawberry Syrup.

 CRIMSON SLIPPER

Over Ice, Pour 1½ oz Cherry Syrup, ½ oz Lemon Syrup. Fill with Soda Water.

 CRYSTAL SPRINGS ORANGE SODA

Over Ice, Pour 1 oz each Syrup: Orange, Apple. Fill with Soda Water. Splash with Grenadine Syrup.

 CUBA LIBRE

Over Ice, Pour 1 oz Rum Syrup, ⅓ oz Lime Syrup. Fill with Cola.

 CUBAN HOT COFFEE

Pour ½ oz Rum Syrup, ¼ oz Creme de Cacao Syrup. Add Hot Water to 1" from top of cup. Top with a double shot of Espresso.

D

 DAIQUIRI COOLER
Over Ice, Pour ⅓ oz
Rum Syrup, ⅔ oz Lime
Syrup. Fill with Soda
Water. Splash with
Lime Syrup.

 DATE NUT DREAM CREAM
Over Ice, Pour 1 oz
each Syrup: Tamarindo,
Hazelnut. Add Soda
Water to ½" from top
of cup. Fill with Half-
and-Half.

 DEMPSEY COOLER
Over Ice, Pour 1½ oz
Apple Syrup, ½ oz
Anisette Syrup. Fill
with Soda Water.
Splash with Grenadine
Syrup.

 DENISE
Pour a triple shot of
Espresso. Add Ice. Add
1 oz Vanilla Syrup. Fill
with 1% Milk.

DEPTH CHARGE
Triple shot of Espresso.

DOPPIO
Double shot of
Espresso with 1
measure (shot) of
Water.

 DOUBLE
Double measure of
Espresso with double
measure of Water.

DOUBLE DECADENCE
Pour ½ oz Thick
Chocolate Syrup, ¾ oz
Caramel Syrup. Add
Espresso. Stir. Fill with
Foamed/Steamed
Chocolate Milk. Top
with Whipped Cream,
and Thin Threads of
Thick Chocolate
Syrup.

 DOUBLE DECADENT DELIGHT
Over Ice, Pour 1 oz
Mocha Syrup, 1 oz
Caramel Syrup. Add 2
shots, Espresso. Fill
with Half-and-Half.
Top with Whipped
Cream and Chopped
Nuts.

D

DOUBLE NO FUN

A latte made with a double shot of Decaf Espresso and Nonfat Milk.

DOUBLE SHORT HARMLESS FOAMLESS

In an 8 oz cup, Pour double shot Decaf Espresso. Fill with Steamed Milk, no Foam.

DOUBLE STANDARD

A latte made with Decaf Espresso and Foamed/Steamed Half-and-Half.

DOUBLE TALL SKINNY BILLIARD BALL

Same as a "Double Tall Skinny Foamless."

DOUBLE TALL SKINNY FOAMLESS

A tall latte made with a double shot of Espresso and Nonfat Steamed Milk. No Foam.

DOUBLE TALL SKINNY LATTE

A tall latte made with a double shot of Espresso and Nonfat Milk.

DOUBLE TALL SPLIT

Pour 1 Shot of Regular Espresso and 1 Shot of Decaf Espresso. Fill with Foamed/ Steamed Milk.

DOUBLE TALL TWO

A tall latte made with a double shot of Espresso and 2% Milk.

DOUBLE TALL WHIPLESS

A tall mocha with a double shot of Espresso and no Whipped Cream.

DOUBLE TALL

A tall latte with a double shot of Espresso.

D

DUTCH COFFEE

Pour ¾ oz Chocolate Mint Syrup. Add Espresso and 6 oz Hot Water. Top with Whipped Cream.

DUTCH KOFFIE

To 1 shot Espresso add 6 oz Hot Water. Top with 1 pat, Butter. Garnish with Cinnamon Stick and serve with Sugar.

DOUG'S DOWNUNDER

Over Ice, Pour ⅔ oz each Syrup: Kiwi, Passion Fruit, Coconut. Fill with Soda Water.

DREAM CREAM— CREAM SODA

Over Ice, Pour 1⅓ oz Orange Syrup, ⅔ oz Vanilla Syrup. Add 3 oz Soda Water. Fill with Half-and-Half.

DREAM CREAM ITALIAN SODA

Over Ice, Pour 1⅓ oz Orange Syrup, ⅔ oz Vanilla Syrup. Fill with Soda Water.

DREAM CREAM STEAMER

Pour ½ oz each Syrup: Orange, Vanilla. Fill with Foamed/Steamed Milk. Top with Whipped Cream. Dust with Vanilla Powder.

DROP KICK

Pour 5 oz Hot Water. Top with double shot of Espresso.

DRY CAPPUCCINO

First foam and steam Milk. Set pitcher aside. Pour Espresso. Reach into pitcher with spatula and pull out dense Foam to fill and top with 2" "cap" of Foam. Dust with Chocolate Powder or Nutmeg.

DUTCH CHOCOLATE ALMOND LATTE

Pour ½ oz each Syrup: Chocolate Mint, Almond. Add Espresso. Fill with Foamed/ Steamed Milk.

E

DUTCH COFFEE

Pour ¾ oz Chocolate Mint Syrup. Add Espresso and 6 oz Hot Water. Top with Whipped Cream.

DUTCH KOFFIE

To 1 shot Espresso add 6 oz Hot Water. Top with 1 pat, Butter. Garnish with Cinnamon Stick and serve with Sugar.

EAST INDIA COOLER

Over Ice, Pour ⅔ oz each Syrup: Coffee, Orange, Pineapple. Fill with Soda Water.

EASTER EGG HATCH

Over Ice, Pour ⅓ oz each Syrup: Irish Cream, Vanilla, Orange. Fill with Egg Nog. Sprinkle with Nutmeg.

EGG NOG CAPPUCCINO

Fill steam pitcher ⅓ full with equal parts of Egg Nog and Milk. Foam and steam Egg Nog-Milk mixture. Set pitcher aside. Pour Espresso. Allow steamed Egg Nog-Milk mixture to pour under foam to ½" from top of cup. Top with 2" "cap" of dense Foam. Dust with Chocolate Powder or Nutmeg.

EGG NOG LATTE

Pour Espresso. Fill with Foamed/Steamed Egg Nog. Dust with Cinnamon or Nutmeg Powder.

EGG NOG MOCHA

Pour 1½ oz Thick Chocolate Syrup. Add Espresso. Stir. Fill with Foamed/Steamed Egg Nog. Dust with Nutmeg.

E

EGG NOG STEAMER

Fill with Foamed/ Steamed Egg Nog. Top with Whipped Cream. Sprinkle with Nutmeg.

EL PRESIDENTE COOLER

Over Ice, Pour ⅔ oz each Syrup: Lime, Pineapple, Cherry. Fill with Soda Water.

EMERALD ZOMBIE

Over Ice, Pour ½ oz each Syrup: Melon, Mint, Coconut, Pineapple. Fill with Soda Water.

ESPRESSO

Pour Espresso in a short cup.

ESPRESSO CHERRY FLIP

Pour ¾ oz Cherry Syrup. Add 8 oz Hot Water. Top with Espresso and Whipped Cream.

ESPRESSO COLA FIZZ

Over Ice, Pour 1 oz Rum Syrup, ½ oz Lemon Juice. Add espresso. Fill with Cola.

ESPRESSO CON GHIACCIO

In an 8 oz cup, Pour Espresso. Fill to ½" from top with Ice. Add 1½ oz of Cold Milk.

ESPRESSO CON GHIACCIO E LATTE

Pour Ice into short cup and add 2 oz Cold Milk. In separate short cup, Pour Espresso.

ESPRESSO CON PANNA

Pour Espresso in a short cup. Top with a dollop of Whipped Cream.

ESPRESSO EGG NOG

Pour Espresso. Add Ice. Fill with Egg Nog. Stir. Dust with Powdered Nutmeg.

E

ESPRESSO GRAND ROYAL

Pour ½ oz each Syrup: Orange, Lemon. Add Espresso. Add lots of Steamed Milk and a short layer of Foamed Milk. Top with Whipped Cream. Splash with Cherry Syrup.

ESPRESSO MANDARINO

Pour ½ oz Mandarino Syrup. Add Espresso.

ESPRESSO NUDGE

Pour ½ oz Creme de Cacao Syrup, ¼ oz Mandarino Syrup, 2 oz Hot Water. Add a double shot Espresso. Dust with Cinnamon and Nutmeg. Add Cinnamon Stick.

ESPRESSO ROMANO

Pour Espresso. Add a Twist of Lemon in a short cup.

ESPRESSO SHOOTER

Pour Espresso in a short cup.

ESPRESSO SPICED APPLE

Pour ½ oz Apple Syrup, ¼ oz Cinnamon Syrup. Add 8 oz Hot Water. Top with Espresso.

ESPRESSO TROPICANA

Pour a double shot of Espresso. Add Ice. Add 1½ oz Rum Syrup, ½ oz Coconut Syrup. Add 2 oz Half-and-Half. Top with Soda Water.

ESPRESSO WITH A TWIST

Pour ½ oz Orange Syrup. Add Espresso. Garnish with Orange Peel.

EYE-OPENER

Pour ¾ oz Anisette Syrup. Add a double shot Espresso. Fill with Foamed/Steamed Milk.

F

 FANTASIA

Pour 1 oz of any Flavored Syrup. Fill with Foamed Milk. Dust with Nutmeg.

 FERRARI

Over Ice, Pour 1½ oz Cherry Syrup, ½ oz Amaretto Syrup. Fill with Soda Water.

 FIFTH AVENUE COOLER

Over Ice, Pour 1 oz each Syrup: Apricot, Creme de Cacao. Fill with Soda Water to ½" from top of cup. Top with Half-and-Half.

FLAMINGO CANARY

Over Ice, Pour 1⅓ oz Strawberry Syrup, ⅔ oz Lemon Syrup. Fill with Soda Water.

 FLAMINGO FLAME SODA

Over Ice, Pour ½ oz Apple Syrup. Add Grapefruit Juice to ½" from top of cup. Top with ⅓ oz Cherry Syrup.

FLAVORED CAPPUCCINO

Pour 1 oz Flavored Syrup into a steaming pitcher. Add 6-8 oz Cold Milk. Foam and steam the Milk-Syrup mixture. Set pitcher aside. Pour Espresso. Allow flavored Steamed Milk to pour under Foam to ½" from top of cup. Top with 2" "cap" of Foam. Dust with any Flavored Powder.

FLAVORED MOCHA

Pour ¾ oz Macadamia Nut Syrup. Add 1 tsp Sweetened Ground Chocolate. Add Espresso. Fill with Steamed/Foamed Milk. Top with Whipped Cream.

 FLORADORA COOLER

Over Ice, Pour 1 oz each Syrup: Lime, Orange. Fill with Soda Water. Splash with Grenadine Syrup.

F

 FLYING GRASSHOPPER

Over Ice, Pour 1⅓ oz Creme de Menthe Syrup, ½ oz Creme de Cacao Syrup. Fill with Soda Water.

 FLYING KANGAROO

Over Ice, Pour ½ oz each Syrup: Coconut, Pineapple, Orange; ¼ oz each Syrup: Banana, Rum. Add Soda Water to ½" from top of cup. Fill with Half-and-Half.

 FOG CUTTER

Over Ice, Pour ⅔ oz each Syrup: Creme de Cacao, Orange, Almond. Fill with Soda Water.

 FRAPPE

Over Ice, Pour 2 oz any Flavored Syrup. Fill glass halfway with Soda Water.

 FRENCH COLADA

Over Ice, Pour ⅔ oz each Syrup: Coconut, Pineapple; ⅓ oz each Syrup: Creme de Cassis, Rum. Add Soda Water to ½" from top of cup. Fill with Half-and-Half.

 FRENCH STALLION

Pour ½ oz Hazelnut Syrup, ¼ oz Coffee Syrup. Add Espresso and 6 oz Hot Water. Top with Whipped Cream and Mixed Sprinkles.

 FRENCH VANILLA LATTE

Pour ½ oz Vanilla Syrup, ¼ oz Hazelnut Syrup. Add Espresso. Fill with Foamed/ Steamed Milk and top with Whipped Cream. Dust with Vanilla Powder.

 FRITZER

Over Ice, Pour 1 oz Lemon Syrup. Fill with Soda Water or Ginger Ale. Splash with Grenadine Syrup.

FROSTED MINT LATTE

Pour ¾ oz Mint Syrup. Add Espresso. Fill with Foamed/Steamed Milk.

 **FRUIT FANTASIA**

Over Ice, Pour ⅔ oz each Syrup: Watermelon, Pineapple, Coconut. Add Soda Water to ½" from top of cup. Fill with Half-and-Half. Splash with Grenadine Syrup.

 FUZZY LEMON FIZZ

Over Ice, Pour 1½ oz Lemon Syrup, ½ oz Peach Syrup. Fill with Soda Water. Splash with Grenadine Syrup.

 FUZZY NAVEL

Over Ice, Pour 1¼ oz Peach Syrup, ¾ oz Orange Syrup. Fill with Soda Water. Splash with Grenadine Syrup.

 GENTLE SEA BREEZE

Over Ice, Pour 1 oz Cranberry Syrup. Fill with Grapefruit Juice. Splash with Cranberry Syrup.

 GEORGIA DREAM CREAM SODA

Over Ice, Pour 1¼ oz Peach Syrup, ½ oz Vanilla Syrup, ¼ oz Lemon Syrup. Add Soda Water to ½" from top of cup. Fill with Half-and-Half. Splash with Lime Syrup.

 GEORGIA MINT JULEP

Over Ice, Pour 1¾ oz Peach Syrup, ¼ oz Mint Syrup. Fill with Milk. Top with Whipped Cream. Splash with Mint Syrup.

G

 GEORGIA RUM COOLER

Over Ice, Pour 1¼ oz Rum Syrup, ½ oz Grenadine Syrup, ¼ oz Lemon Syrup. Fill with Soda Water. Splash with Praline Syrup.

 GERMAN CHOCOLATE CAKE MOCHA

Pour ¼ oz Macadamia Nut Syrup, ¼ oz Hazelnut Syrup, ½ oz Coconut Syrup. Add Espresso. Fill with Foamed/Steamed Chocolate Milk. Top with Whipped Cream. Garnish with Chocolate Sprinkles and Vanilla Sprinkles.

 GERMAN CHOCOLATE MOCHA

Pour ½ oz Thick Chocolate Syrup, ¼ oz Thick Caramel Syrup. Add ¼ oz each Syrup: Coconut, Hazelnut. Add Espresso. Stir. Fill with Foamed/Steamed Milk. Top with Whipped Cream and Chocolate Sprinkles.

 GERMAN KIRSCH COFFEE

Pour ¼ oz Cherry Syrup. Add Espresso and 2 tsp Brown Sugar. Fill with Hot Water. Top with Whipped Cream.

 GINGER LEMON SODA

Over Ice, Pour 1 oz each Syrup: Ginger, Lemon. Fill with Soda Water.

GINGER MINT COOLER

Over Ice, Pour 1 oz Mint Syrup. Add 4 oz Ginger Ale. Fill with Soda Water.

G

 GINGER ORANGE CREAM

Over Ice, Pour 1 oz Orange Syrup. Add Ginger Ale to ½" from top of cup. Fill with Half-and-Half.

 GLACIER SODA

Over Ice, Pour 1¼ oz Anisette Syrup, ¾ oz Peppermint Syrup. Fill with Soda Water.

 GLOOM LIFTER

Pour Espresso. Add Ice. Pour 1 oz Raspberry Syrup, ½ oz Lemon Syrup. Fill with Milk.

 GOING APE

Pour ¾ oz Thick Chocolate Syrup. Add ⅓ oz Banana Syrup. Add Espresso. Stir. Fill with Foamed/Steamed Milk and top with Whipped Cream and Chocolate Sprinkles.

 GOLDEN DAWN

Over Ice, Pour 1 oz Apple Syrup. Add ½ oz each Syrup: Apricot, Orange. Fill with Soda Water. Splash with Grenadine Syrup.

 GOLDEN FLAMINGO FIZZ

Over Ice, Pour 1½ oz Cherry Syrup. Fill to ¼" from top of cup with Soda Water. Top with ½ oz Lemon Syrup.

 GOLDEN SLIPPER

Over Ice, Pour ⅔ oz Lemon Syrup, 1⅓ oz Apricot Syrup. Fill with Soda Water.

 GOLDEN SOMBRERO FIZZ

Pour 1½ oz Apple Syrup, ½ oz Cinnamon Syrup, ½ oz Honey. Stir. Add Ice. Fill with Soda Water. Splash with Lemon Syrup.

G

 GRAND ROYAL FIZZ

Over Ice, Pour ½ oz each Syrup: Coffee, Lemon, Maraschino, Orange. Add Half-and-Half to ½" from top of cup. Fill with Soda Water.

 GRANDMA EVE'S ICED APPLECCINO

Over Ice, Pour 2 oz Apple Syrup, ½ oz Cinnamon Syrup. Add 2 shots, Espresso. Fill with Half-and-Half. Top with Whipped Cream or Milk Foam. Garnish with Grated Nutmeg.

 GRANITA

A machine-made slush drink flavored with sugar and either a coffee or fruit essence. A milk or nondairy cream base can be added.

 GRANOLA BAR LATTE

Pour ⅓ oz each Thick Syrup: Honey, Molasses. Add ½ oz Coconut Syrup. Add Espresso. Stir. Fill with Foamed/Steamed Milk and Whipped Cream.

 GRAPE & LIME COOLER

Over Ice, Pour 1 oz each Syrup: Grape, Lime. Fill with Soda Water.

 GRAPE BERRY CREAM SODA

Over Ice, Pour 1 oz each Syrup: Grape, Blueberry. Add Soda Water to ½" from top of cup. Fill with Half-and-Half.

 GRAPE CREAM SODA

Over Ice, Pour 1 oz each Syrup: Grape, Vanilla. Add Soda Water to ½" from top. Fill with Half-and-Half.

GRAPE CRUSH
Over Ice, Pour 1⅓ oz
Grape Syrup. Add ⅓ oz
each Syrup: Cranberry,
Lime. Fill with Soda
Water.

 GRAPE NUT LATTE
Pour ½ oz each Syrup:
Grape, Almond. Add
Espresso. Fill with
Foamed/Steamed Milk.

 **GRAPEFRUIT KIWI
SODA**
Over Ice, Pour 1 oz
each Syrup: Grapefruit,
Kiwi. Fill with Soda
Water.

 **GRASSHOPPER
CREAM COOLER**
Over Ice, Pour 1⅓ oz
Creme de Menthe
Syrup, ⅔ oz Creme de
Cacao Syrup. Add 3 oz
Soda Water. Fill with
Half-and-Half.

 **GREEN DEVIL
COOLER**
Over Ice, Pour 1½ oz
Creme de Menthe Syrup,
½ oz Lime Syrup. Fill
with Soda Water.

 **GREEN DRAGON
COOLER**
Over Ice, Pour 1½ oz
Creme de Menthe
Syrup, ½ oz Lemon
Syrup. Fill with Soda
Water.

 GREEN OPAL
Over Ice, Pour 1½ oz
Lime Syrup, ½ oz
Anisette Syrup. Fill
with Soda Water.

 HAMMERHEAD
Pour a double shot of
Espresso. Add 5 oz
French-roast Coffee.

 HARLEM COOLER
Over Ice, Pour 1½ oz
Pineapple Syrup, ½ oz
Maraschino Syrup. Fill
with Soda Water.

 HARVARD COOLER
Over Ice, Pour 2 oz
Apple Syrup. Fill with
Soda Water.

H

 HAVANA CREAM COOLER

Over Ice, Pour ⅔ oz each Syrup: Coffee, Pineapple, Lime. Fill with Soda Water to ½" from top of cup. Top with 2 oz Half-and-Half.

 HAVANA SPECIAL

Over Ice, Pour 1¼ oz Pineapple Syrup, ¾ oz Rum Syrup. Fill with Soda Water. Splash with ¼ oz Grenadine Syrup.

 HAWAIIAN CHILL

Over ice, Pour ¼ oz each Syrup: Mango, Orange. Fill with Soda Water to ¼" from top of cup. Top with ½ oz Kiwi Syrup.

 HAWAIIAN COFFEE

Pour 1 oz Coconut Syrup. Add Espresso. Fill with Foamed/ Steamed Milk. Garnish with Toasted Coconut.

 HAWAIIAN DELIGHT

Over Ice, Pour 1 oz each Syrup: Pineapple, Coconut. Fill with Soda Water to ½" from top of cup. Top with Half-and-Half.

 HAWAIIAN ESPRESSO

Pour Espresso. Into a steaming pitcher, Pour 1 oz Coconut Syrup and 6 oz Cold Milk. Foam and steam the Flavored Milk. Top the Espresso with equal parts of Steamed and Foamed Flavored Milk.

 HAWAIIAN ICED COFFEE

Pour Espresso. Add Ice. Add ⅔ oz each Syrup: Pineapple, Passion Fruit, Coconut. Fill with Milk. Top with Whipped Cream.

H

HAZELNUT DIVINITY LATTE

Pour ½ oz Hazelnut Syrup, ¼ oz Creme de Cacao Syrup. Stir in 1 teaspoon Dutch Chocolate Powder. Pour Espresso. Stir. Fill with Foamed/Steamed Milk.

HAZLENUT FUDGE LATTE

Pour ½ oz each Syrup: Hazelnut, Chocolate Fudge. Add Espresso. Stir. Fill with Foamed/Steamed Milk. Top with Whipped Cream and Chocolate Sprinkles.

HAZLENUT HAMMER

Pour ½ oz Hazelnut Syrup, ½ oz Chocolate Syrup. Fill with Foamed/Steamed Milk. Top with Whipped Cream and Chocolate Powder.

HAZELNUT HOT CHOCOLATE

Pour 1¼ oz Thick Chocolate Syrup, ¼ oz Hazelnut Syrup. Fill with Foamed/Steamed Milk. Stir. Top with Whipped Cream. Dust with Chocolate Powder.

HAZELNUT LATTE

Pour ¾ oz Hazelnut Syrup. Add Espresso. Fill with Foamed/Steamed Milk.

HAZLENUT MELT

Pour ¾ oz Hazelnut Syrup. Add Espresso. Add Hot Water to ½" from top of cup. Top with 15 Miniature Marshmallows. Let stand for 1-2 minutes to allow Marshmallows to melt.

HAZELNUT TRUFFLE LATTE

Pour ½ oz Thick Chocolate Syrup, ½ oz Hazelnut Syrup. Add Espresso. Stir. Fill with Foamed/Steamed Milk.

H

 HIGHBALL SODA
Over Ice, Pour 1 oz each Syrup: Lemon, Mint. Fill with Soda Water.

 HONEY-CREAM COFFEE
Pour 1 oz Brandy Syrup. Add Espresso and 6 oz Hot Water. Top with Whipped Cream sweetened with Honey and a dash of Cloves.

 HONEY ESPRESSO
Pour 1¼ oz Honey. Add 8 oz Hot Water and stir. Top with Espresso.

 HONEY ICED ESPRESSO
In 8 oz cup, Pour Espresso. Add Ice. Add 2 oz of Half-and-Half. Add tablespoon of Honey. Stir.

 HONEY ICED ESPRESSO II
Over Ice or Frozen Americano Cubes, Pour 2 shots Espresso and 4 oz Half-and-Half. Add ½ oz Honey.

 HONEY RUM COFFEE
Pour ½ oz Rum Syrup and ½ tsp Honey. Add Espresso, 6 oz Hot Water and 1 oz Half-and-Half. Garnish with Nutmeg.

 HONEY VANILLA CREAM LATTE
Pour ¾ oz Honey, ⅓ oz Vanilla Syrup. Add Espresso. Stir. Fill with Foamed/Steamed Milk.

 HONOLULU COOLER
Over Ice, Pour ⅔ oz each Syrup: Orange, Pineapple, Passion Fruit. Fill with Soda Water.

 HOT AFTER DINNER MINT STEAMER
Pour ½ oz each Syrup: Creme de Menthe, Chocolate. Fill with Foamed/Steamed Milk. Top with Whipped Cream.

H

HOT APPLE PIE

Pour ¾ oz Apple Syrup. Add ¼ oz each Syrup: Hazelnut, Cinnamon. Add 6 oz Hot Water. Add Espresso.

HOT BRICK TODDY

Pour ¾ oz Praline Syrup. Add Espresso. Fill with Foamed/ Steamed Milk.

HOT BUTTERED RUM LATTE

Pour ½ oz Rum Syrup, ¼ oz Thick Butterscotch Syrup. Add Espresso. Stir. Fill with Foamed/Steamed Milk.

HOT BUTTERED COFFEE

Place 1 tablespoon Brown Sugar, 1 tablespoon Soft Butter in cup. Add pinch of Cinnamon, and a pinch of Nutmeg Powder. Add Hot Water to 1" from top of cup. Stir. Top with Espresso.

HOT CHOCOLATE

Pour 2 oz Thick Chocolate Syrup. Fill with Foamed/Steamed Milk. Stir. Top with Whipped Cream and dust with Chocolate Powder.

HOT CHOCOLATE BANANA

Pour ½ oz each Syrup: Chocolate, Banana. Fill with Foamed/Steamed Milk and top with Whipped Cream and Powdered Chocolate.

HOT CHOCOLATE MOCHA

Pour ⅓ oz Rum Syrup, ½ oz Crème de Cacao Syrup, ⅓ oz Almond Syrup. Add 2 shots, Espresso. Fill with Steamed/Foamed Chocolate Milk. Top with Whipped Cream. Garnish with Cinnamon, Nutmeg, Chocolate Shavings.

H

HOT COCONUT COFFEE

Pour ¾ oz Coconut Syrup. Add Hot Water to ½" from top of cup. Top with Espresso.

HOT COCONUT COFFEE II

Pour 1 oz Coconut Syrup. Add Espresso and 6 oz Hot Water. Top with Whipped Cream.

HOT GOLD

Pour ½ oz each Syrup: Amaretto, Orange. Add Espresso. Fill with Foamed/Steamed Milk.

HOT MOCHA HONEY

Pour ¾ oz Thick Chocolate Syrup. Add ¾ oz Honey. Add Espresso. Stir. Fill with Foamed/Steamed Milk. Top with Whipped Cream and Chocolate Powder.

HOT SPICED CRANBERRY

In an 8 oz cup, Pour ½ oz each Syrup: Cranberry, Rum. Add ¼ oz Cinnamon Syrup. Fill with Hot Water. Dust with Nutmeg.

HOT SPRINGS COOLER

Over Ice, Pour 2 oz Pineapple Syrup. Fill with Soda Water. Splash with Maraschino Syrup.

HOT TODDY

Steam 8 oz Apple Juice. Pour into cup. Add ½ teaspoon Brown Sugar. Stir. Dust with Cinnamon.

HUMMER

Over Ice, Pour ⅔ oz each Syrup: Chocolate, Coffee, Rum. Add Soda Water to ½" from top of cup. Fill with Half-and-Half.

I

HURRICANE SODA
Over Ice, Pour 1 oz each Syrup: Apple, Pineapple. Fill with Soda Water. Splash with Grenadine Syrup.

ICED BREVÉ
Pour Espresso. Add Ice. Fill with Half-and-Half.

ICED CAPPUCCINO
Pour Espresso. Add Ice. Fill with Milk. Top with Whipped Cream. Dust with Nutmeg.

ICED CHOCOLATE ALMOND MOO
Over Ice, Pour 1 oz each Syrup: Chocolate, Almond. Fill with Cold Milk. Dust with Chocolate Powder.

ICED CHOCOLATE ESPRESSO
Pour 1½ oz Chocolate Syrup. Add Espresso. Fill with Ice. Add Cold Milk to ½" from top of cup. Top with Whipped Cream. Place one Chocolate-covered Coffee Bean on top.

ICED COFFEE
Over Ice, Pour Espresso. Fill with Cold Water.

ICED COFFEE À LA REINE
Over Ice, Pour 1 oz Kahlua Syrup, 3 oz Half-and-Half. Add 2 shots, Espresso. Fill with Club Soda.

ICED COFFEE ROYALE
Over Ice, Pour 1 oz Coffee Syrup, ½ oz Chocolate Syrup, ¼ oz each Syrup: Coconut, Vanilla. Fill to ¼" from top of cup with Soda Water. Top with Half-and-Half.

ICED BREVÉ LATTE
Pour Espresso. Fill with Ice. Top with Half-and-Half.

I

 ICED BREVÉ MOCHA

Pour 2 oz Thick Chocolate Syrup. Add Espresso. Stir. Fill with Ice. Pour Half-and-Half to ½" from top of cup. Top with Whipped Cream and Chocolate Sprinkles.

 ICED ALMOND LATTE

Pour 1 oz Almond Syrup. Add Espresso and Ice. Fill with Milk. Top with Whipped Cream.

 ICED BANANA MOCHA

Pour ¾ oz Banana Syrup, ¼ oz Chocolate Syrup. Add Espresso and Ice. Fill with Cold Milk. Top with Whipped Cream and Chocolate Sprinkles.

 ICED CINNAMON COFFEE

Over Ice, pour Espresso pulled with 2 tsp Ground Cinnamon and 2 tsp Cloves. Add 1 tsp Brown Sugar. Fill with Half-and-Half.

 ICED DOUBLE TALL CAFE AMORÈ

Over Ice, Pour 1 oz Tiramisu Syrup, ⅛ oz Orange Syrup. Add 2 shots, Espresso. Fill with Milk. Stir. Top with Whipped Cream.

 ICED ESPRESSO

Use a short cup. Pour Espresso. Add Ice.

 ICED GINGER COFFEE CREAM

Pour ¾ oz Ginger Syrup. Add Espresso and Ice. Fill with Cold Water to ½" from top of cup. Top with 2 oz Heavy Cream.

I

 ICED IRISH COCONUT COFFEE

Over Ice, Pour, ½ oz each Syrup: Irish Cream, Coconut. Add Espresso. Fill with Cold Milk. Top with Whipped Cream.

 ICED LATTE

Pour Espresso. Add Ice. Fill with Milk.

 ICED MOCHA

Pour 2 oz Thick Chocolate Syrup. Add Espresso. Stir. Add Ice. Fill with Milk. Top with Whipped Cream and Chocolate Sprinkles.

 ICED RUM COFFEE

Pour 1½ oz Rum Syrup. Add Espresso. Fill with Ice. Fill with Milk. Splash with Coffee Syrup.

 ICED VANILLA MOCHA

Over Ice, Pour ½ oz Vanilla Syrup, 1 oz Chocolate Syrup. Add Espresso. Fill with Milk. Top with Whipped Cream.

 ICY MINTY MOCHA

Pour 1½ oz Thick Chocolate Syrup, 1 oz Mint Syrup. Add Espresso. Stir. Add Ice. Fill with Milk. Top with Whipped Cream and Chocolate Sprinkles.

 IMPERIAL EGG NOG

Over Ice, Pour 1 oz Amaretto Syrup. Fill with Cold Egg Nog. Stir. Dust with Powdered Nutmeg.

 INDIAN SUMMER

Over Ice, Pour 2 oz Apple Syrup. Fill with Soda Water. Add Cinnamon Stick.

I

 INDIAN SUMMER 2
Over Ice, Pour 1 oz
Vanilla Syrup. Add
Apple Cider to ½"
from top of cup. Fill
with Soda Water. Add
Cinnamon Stick.

 **INNOCENT
PASSION**
Over Ice, Pour 1 oz
Passion Fruit Syrup,
½ oz each Syrup:
Cranberry, Lemon. Fill
with Soda Water.

 IRISH COFFEE
Pour ¾ oz Irish Cream
Syrup. Add Espresso.
Fill with Hot Water.
Top with Whipped
Cream.

 **IRISH COW
STEAMER**
Pour 1 oz Irish Cream
Syrup. Fill with
Foamed/Steamed Milk.
Top with Whipped
Cream.

**IRISH CREAM
BREVÉ**
Pour ¾ oz Irish Cream
Syrup. Add Espresso. Fill
with Foamed/Steamed
Half-and-Half.

**IRISH CREAM
BROWNIE LATTE**
Pour ¾ oz Thick
Chocolate Syrup, 1/3 oz
Irish Cream Syrup. Add
Espresso. Stir. Fill with
Foamed/Steamed Milk.

**IRISH CREAM EGG
NOG LATTE**
Pour ¾ oz Irish Cream
Syrup. Add Espresso.
Fill with Foamed/
Steamed Egg Nog.
Dust with Chocolate
Powder.

IRISH ESPRESSO
Pour ¾ oz Irish Cream
Syrup. Add 8 oz Hot
Water. Top with Espresso.

IRISH NUT
Pour ½ oz each Syrup:
Hazelnut, Irish Cream.
Add Espresso. Fill with
Steamed Milk. Dust
with Nutmeg.

I.R.S. CREAM SODA

Over Ice, Pour ⅔ oz each Syrup: Cherry, Lime, Pineapple. Add Soda Water to ½" from top of cup. Fill with Half-and-Half. Top with Whipped Cream. Garnish with Money Umbrella.

 ISLAND COOLER

Over Ice, Pour ½ oz each Syrup: Orange, Mango, Passion Fruit, Pineapple. Fill with Soda Water. Splash with Cranberry Syrup.

 ITALIAN COLADA

Over Ice, Pour ⅔ oz each Syrup: Coconut, Pineapple, ⅓ oz each Syrup: Amaretto, Rum. Add Soda Water to ½" from top of cup. Fill with Half-and-Half.

 ITALIAN COFFEE

Pour ¾ oz Amaretto Syrup. Add Hot Water to 1" from top of cup. Top with double shot of Espresso.

 ITALIAN CREAM SODA

Over Ice, Pour 2 oz of any Flavored Syrup. Add Soda Water to ½" from top of cup. Fill with Half-and-Half.

 ITALIAN SODA

Over Ice, Pour 2 oz of any Flavored Syrup. Fill with Soda Water.

 ITALIAN SOMBRERO

Pour ¾ oz Amaretto Syrup. Add Espresso. Fill with Foamed/ Steamed Half-and-Half.

 JAMAICA FEVER

Over Ice, Pour ½ oz each Syrup: Pineapple, Mango, Cherry, Rum. Fill with Soda Water. Splash with Lime Syrup.

 JAMAICA HOP

Pour ½ oz each Syrup: Coffee, Creme de Cacao. Add a double shot Espresso. Fill with Foamed/Steamed Milk.

J

JAMAICAN BANANA CREAM LATTE

Pour ½ oz Banana Syrup, ¼ oz each Syrup: Rum, Coconut. Add Espresso. Fill with Foamed/Steamed Milk. Splash with Creme de Cacao Syrup.

JAMAICAN COFFEE

Pour ½ oz Coffee Syrup, ¼ oz Praline Syrup, 5 oz Hot Water. Add Espresso. Top with Whipped Cream. Dust with Nutmeg.

JAMAICAN COOLER

Over Ice, Pour 1 oz Rum Syrup. Add Espresso. Fill with Water. Top with Whipped Cream.

JAMAICAN LATTE

Pour ½ oz each Syrup: Cinnamon, Creme de Cacao. Add Espresso. Fill with Foamed/Steamed Milk.

JAMOCHA

Pour 1 oz Rum Syrup. Add pinch, Cinnamon. Add Espresso and 6 oz Hot Water. Top with Whipped Cream.

JAPANESE LATTE

Pour ⅓ oz each Syrup: Cherry, Orange, Almond. Add Espresso. Fill with Foamed/Steamed Milk.

JELLY BEAN LATTE

Pour ½ oz each Syrup: Anisette, any Fruit Flavor. Add Espresso. Fill with Foamed/Steamed Milk.

JELLY BEAN SODA

Over Ice, Pour 1 oz each Syrup: Anisette, any Fruit Flavor. Fill with Soda Water.

JOE BENTI SPECIAL TECHNIQUE

Pull 2 shots, Espresso. Combine with 4 oz Milk. Steam Espresso and Milk together. Top with Whipped Cream and Chocolate Shavings.

K

KAFFEE MILCH

A German latte, made with Viennese roast. The espresso and steamed milk are generally poured into a large ceramic mug simultaneously.

KAHLUA BAVARIAN COFFEE

Pour 1 oz Kahlua Syrup, ½ oz Peppermint Syrup. Add Espresso and 6 oz Hot Water. Top with Whipped Cream.

KAHLUA EGG CREAM

Over Ice, Pour 2 oz Coffee Syrup. Add Cold Milk to 1" from top of cup. Fill with Soda Water.

KAHLUA ALMOND FUDGE LATTE

Pour ½ oz each Syrup: Almond, Chocolate. Add Espresso. Fill with Foamed/Steamed Milk. Dust with Chocolate Powder.

KAHLUA ALMOND FUDGE SODA

Over Ice, Pour ⅔ oz each Syrup: Coffee, Almond, Chocolate. Fill with Soda Water.

KAHLUA COFFEE

Pour ¾ oz Creme de Cacao Syrup. Add 5 oz Hot Water. Add Espresso. Top with Whipped Cream. Dust with Nutmeg.

KAHLUA & CREAM

Pour ¾ oz Creme de Cacao Syrup. Add Espresso. Fill with Foamed/Steamed Half-and-Half.

KAHLUA & CREAM COOLER

Pour Espresso. Add Ice. Pour 1½ oz Creme de Cacao Syrup. Fill with Half-and-Half.

KAHLUA EGG NOG LATTE

Pour ¾ oz Creme de Cacao Syrup. Add Espresso. Fill with Foamed/Steamed Egg Nog. Dust with Chocolate Powder or Nutmeg.

K

KAHLUA LATTE

Pour ¾ oz Coffee Syrup. Add Espresso. Fill with Foamed/Steamed Milk.

KAHLUA-MINT COFFEE

Pour ⅓ oz Kahlua Syrup, ⅓ oz Mint Syrup, ⅓ oz Irish Cream Syrup. Add Espresso and 6 oz Hot Water. Top with Whipped Cream.

KAHLUA MOCHA

Pour 1 oz Chocolate Syrup, ½ oz Kahlua Syrup. Add Espresso. Fill with Steamed/Foamed Milk. Top with Whipped Cream.

KAHLUA-N-CREAM BREVÉ

Pour ¾ oz Coffee Syrup. Add Espresso. Fill with Foamed/Steamed Half-and-Half. Top with Whipped Cream and splash with Coffee Syrup.

KAHLUA PEACHES AND CREAM

Over Ice, Pour 1 oz Kahlua Syrup, 1 oz Peach Syrup. Add Espresso. Fill with Half-and-Half.

KAHLUA STRAWBERRIES AND CREAM

Over Ice, Pour 1 oz Kahlua Syrup, 1 oz Strawberry Syrup. Add Espresso. Fill with Half-and-Half. Garnish with Strawberry.

KAHLUA TOASTED ALMOND

Over Ice, pour ½ oz Kahlua Syrup, ¼ oz Amaretto Syrup. Add Espresso. Fill with Half-and-Half.

KEOKE COFFEE

Pour ¼ oz Brandy Syrup, ¼ oz Kahlua Syrup, ¼ oz Crème de Cacao Syrup. Add Espresso and 6 oz Hot Water.

L

 KEY LIME CREAM SODA

Over Ice, Pour 1½ oz Lime Syrup, ½ oz Vanilla Syrup. Add Soda Water to ½" from top of cup. Top with Half-and-Half and Whipped Cream.

 KIWI & CREAM SODA

Over Ice, Pour 1 oz each Syrup: Kiwi, Vanilla. Add Soda Water to ½" from top of cup. Fill with Half-and-Half.

 KIWI & GINGER SPRITZER

Over Ice, Pour 1 oz Kiwi Syrup. Fill with equal parts Ginger Ale and Soda Water.

 KLONDIKE COOLER

Over Ice, Pour ⅓ oz each Syrup: Orange, Apricot, Pineapple. Fill with Ginger Ale.

 LACCINO

A latte-cappuccino combination, with less milk and more foam than a standard latte.

 LAKE BREEZE

Over Ice, Pour ⅔ oz each Syrup: Strawberry, Cranberry. Add ⅓ oz each syrup: Lemon, Pineapple. Fill with Soda Water.

 LATTE

Pour Espresso. Fill with Foamed/Steamed Milk.

LATTE CALDO

Fill cup with Hot Steamed Milk.

LATTE MACCHIATO

Pour Steamed Milk to ½" from top of cup. Top with Peak of Foamed Milk. Pour Espresso through Milk leaving a telltale marking.

L

☕ LATTE ROYALE
Pour ¾ oz any Flavored Syrup. Add Espresso. Fill with Steamed Milk to ¼" from top of cup. Top with Flavored Whipped Cream and any garnish.

☕ LATTECCINO
Pour Espresso. Fill with ⅔ Steamed Milk and ⅓ Foamed Milk.

LEMON AND LIME SODA
Over Ice, Pour 1 oz each Syrup: Lemon, Lime. Fill with Soda Water.

LEMON CHIFFON CREAM PIE SODA
Over Ice, Pour 1⅓ oz Lemon Syrup, ⅔ oz Vanilla Syrup. Fill with Soda Water to ½" from top of cup. Top with Half-and-Half and Whipped Cream.

KIWI MELON SODA
Over Ice, Pour 1 oz each Syrup: Kiwi, Melon. Fill with Soda Water.

LATANGO
Over Ice, Pour ⅔ oz Chocolate Syrup, ½ oz Rum Syrup, ½ oz Coconut Syrup. Add 2 shots, Espresso. Fill with Milk.

☕ LAYERED RASPBERRY LATTE
Foam/Steam with Milk 1 oz Raspberry Syrup. Through this mixture, add Espresso. Top with Foam and dash, Raspberry Syrup

LEMON CHILL
Over Ice, Pour 2 oz Lemon Syrup. Fill with Soda Water.

☕ LEMON ESPRESSO
Pour ¼ oz Lemon Syrup in cup. Add a double shot of Espresso.

LEMON FIZZ
Over Ice, Pour 1¾ oz Lemon Syrup, ¼ oz Mint Syrup. Fill with Soda Water.

L

LEMON RUM COFFEE

Pour ⅓ oz each Syrup: Lemon, Rum. Add Hot Water to 1" from top of cup. Top with Espresso.

LEPRECHAUN

Pour ½ oz Irish Cream Syrup, ¼ oz Mint Syrup. Add Espresso. Fill with Foamed/Steamed Milk. Top with Whipped Cream.

LICORICE COFFEE

Over Ice, Pour ½ oz Licorice Syrup. Add Espresso and 6 oz Water. Top with Whipped Cream and Chocolate Shavings.

LICORICE SPICE LATTE

Pour ¼ oz Anisette Syrup, ¼ oz Cinnamon Syrup, ¼ oz Orange Syrup. Add Espresso. Fill with Foamed/Steamed Milk.

LIME & MINT JULEP

Over Ice, Pour 1 oz each Syrup: Lime, Mint. Fill with Soda Water.

LIME COLA COOLER

Over Ice, Pour ½ oz Lime Syrup. Fill with Cola.

LIME COOLER

Over Ice, Pour 2 oz Lime Syrup. Fill with Soda Water.

LIME RICKEY

Over Ice, Pour 2 oz Lime Syrup. Fill with Soda Water. Splash with Cherry Syrup.

LUNGO (Long Pour)

Pour 1½ oz Water through a Single Measure of Espresso—7 grams.

LUG NUT LATTE

Pour ½ oz Hazelnut Syrup. Add 1 tbs Peanut Butter and Espresso. Stir. Fill with Foamed/Steamed Milk.

M

MACADAMIA NUT LATTE

Pour ¾ oz Macadamia Nut Syrup. Add Espresso. Fill with Foamed/Steamed Milk.

MACCHIATO

Pour Espresso. Top with a dollop of Foamed Milk in a small cup.

MADRAS COOLER

Over Ice, Pour 1 oz each Syrup: Orange, Cranberry. Fill with Soda Water.

MAI TAI COOLER

Over Ice, Pour 1 oz Rum Syrup. Add ¼ oz each Syrup: Almond, Orange, Lime. Fill with Soda Water to ½" from top of cup. Top with ¼ oz Grenadine Syrup.

MAIDEN'S BLUSH SODA

Over Ice, Pour 1 oz each Syrup: Mango, Lemon. Fill with Soda Water. Splash with Grenadine Syrup.

THE MAIN ISLAND SODA

Over Ice, Pour 1 oz each Syrup: Banana, Pineapple. Fill with Soda Water. Splash with Strawberry Syrup.

MALTACCINO

Place heaping tsp Malt Powder in cup. Foam and Steam Milk. Set pitcher aside. Pour Espresso. Stir. Allow Steamed Milk to pour under foam to ½" from top of cup. Top with 2" "cap" of Dense Foam.

MALTED MOCHA

Pour 1 heaping teaspoon of Malt Powder into a cup. Add 1 oz Thick Chocolate Syrup. Add Espresso. Stir. Fill with Foamed/Steamed Milk. Top with Whipped Cream and Chocolate Sprinkles.

M

 MANDARINO LIME SODA

Over Ice, Pour 1⅓ oz Mandarino Syrup, ⅔ oz Lime Syrup. Fill with Soda Water.

 MANGO & COCONUT CREAM SODA

Over Ice, Pour 1 oz each Syrup: Mango, Coconut. Add Soda Water to ½" from top of cup. Fill with Half-and-Half. Splash with Grenadine Syrup.

 MANGO COOLER

Over Ice, Pour 2 oz Mango Syrup. Fill with Soda Water.

 MANGO MELBA

Over Ice, Pour ⅔ oz each Syrup: Mango, Banana, Raspberry. Add Soda Water to ½" from top of cup. Fill with Half-and-Half.

 MANGO MANDARINO SODA

Over Ice, Pour 1 oz each Syrup: Mango, Mandarino. Fill with Soda Water.

 MANGO NUT LATTE

Pour ½ oz each Syrup: Mango, Hazelnut. Add Espresso. Fill with Foamed/Steamed Milk.

 MANGO ORANGE CREAM SODA

Over Ice, Pour 1 oz each Syrup: Mango, Orange. Fill with Soda Water to ½" from top of cup. Top with Half-and-Half. Splash with Mango Syrup.

 MANILA FIZZ

Over Ice, Pour ¾ oz Lime Syrup. Add Egg Nog to 1" from top of cup. Fill with Root Beer.

M

MAPLE LATTE
Pour ¾ oz Maple Syrup. Add Espresso. Fill with Foamed/Steamed Milk.

MAPLE MOCHA
Pour ½ oz Maple Syrup, ¾ oz Thick Chocolate Syrup. Add Espresso. Stir. Fill with Foamed/Steamed Milk. Top with Whipped Cream and Chocolate Sprinkles.

MAPLE NUT FUDGE LATTE
Pour ½ oz Chocolate Fudge Syrup, ¼ oz each Syrup: Maple, Hazelnut. Add Espresso. Stir. Fill with Foamed/Steamed Milk. Top with Whipped Cream and Chocolate Sprinkles.

MARADONA CREAM COOLER
Over Ice, Pour 1¾ oz Passion Fruit Syrup, ¼ oz Coconut Syrup. Add Soda Water to ½" from top of cup. Fill with Half-and-Half.

MARVIN'S CAPPUCCINO NEAPOLITAN
Pour ½ oz each Syrup into steaming pitcher: Strawberry, Vanilla. Add Milk to pitcher until ⅓ full. Foam and steam Milk-Syrup. Set pitcher aside. Pour ⅓ oz Chocolate Syrup into cup. Add Espresso to cup. Stir. Allow steamed Milk-Syrup to pour under foam to ½" from top of cup. Top with 2" "cap" of Dense Foam. Dust with Chocolate Powder.

MARZIPAN ORANGE BREVÉ
Pour ¾ oz Orange Syrup, ¼ oz Amaretto Syrup. Add Espresso. Top with Foamed/Steamed Half-and-Half.

M

 MAUI COOLER

Over Ice, Pour ⅔ oz Pineapple Syrup, ½ oz Vanilla Syrup. Add Soda Water to ½" from top of cup. Fill with Orange Juice. Splash with Grenadine Syrup.

 MAY BLOSSOM FIZZ

Over Ice, Pour ⅔ oz each Syrup: Cherry, Almond, Strawberry. Fill with Soda Water. Splash with Lemon Syrup.

 MAZAGRAN (SPANISH ICED COFFEE)

Over Ice, Pour ½ oz Brandy Syrup. Add 1 tsp Sugar, and ½ tsp Lemon Juice. Add Espresso. Fill with Water.

 MAZAGRAN AMERICANO

Pour ¾ oz Lemon Syrup. Add Espresso. Add Ice. Fill with Soda Water.

 MacINTOSH APPLE SODA

Over Ice, Pour 1 oz each Syrup: Apple, Lemon. Fill with Soda Water. Splash with Cherry Syrup.

 **MEDITERRANEAN COFFEE**

Pour ¼ oz each Syrup: Chocolate, Anisette. Add 4 oz Hot Water. Add Espresso. Top with Whipped Cream.

MEGA MOCHA

A standard mocha with a double shot espresso in a 16 oz cup.

MELANGE

Pour Espresso. Add 4 oz Hot Water. Fill with Steamed Milk.

MELLOW YELLOW CREAM SODA

Over Ice, Pour 1 oz each Syrup: Lemon, Vanilla. Add Soda Water to ½" from top of cup. Fill with Half-and-Half. Splash with Banana Syrup.

M

 MELON BALL
Over Ice, Pour 1 oz each Syrup: Melon, Pineapple. Fill with Soda Water.

 MELON JAMAICAN
Over Ice, Pour ½ oz Kahlua Syrup, ½ oz Rum Syrup, ½ oz Melon Syrup, ½ oz Piña Colada Syrup. Add 2 shots, Espresso. Fill with Water.

 MELON MELANGE
Over Ice, Pour 1 oz Melon Syrup. Add ½ oz each Syrup: Orange, Lime. Fill with Soda Water.

 MELONADE
Over Ice, Pour 1 oz Melon Syrup. Add ½ oz each Syrup: Orange, Lime. Fill with Soda Water.

 MERRY WIDOW FIZZ
Over Ice, Pour ⅓ oz each Syrup: Lemon, Orange. Add ⅔ oz Cherry Syrup. Add Egg Nog to 1" from top of cup. Fill with Soda Water. Splash with Grenadine Syrup.

 MEXICAN COFFEE
Pour double shot of Espresso. Fill with Steamed Milk. Dust with Cinnamon.

 MEXICAN COFFEE 2
Pour ¾ oz Coffee Syrup. Fill to ½" from top with Hot Water. Top with Espresso and Whipped Cream. Dust with Mexican Chocolate Powder.

 MEXICAN COLADA
Over Ice, Pour ⅔ oz each Syrup: Coconut, Pineapple; ⅓ oz each Syrup: Creme de Cacao, Rum. Add Soda Water to ½" from top of cup. Fill with Half-and-Half.

M

MEXICAN HOT CHOCOLATE

Same as hot chocolate except with Mexican chocolate mix (a blend of chocolate, cinnamon, nutmeg, and almonds).

MEXICAN MELANGE LATTE

Pour ¼ oz each Syrup: Amaretto, Coconut, Banana, Cinnamon. Add Espresso. Fill with Foamed/Steamed Milk.

MEXICAN MOCHA

Pour 1 oz Thick Chocolate Syrup. Add 1 tablespoon Mexican Chocolate Powder. Add Espresso. Stir. Fill with Foamed/Steamed Milk. Top with Whipped Cream and Mexican Chocolate Powder.

MEXICAN MUDSLINGER

Pour ½ oz Creme de Cacao Syrup, ¼ oz Coffee Syrup. Add Espresso. Fill with Foamed/Steamed Half-and-Half. Splash with Coffee Syrup.

MEXICAN ROOT BEER

Over Ice, Pour 1½ oz Root Beer Syrup, ½ oz Kahlua Coffee Syrup. Fill with Soda Water.

MEXICOLA

Over Ice, Pour ½ oz Lime Syrup. Fill with Cola. Splash with Lime Syrup.

MIDNIGHT SILK MOCHA

Pour ½ oz each Syrup: Anisette, Chocolate. Add Espresso. Add Foamed/Steamed Milk. Top with Whipped Cream.

M

MILE HIGH BANANA CREAM CAPPUCCINO

Pour ½ oz Banana Syrup into serving cup. Pour ¾ oz Banana Syrup into steaming pitcher. Add 6 oz Cold Milk. Foam and steam Milk-Syrup mixture. Set pitcher aside. Pour Espresso. Allow Flavored Steamed Milk to pour under foam to ½" from top of cup. Top with 2" "cap" of Dense Foam.

MILE HIGH ORANGE BANANA CREAM

Over Ice, Pour 1 oz each Syrup: Orange, Banana. Add Soda Water to ½" from top of cup. Fill with Half-and-Half. Top with lots of Whipped Cream. Splash with Grenadine Syrup.

MILKY WAY ICED

Over Ice, Pour 1 oz each Syrup: Caramel, Chocolate. Fill with Soda Water to ½" from top of cup. Top with Half-and-Half and Whipped Cream.

MILKY WAY

Pour ¾ oz of each Thick Syrup: Caramel, Chocolate. Add Espresso. Stir. Fill with Foamed/Steamed Milk. Top with Whipped Cream and Chocolate Sprinkles.

MIMOSA

Over Ice, Pour 1 oz each Syrup: Orange, Apple. Fill with Soda Water.

MINT COOLER

Over Ice, Pour 2 oz Creme de Menthe Syrup. Fill with Soda Water.

M

 MINT CREAM COLADA

Over Ice, Pour ¾ oz each Syrup: Coconut, Pineapple. Add Soda Water to ½" from top of cup. Fill with Half-and-Half. Splash with ¼ oz Mint Syrup.

 MINT CREAM SODA

Over Ice, Pour 2 oz Creme de Menthe Syrup, 3 oz Soda Water. Fill with 2 oz Half-and-Half. Top with Whipped Cream.

 MINT DREAM TEAM

Over Ice, Pour 2 oz Creme de Menthe Syrup. Fill to ½" from top with Soda Water. Top with Half-and-Half and Whipped Cream.

 MINT JULEP

Over Ice, Pour 2 oz Mint Syrup. Fill with Milk. Top with Whipped Cream. Splash with Mint Syrup.

 MINT PATTY

Pour ½ oz each Syrup: Creme de Cacao, Creme de Menthe. Fill with Hot Water to ½" from top of cup. Add Espresso. Top with Whipped Cream.

 MINTY LEMON ESPRESSO

Pour ⅓ oz each Syrup: Lemon, Mint. Add Hot Water to 1" from top of cup. Top with Espresso.

 MIXED FRUIT SMOOTHY

Over Ice, Pour 1 oz each Syrup: Orange, Peach. Add Soda Water to ½" from top of cup. Fill with Half-and-Half. Splash with Vanilla Syrup.

M

MOCHA
Pour 1 oz Thick
Chocolate Syrup. Add
Espresso. Stir. Fill with
Foamed/Steamed Milk.
Top with Whipped
Cream and Chocolate
Sprinkles.

MOCHA & CREAM
Over Ice, Pour 1¼ oz
Coffee Syrup, ¾ oz
Creme de Cacao Syrup.
Fill with Half-and-
Half. Top with
Whipped Cream.

MOCHA CREAM COOLER
Over Ice, Pour 1 oz
Creme de Cacao Syrup.
Add Espresso and 3 oz
Soda Water. Fill with
Half-and-Half. Top
with Whipped Cream.

MOCHA FROST
Over Ice, Pour 2 oz
Licorice Syrup. Add
Double Ristretto
Espresso. Fill to near
top with Chocolate
Milk, then to top with
Nonfat Milk. Float
with Whipped Cream
and garnish with
Frozen Licorice Stick.

MOCHA FROTH
Pour 1 oz Thick
Chocolate Syrup. Add
Espresso. Stir. Fill with
Foamed Milk. Dust
with Chocolate Powder.

MOCHA LITE
Pour 1 heaping
tablespoon of Sugarfree
Cocoa into cup. Add
Espresso. Stir. Fill with
Foamed/Steamed
Nonfat Milk.

MOCHA MINT
Pour ¾ oz Thick
Chocolate Syrup, ¼ oz
Creme de Menthe
Syrup. Add Espresso.
Stir. Fill with Foamed/
Steamed Milk. Top with
Whipped Cream and
Chocolate Sprinkles.

MOCHA MINT LATTE
Pour ¾ oz Thick
Chocolate Syrup, ⅓ oz
Creme de Menthe
Syrup. Add Espresso.
Stir. Fill with Foamed/
Steamed Milk. Top with
Whipped Cream and
Chocolate Sprinkles.

M

 MOCHA MOO

Pour ⅓ oz Almond Syrup, ¾ oz Thick Chocolate Syrup. Add Espresso. Stir. Fill with Foamed/Steamed Milk. Top with Whipped Cream and Chocolate Sprinkles.

 MOCHA NOG

Over Ice, Pour 1 oz Chocolate Syrup. Add Espresso. Fill with ½ cup Eggnog and ½ cup Milk. Garnish with Grated Nutmeg.

 MOCHA STEAMER

Pour 1 oz Creme de Cacao Syrup. Fill with Foamed/Steamed Milk. Top with Whipped Cream and dust with Chocolate Powder.

 MOCHAMALLOW

Pour 1 oz Chocolate Syrup. Add Espresso. Fill with Foamed/Steamed Milk. Top with Marshmallows, Cinnamon, or splash of Vanilla Syrup.

 MOCK MOOSE MILK

Pour 1 oz Rum Syrup, ½ oz Almond Syrup. Fill with Foamed/Steamed Milk.

 MOONLIGHT SODA

Over Ice, Pour 1⅓ oz Apple Syrup, ⅔ oz Lemon Syrup. Fill with Soda Water.

 MORIR Y SONANDOR

Over Ice, Pour 2 oz Orange Syrup. Add Espresso. Fill with Cold Milk. Top with Whipped Cream.

 MORNING GLORY FIZZ

Over Ice, Pour 1¼ oz Lemon Syrup, ¾ oz Anisette Syrup. Fill with Soda Water.

 MOUNDS® BAR

Over Ice, Pour 1 oz each Syrup: Chocolate, Coconut. Add 2 oz Soda Water. Fill with Half-and-Half. Stir.

M

🎵 MOUNDS® BAR LATTE

Pour 1 oz Thick Chocolate Syrup, ⅓ oz Coconut Syrup. Add Espresso. Stir. Fill with Foamed/Steamed Milk. Top with Whipped Cream and thin threads of Thick Chocolate Syrup.

🎵 MR. SANDMAN

Pour ½ oz Cream de Cocoa, ½ oz Irish Cream. Fill with Foamed/Steamed Milk. Top with Whipped Cream and Chocolate Powder.

🎵 MT. ST. HELENS

In an 8-oz cup, Pour a triple shot of Espresso. Top with Whipped Cream.

🎵 MUD SLIDE

Pour 1½ oz Thick Chocolate Syrup. Add a double shot of Espresso. Stir. Fill with Steamed Milk. Top with Whipped Cream and Chocolate Sprinkles.

🎵 MUNICH MADNESS

Pour ⅓ oz, Coconut Syrup, ⅓ oz Caramel Syrup, 1/6 oz Hazelnut Syrup. Add Espresso. Fill with Foamed/Steamed Chocolate Milk. Top with Whipped Cream.

🎵 NEW ORLEANS COFFEE

(Use a very Dark Roast, or Chicory Blend, Coffee.) Pour double shot of Espresso. Fill with Steamed Milk.

🎵 NEWTON SPRITZER

Over Ice, Pour 2 oz Apple Syrup. Fill with Soda Water. Splash with Lemon Syrup.

🎵 NIENTA

First foam and steam Nonfat Milk. Set pitcher aside. Pour Decaf Espresso. Allow Steamed Milk to pour under Foam to ½" from top of cup. Top with 2" "cap" of dense Foam. Dust with Chocolate Powder or Nutmeg.

N

NO FUN
A latte with Decaf Espresso.

NUTTIN' HONEY LATTE
Pour 1 tablespoon Honey, ½ oz Hazelnut Syrup. Add Espresso. Stir. Fill with Foamed/Steamed Milk. Dust with Nutmeg Powder.

NUTTY BUDDY
Pour ¾ oz Thick Chocolate Syrup and ⅓ oz Hazelnut Syrup. Add Espresso. Stir. Fill with Foamed/Steamed Milk.

NUTTY CARAMEL COFFEE
Pour ½ oz Caramel Syrup, ¼ oz Hazelnut Syrup. Add 4 oz Hot Water and top with Espresso.

NAPOLEON
Over Ice, Pour 1 oz Crème de Cacao. Add 2 shots, Espresso. Fill with Water.

NIENTA
Foam and steam Nonfat Milk. Set pitcher aside. Pour Espresso. Allow Steamed Milk to pour under foam to ½" from top of cup. Top with 2" "cap" of Dense Foam. Dust with Chocolate Powder or Nutmeg.

NUTTIE BRITANNIO LATTE
Pour ½ oz English Toffee Syrup, ½ oz Toasted Walnut Syrup. Add Espresso. Fill with Foamed/Steamed Milk. Top with Whipped Cream.

NUTTY COCADA CREAM SODA
Over Ice, Pour ⅔ oz each Syrup: Amaretto, Coconut, Pineapple. Add Soda Water to ½" from top of cup. Top with Half-and-Half.

O

 NUTTY IRISH CREAM

Pour ⅓ oz Hazelnut Syrup, ⅔ oz Irish Cream Syrup. Add Espresso. Fill with Foamed/Steamed Milk.

 OLD FASHIONED AMERICAN SODA

Over Ice, Pour 1 oz Vanilla Syrup and 1 oz of any other Flavored Syrup. Fill with Soda Water.

OLD FASHIONED COBBLER CREAM SODA

Over Ice, Pour ⅔ oz each Syrup: Apple, Peach. Add ½ oz Cinnamon Syrup and 3 oz Soda Water. Fill with Half-and-Half. Top with Whipped Cream.

 OLYMPIC GOLD SODA

Over Ice, Pour 1¼ oz Passion Fruit Syrup, ¾ oz Strawberry Syrup. Fill with Soda Water.

 ORANGE ALMOND LATTE

Pour ½ oz each Syrup: Orange, Almond. Add Espresso. Fill with Foamed/Steamed Milk.

 ORANGE ALMOND MOCHA

Pour ¾ oz Thick Chocolate Syrup. Add ¼ oz each Syrup: Orange, Almond. Add Espresso. Stir. Fill with Foamed/Steamed Milk. Top with Whipped Cream and Chocolate Sprinkles.

ORANGE BANANA CREAM SODA

Over Ice, Pour ¾ oz each Syrup: Orange, Banana. Add ½ oz Vanilla Syrup. Add Soda Water to ½" from top of cup. Fill with Half-and-Half.

 ORANGE BRANDY LATTE

Pour ½ oz Orange Syrup, ¼ oz Amaretto Syrup. Add Espresso. Fill with Foamed/Steamed Milk.

O

ORANGE CAPPUCCINO

Pour ½ oz Chocolate Syrup, ½ oz Orange Syrup. Foam and steam Milk. Set pitcher aside. Pour Espresso. Stir. Allow Steamed Milk to Pour under Foam to ½" from top of cup. Top with 2" "cap" of Dense Foam. Top with Grated Orange Peel.

ORANGE COFFEE

Pour ¾ oz Orange Syrup. Add Hot Water to ½" from top of cup. Top with Espresso.

ORANGE DROP ITALIAN SODA

Over Ice, Pour ¾ oz each Syrup: Cherry, Lemon, ½ oz Orange Syrup. Fill with Soda Water.

ORANGE EGG NOG LATTE

Pour ¾ oz Orange Syrup. Add Espresso. Fill with Foamed/ Steamed Egg Nog and top with Whipped Cream.

ORANGE FIZZ

Over Ice, Pour 1½ oz Orange Syrup, ½ oz Lime Syrup. Fill with Soda Water.

ORANGE FLOWER COOLER

Over Ice, Pour 1 oz Orange Syrup. Add 3 oz Grapefruit Juice. Fill with Soda Water. Splash with Maraschino Syrup.

ORANGE GROG

Pour into steam pitcher, 1 oz Orange Syrup, ½ oz Cinnamon Syrup. Add 9 oz Water. Steam. Pour into cup. Dust with Cinnamon Powder.

ORANGE IRISH CREAM LATTE

Pour ½ oz each Syrup: Orange, Irish Cream. Add Espresso. Fill with Foamed/Steamed Milk.

O

ORANGE MOCHA

Pour ¾ oz Thick Chocolate Syrup, ⅓ oz Orange Syrup. Add Espresso. Stir. Fill with Foamed/Steamed Milk. Top with Whipped Cream and Chocolate Sprinkles.

ORANGE NUT LATTE

Pour ½ oz Orange Syrup, ¼ oz Hazelnut Syrup. Add Espresso. Fill with Foamed/ Steamed Milk.

ORANGE OASIS

Over Ice, Pour 1½ oz Orange Syrup, ½ oz Cherry Syrup. Fill with Soda Water.

DOUBLE TALL ORANGE PECAN MOCHA

Pour ½ oz Orange Syrup, ½ oz Praline Syrup. Add 2 shots, Espresso mixed with ½ tsp Dark Unsweetened Cocoa and ½ tsp Sugar. Fill with Foamed/ Steamed Milk. Top with Whipped Cream.

ORANGE SPARKLER

Over Ice, Pour 1½ oz Orange Syrup, ½ oz Anisette Syrup. Fill with Soda Water.

ORANGE SWIZZLE

Over Ice, Pour 1½ oz Orange Syrup. Add Soda Water to ½" from top of cup. Fill with Ginger Ale. Splash with Grenadine Syrup.

ORANGE VANILLA MOCHA

Pour ¾ oz Chocolate Syrup, ¼ oz Vanilla Syrup. Add Double Ristretto Shot. Top with Milk, Foamed/Steamed with 1 oz Orange Syrup.

OVALTINE LATTE

Pour 1 heaping tablespoon of Ovaltine into cup. Add Espresso. Stir. Fill with Foamed/ Steamed Milk.

OUTRIGGER

Over Ice, Pour ⅔ oz each Syrup: Peach, Lime, Pineapple. Fill with Soda Water.

P

 PAGO PAGO

Over Ice, Pour 1 oz
Rum Syrup, ½ oz
Pineapple Syrup, ¼ oz
each Syrup: Creme de
Cacao, Lime. Fill with
Soda Water. Splash
with Lime Syrup.

 PALISADES SODA

Over Ice, Pour 1 oz
Banana Syrup. Add
Soda Water to 1 ½"
from top of cup. Fill
with Orange Juice.

 **PALM GROVE
COOLER**

Over Ice, Pour ½ oz
each Syrup: Orange,
Mango, Pineapple,
Lime. Fill with Soda
Water. Splash with
Grenadine Syrup.

 PANAMA COOLER

Over Ice, Pour ⅔ oz
each Syrup: Chocolate,
Banana, Coffee. Fill
with Soda Water.

 PANAMA COOLER II

Over Ice, Pour 1 oz
Banana Syrup, 1 oz
Evaporated Milk. Add
Espresso. Fill with
Cream Soda.

 PARADISE COOLER

Over Ice, Pour ½ oz
each Syrup: Orange,
Lemon, Banana, Rum.
Fill with Soda Water.

 **PARK AVENUE
ICED ESPRESSO**

Pour Espresso. Add Ice.
Add 1 oz Vanilla Syrup.
Fill with Soda Water.

 PARISIAN COFFEE

Pour ½ oz Brandy
Syrup. Add Espresso, 6
oz Hot Water, and 1½
oz, Half-and-Half.

 **PASSION FRUIT
SPRITZER**

Over Ice, Pour 2 oz
Passion Fruit Syrup.
Fill with Soda Water.

P

PASSION NUT LATTE

Pour ½ oz Passion Fruit Syrup, ¼ oz Hazelnut Syrup. Add Espresso. Fill with Foamed/Steamed Milk.

PASSIONATE MANGO COOLER

Over Ice, Pour 1 oz each Syrup: Passion Fruit, Mango. Splash with Lime Syrup. Fill with Soda Water.

PEACH & GINGER SPRITZER

Over Ice, Pour 1 oz Peach Syrup. Add Soda Water to ¾" from top of cup. Fill with Ginger Ale.

PEACH & LIME COOLER

Over Ice, Pour 1½ oz Peach Syrup, ½ oz Lime Syrup. Fill with Soda Water.

PEACH BLOSSOM

Over Ice, Pour 1½ oz Peach Syrup, ½ oz Almond Syrup. Fill with Soda Water. Splash with Grenadine Syrup.

PEACH BUNNY

Over Ice, Pour 1 oz each Syrup: Peach, Creme de Cacao. Add Soda Water to ½" from top of cup. Top with Half-and-Half.

PEACH COCONUT FLIP

Over Ice, Pour 1 oz Peach Syrup, ¼ oz Rum Syrup, ¾ oz Coconut Syrup. Add Soda Water to ½" from top of cup. Fill with Half-and-Half.

PEACH MELBA

Over Ice, Pour 1½ oz Peach Syrup, ½ oz Raspberry Syrup. Add Soda Water to ½" from top of cup. Fill with Half-and-Half.

P

 PEACH ORANGE & GINGER FIZZ

Over Ice, Pour ⅔ oz each Syrup: Peach, Orange. Fill with equal parts of Ginger Ale and Soda Water.

 PEACH SANGAREE

Over Ice, Pour 1½ oz Peach Syrup, ½ oz Grape Syrup. Fill with Soda Water. Splash with Lemon Syrup.

 PEACH SCHNAPPS COOLER

Over Ice, Pour 1½ oz Peach Syrup, ½ oz Amaretto Syrup. Fill with Soda Water.

 PEACH SCHNAPPS LATTE

Pour ½ oz Peach Syrup, ¼ oz Amaretto Syrup. Add Espresso. Fill with Foamed/Steamed Milk.

 PEACH-ANISETTE AND LIME COOLER

Over Ice, Pour ⅔ oz each Syrup: Peach, Anisette, Lime. Fill with Soda Water.

 PEACHES-N-CREAM

Over Ice, Pour 2 oz Peach Syrup. Fill with Soda Water to ½" from top of cup. Top with Half-and-Half and Whipped Cream.

 PEACHLIFTER

Over Ice, Pour ¾ oz Peach Syrup. Add ½ oz each Syrup: Apple, Lime, Coconut. Fill with Soda Water.

 PEACHY COLADA

Over Ice, Pour ⅔ oz each Syrup: Coconut, Pineapple, Peach. Fill with Soda Water.

 **PEANUT BAR MOCHA**

Pour ½ oz Thick Chocolate Syrup. Add 1 tablespoon Smooth Peanut Butter. Add Espresso. Stir. Fill with Foamed/Steamed Milk to ¼" from top of cup. Top with Whipped Cream and Thin Threads of Thick Chocolate Syrup.

P

 PEANUT BUTTER CUP

Pour ½ oz Thick Chocolate Syrup. Add 1 tablespoon Peanut Butter. Add Espresso. Stir. Fill with Foamed/Steamed Milk. Top with Whipped Cream and Chocolate Sprinkles.

 PEANUT BUTTER-CARAMEL COFFEE

Pour ⅔ oz Caramel Syrup. Add 1 tablespoon Peanut Butter. Add Espresso. Stir. Add Ice. Fill with Cold Milk.

 PECAN APPLE LATTE

Pour ½ oz each Syrup: Pecan, Apple. Add Espresso. Fill with Foamed/Steamed Milk.

PECAN CARAMEL LATTE

Pour ½ oz each Syrup: Pecan, Caramel. Add Espresso. Fill with Foamed/Steamed Milk. Top with Whipped Cream.

 PEDRO COLLINS

Over Ice, Pour 1⅓ oz Rum Syrup, ⅔ oz Lemon Syrup. Fill with Soda Water.

 PEPPERMINT CREAM TWIST

Over Ice, Pour 1½ oz Peppermint Syrup. Add Soda Water to ½" from top of cup. Fill with Half-and-Half to ¼" from top of cup. Top with ½ oz Cherry Syrup.

 PEPPERMINT PATTY

Over Ice, Pour 1 oz each Syrup: Peppermint, Creme de Cacao. Add Soda Water to ½" from top of cup. Fill with Half-and-Half.

 PEPPERMINT PATTY SODA

Over Ice, Pour 1 oz each Syrup: Peppermint, Creme de Cacao. Fill with Soda Water.

P

 PEPPERMINT PATTY SODA II

Over Ice, Pour 1 oz each Syrup: Frosted Mint (Peppermint may be substituted), White Chocolate. Add Espresso. Fill with Soda Water. Top with Whipped Cream.

 PEPPERMINT VANILLA LATTE

Pour ½ oz each Syrup: Peppermint, Vanilla. Add Espresso. Fill with Foamed/Steamed Milk.

 PEPPY PENGUIN

Pour 1½ oz Thick Chocolate Syrup. Add a double shot of Espresso. Stir. Add Ice. Fill with Half-and-Half.

 PERPETUALLY YOURS

Over Ice, Pour 1½ oz Creme de Cassis, ½ oz Creme de Cacao. Fill with Soda Water.

 PINA COLADA CREAM SODA

Over Ice, Pour 1 oz each Syrup: Coconut, Pineapple. Add 2 oz Soda Water. Fill with Half-and-Half.

 PIÑATA

Over Ice, Pour 1½ oz Banana Syrup, ½ oz Lime Syrup. Add 3 oz Soda Water. Fill with Half-and-Half.

 PINEAPPLE COOLER

Over Ice, Pour 2 oz Pineapple Syrup. Fill with Soda Water. Splash with Grenadine Syrup.

 PINEAPPLE CRANBERRY SPRITZER

Over Ice, Pour 1 oz each Syrup: Pineapple, Cranberry. Fill with equal parts Ginger Ale and Soda Water.

P

 PINEAPPLE MINT COOLER

Over Ice, Pour 1¼ oz Pineapple Syrup, ½ oz Creme de Menthe Syrup, ¼ oz Lemon Syrup. Fill with Soda Water.

 PINEAPPLE RUM FIZZ

Over Ice, Pour 1 oz each Syrup: Pineapple, Rum. Fill with Soda Water.

 PINK ALMOND CREAM SODA

Over Ice, Pour 1 oz each Syrup: Almond, Cherry. Add Soda Water to ½" from top of cup. Fill with Half-and-Half. Splash with Cherry Syrup.

 PINK CREOLE SODA

Over Ice, Pour ⅔ oz each Syrup: Grenadine, Lime, Rum. Fill with Soda Water.

 PINK ELEPHANT

Over Ice, Pour 1 oz Grenadine Syrup. Add ½ oz each Syrup: Lemon, Lime. Fill with Soda Water.

 PINK FLAMINGO

Over Ice, Pour 1 oz Strawberry Syrup. Add ⅓ oz each Syrup: Apple, Lemon, Banana. Fill with Soda Water.

 PINK GRAPEFRUIT LEMON FIZZ

Over Ice, Pour 1½ oz Pink Grapefruit Syrup, ½ oz Lemon Syrup. Fill with Soda Water.

 PINK LADY

Over Ice, Pour 1¾ oz Raspberry Syrup, ¼ oz Lemon Syrup. Fill with Soda Water.

 PINK PANTHER

Over Ice, Pour 1 oz each Syrup: Creme de Cassis, Mandarino. Add Soda Water to ½" from top of cup. Fill with Half-and-Half.

P

PINK PANTHER SODA

Over Ice, Pour 1 oz each Syrup: Cherry, Pineapple. Fill with Soda Water. Splash with Grenadine Syrup.

PINK PUSSY CAT

Over Ice, Fill cup to ½" from top with Grapefruit Juice. Add ½ oz Grenadine Syrup.

PINK SNOWMAN

Over Ice, Pour ⅔ oz each Syrup: Raspberry, Orange, Vanilla. Add Soda Water to ¾" from top of cup. Top with Half-and-Half.

PINK SQUIRREL

Over Ice, Pour 1 oz Cherry Syrup, ⅔ oz Almond Syrup, ⅓ oz Creme de Cacao Syrup. Add 3 oz Soda Water. Fill with Half-and-Half.

PINKY COLADA

Over Ice, Pour ⅔ oz each Syrup: Coconut, Pineapple, Grenadine. Add Soda Water to ½" from top of cup. Fill with Half-and-Half. Splash with Grenadine Syrup.

POCA POLA

Over Ice, Pour 1 oz Tamarindo Syrup. Fill with Ginger Ale. Splash with Lemon Syrup.

POLLYANNA

Over Ice, Pour ⅔ oz each Syrup: Mandarino, Pineapple, Raspberry. Fill with Soda Water.

POLYNESIAN CREAM SODA

Over Ice, pour ¾ oz each Syrup: Rum, Passion Fruit. Pour ½ oz Lime Syrup. Add Soda Water to ½" from top of cup. Top with Half-and-Half. Splash with Lime Syrup.

P

POPSICLE
Over Ice, Pour 1 oz Amaretto Syrup, Add Orange Juice to ½" from top of cup. Fill with Half-and-Half.

POSTEM LATTE
Add 1 heaping teaspoon Postem. Pour 2 oz Hot Water. Stir. Fill with Foamed/Steamed Milk.

POUSSE CAFE
Pour ½ oz Crème de Cacao, ⅓ oz Brandy Syrup, ⅓ oz Licorice Syrup. Add Espresso and 6 oz Hot Water.

PRALINE LATTE
Pour ¾ oz Praline Syrup. Add Espresso. Fill with Foamed/Steamed Milk.

PRALINE MOCHA
Pour ¾ oz Thick Chocolate Syrup, ⅓ oz Praline Syrup. Add Espresso. Stir. Fill with Foamed/Steamed Milk. Top with Whipped Cream and Chocolate Sprinkles.

PRALINE SPRITZER
Over Ice, Pour 2 oz Praline Syrup. Fill with Soda Water. Splash with Orange Syrup.

PRALINES & CREAM LATTE
Pour ½ oz Praline Syrup, ¼ oz Vanilla Syrup. Add Espresso. Fill with Foamed/Steamed Milk.

PRESBYTERIAN
Over Ice, Pour 1½ oz Irish Cream Syrup. Fill with equal parts of Ginger Ale and Soda Water.

PRETTY MAMA
Over Ice, Pour 1 oz each Syrup: Apricot, Pineapple. Add Soda Water. Splash with Grenadine Syrup.

P

PRETTY MAMA CREAM SODA

Over Ice, Pour 1 oz each Syrup: Apricot, Pineapple. Add Soda Water to ½" from top of cup. Fill with Half-and-Half. Splash with Cherry Syrup.

PRINCESS CREAM SODA

Over Ice, Pour 2 oz Apricot Syrup. Add 3 oz. Soda Water. Fill with Half-and-Half. Top with Whipped Cream.

PUERTO APPLE CREAM SODA

Over Ice, Pour ¾ oz Apple Syrup, ¼ oz Lime Syrup, ½ oz each Syrup: Rum, Almond. Add Soda Water to ½" from top of cup. Fill with Half-and-Half.

PUMPKIN LATTE

Place 1 tablespoon of Pumpkin based mix in a cup. Add Espresso. Stir. Fill with Foamed/Steamed Milk. Splash with Praline Syrup.

PUPPY'S NOSE

Pour ¼ oz Peppermint Syrup, ¼ oz Brandy Syrup, ¼ oz Irish Cream Syrup. Add 2 shots, Espresso and 6 oz Hot Water.

PURPLE CLOUD COOLER

Over Ice, Pour 1½ oz Grape Syrup, ½ oz Almond Syrup. Fill with Soda Water.

PURPLE COW

Over Ice, Pour 1½ oz Grape Syrup, ½ oz Banana Syrup. Add Soda Water to ¾" from top of cup. Fill with Half-and-Half. Top with Whipped Cream. Splash with Grape Syrup.

PURPLE HAZE COOLER

Over Ice, Pour 1⅓ oz Creme de Cassis Syrup, ⅔ oz Creme de Cacao Syrup. Fill with Soda Water.

R

 PURPLE PASSION

Over Ice, Pour 1½ oz Grape Syrup. Add ¼ oz each Syrup: Lemon, Pineapple. Fill with Soda Water. Splash with Creme de Cassis Syrup.

 PURPLE PASSION COOLER

Over Ice, Pour Grapefruit Juice to 1" from top of cup. Add 2 oz Soda Water. Top with ¾ oz Grape Syrup.

 QUAD TALL WHIPLESS FOAMLESS

A tall mocha with 4 shots of espresso, all steamed milk, and no foamed milk or whipped cream.

 R & R SODA

Over Ice, Pour 1 oz each Syrup: Rum, Raspberry. Fill with Soda Water.

 RACEHORSE

A latte made with 5 shots of espresso in a 16 oz cup.

 RAMBLING ROSE

Over Ice, Pour ⅓ oz each Syrup: Strawberry, Raspberry, Lime. Add Ginger Ale to ½" from top of cup. Fill with Soda Water.

 RASPBERRY BANANA COOLER

Over Ice, Pour 1 oz each Syrup: Raspberry, Banana. Fill with Soda Water.

 RASPBERRY BRANDY LATTE

Pour ¾ oz Raspberry Syrup, ¼ oz Amaretto Syrup. Add Espresso. Fill with Foamed/ Steamed Milk.

 RASPBERRY CAPPUCCINO

Pour 1 oz Raspberry Syrup and 2 tbs Whipping Cream. Foam and steam Milk. Set pitcher aside. Pour Espresso. Stir. Allow Steamed Milk to Pour under Foam to ½" from top of cup. Top with 2" "cap" of Dense Foam. Top with Chocolate Shavings.

RASPBERRY COFFEE LATTE

Pour ½ oz Raspberry Syrup, ¼ oz Coffee Syrup. Add Espresso. Fill with Foamed/ Steamed Milk.

 RASPBERRY CREAM

Over Ice, Pour 1½ oz Raspberry Syrup, ½ oz Creme de Cacao Syrup. Fill with Half-and-Half. Top with Whipped Cream and Splash of Raspberry Syrup.

 RASPBERRY DAISY

Over Ice, Pour 1½ oz Raspberry Syrup, ½ oz Lemon Syrup. Fill with Soda Water.

 RASPBERRY LICORICE COFFEE CREAM SODA

Over Ice, Pour ⅔ oz each Syrup: Raspberry, Licorice, Coffee. Fill with Soda Water to ½" from top of cup. Top with Half-and-Half and Whipped Cream.

 RASPBERRY MOCHA

Pour ¾ oz Thick Chocolate Syrup, ½ oz Raspberry Syrup. Add Espresso. Stir. Fill with Foamed/Steamed Milk. Top with Whipped Cream and Chocolate Sprinkles.

 RASPBERRY MOCHA CREAM SODA

Over Ice, Pour 1 oz each Syrup: Raspberry, Creme de Cacao. Add Soda Water to ½" from top of cup. Fill with Half-and-Half. Top with Whipped Cream.

 RASPBERRY MOCHA SODA

Over Ice, Pour 1¼ oz Raspberry Syrup, ¾ oz Creme de Cacao Syrup. Fill with Soda Water.

R

 RASPBERRY MOCHA STEAMER

Pour ⅔ oz Raspberry Syrup, ⅓ oz Creme de Cacao Syrup. Fill with Foamed/Steamed Milk. Top with Whipped Cream and dust with Chocolate Powder.

 RASPBERRY NUT MOCHA

Pour ½ oz Thick Chocolate Syrup, ¼ oz each Syrup: Raspberry, Almond. Add Espresso. Stir. Fill with Foamed/Steamed Milk. Top with Whipped Cream. Splash with Raspberry Syrup.

 RASPBERRY PEAR COOLER

Over Ice, Pour 1 oz each Syrup: Raspberry, Pear. Fill with Soda Water.

RASPBERRY RICKEY

Over Ice, Pour 1¼ oz Raspberry Syrup, ¾ oz Lime Syrup. Fill with Soda Water. Splash with Lime Syrup.

 RASPBERRY SODA

Over Ice, Pour 1¾ oz Raspberry Syrup, ¼ oz Vanilla Syrup. Fill with Soda Water.

 RASPBERRY SOUR CREAM PIE CREAM SODA

Over Ice, Pour 1¼ oz Raspberry Syrup, ¾ oz Lemon Syrup. Add 3 oz Soda Water. Fill with Half-and-Half and top with Whipped Cream.

 RASPBERRY TORTE BREVÉ

Pour ½ oz each Syrup: Raspberry, Chocolate. Add Espresso. Fill with Foamed/Steamed Half-and-Half. Top with Whipped Cream. Dust with Chocolate Sprinkles.

 RASPBERRY TRUFFLE LATTE

Pour ¾ oz Thick Chocolate Syrup, ½ oz Raspberry Syrup. Add Espresso. Stir. Fill with Foamed/Steamed Milk. Top with Chocolate Sprinkles and splash with Raspberry Syrup.

R

 RASPBERRY VANILLA CREAM SODA

Over Ice, Pour 1 oz each Syrup: Raspberry, Vanilla. Add Soda Water to ½ oz from top of cup. Fill with Half-and-Half. Splash with Raspberry Syrup.

 RAZZ-MA-TAZZ

Pour ½ oz each Syrup: Chocolate, Raspberry. Add Espresso. Fill with Foamed/Steamed Milk.

 RED APPLE CREAM SODA

Over Ice, Pour 1 oz Apple Syrup, ¼ oz Cinnamon Syrup, ¾ oz Raspberry Syrup. Add Soda Water to ½" from top of cup. Fill with Half-and-Half.

 RED CLOUD SODA

Over Ice, Pour 1 oz Apricot Syrup, ¼ oz Lemon Syrup, ¾ oz Strawberry Syrup. Fill with Soda Water. Splash with Strawberry Syrup.

 RED DAWN COOLER

Over Ice, Pour 1 oz each Syrup: Cherry, Grape. Fill with Soda Water.

 RED DEVIL

Over Ice, Pour 1¾ oz Cherry Syrup. Fill to ¼" from top of cup with Soda Water. Top with ¼ oz Cinnamon Syrup.

 RED DEVIL SODA

Over Ice, Pour 1¼ oz Cherry Syrup, ¾ oz Cinnamon Syrup. Fill with Soda Water.

 RED LICORICE LATTE

Pour ½ oz each Syrup: Licorice, Raspberry. Add Espresso. Fill with Foamed/Steamed Milk. Splash with Raspberry Syrup.

 RED SLED

Over Ice, Pour 1 oz each Syrup: Peach, Cranberry. Add Soda Water to ½" from top of cup. Fill with Half-and-Half.

R

 RED STAR SPLASH

 Over Ice, Pour 1½ oz
Cranberry Syrup, ¼ oz
each Syrup: Grenadine,
Lime. Fill with Soda
Water.

 **RICH'S HONEY BEE
LATTE**

Pour ½ oz Honey, ¼ oz
any flavor Syrup. Add
Espresso. Stir. Fill with
Foamed/Steamed Milk.

RICO BREVÉ

Pour ¾ oz Cinnamon
Syrup, ¼ oz Orange
Syrup. Add Espresso. Fill
with Foamed/Steamed
Half-and-Half.

 **RISTRETTO (Short
Pour)**

Pour ¾-1 oz Water
through a Single
Measure of Coffee—
7 grams.

 **RICHLAND
BOMBER**

Pour ¾ oz B-52 Syrup,
¼ oz Cherry Syrup.
Add a triple shot
Ristretto. Top with
Foamed/Steamed Half-
and-Half. Garnish with
a Maraschino Cherry.

 ROCKET

Pour a double shot of
Espresso. Add Ice. Add
Soda Water to ½ full.
Fill with Milk. Top
with Whipped Cream.

 ROCCA PEEL

Pour ½ oz Almond
Rocca® Syrup, ½ oz
Orange Syrup. Foam/
Steam with Milk. Add
2 shots, Espresso. Top
with Sliced Almonds
and Twist of Orange.

R

 ROCKY ROAD

Pour ½ oz of each
Thick Syrup:
Chocolate,
Marshmallow. Add
¼ oz Almond Syrup.
Add Espresso. Stir. Fill
with Foamed/Steamed
Milk. Top with
Whipped Cream and
Chocolate Sprinkles.

 ROOT BEER FLOAT

Over Ice, Pour 2 oz
Root Beer Syrup. Add
3 oz Soda Water. Top
with Half-and-Half and
Whipped Cream.

**ROSE'S RUBY
HEART**

Over Ice, Pour 1¾ oz
Strawberry Syrup, ¼ oz
Lime Syrup. Add Soda
Water to ½" from top
of cup. Top with Half-
and-Half.

 ROSEY O'TOOLE

Over Ice, Pour 1 oz
each Syrup: Irish
Cream, Strawberry.
Add 2 oz Soda Water.
Top with Half-and-
Half. Splash with
Creme de Menthe
Syrup.

 ROSY PIPPIN

Over Ice, Pour ½ oz
Apple Syrup, ¼ oz
Lemon Syrup. Add
3 oz Soda Water. Fill
with Ginger Ale. Splash
with Grenadine Syrup.

 **ROYAL STREET
COFFEE**

Pour ½ oz Amaretto
Syrup, ⅓ oz Creme de
Cacao Syrup. Add Hot
Water to 1" from top of
cup. Top with Espresso
and Whipped Cream.

 RUBY FIZZ

Over Ice, Pour 1½ oz
Raspberry Syrup, ½ oz
Blackberry Syrup. Fill
with Soda Water.
Splash with Lemon
Syrup.

R

 RUM ALEXANDER
Over Ice, Pour 1¼ oz
Rum Syrup, ¾ oz
Creme de Cacao Syrup.
Top with 3 oz Half-
and-Half. Dust with
Powdered Nutmeg.

 **RUM AND
COCONUT
COOLER**

Over Ice, Pour 1 oz
each Syrup: Rum,
Coconut. Fill with
Soda Water.

 RUM MOCHA
Pour ¾ oz Thick
Chocolate Syrup, 1/3
oz Rum Syrup. Add
Espresso. Stir. Fill with
Foamed/Steamed Milk.
Top with Whipped
Cream and Chocolate
Sprinkles.

 **RUM AND
PINEAPPLE
COOLER**

Over Ice, Pour 1 oz
each Syrup: Rum,
Pineapple. Fill with
Soda Water.

 RUM COFFEE SODA
Over Ice, Pour 1 oz each
Syrup: Rum, Coffee.
Add Half-and-Half to 1"
from top of cup. Fill
with Soda Water.

 **RUM
SCREWDRIVER**

Over Ice, Pour ¾ oz
Rum Syrup. Fill with
Orange Juice.

 RUMETTO
Pour ½ oz each Syrup:
Rum, Amaretto. Add
Espresso. Fill with
Foamed/Steamed Milk.

 SACRED COW
Over Ice, Pour 1 oz
Cream de Cocoa. Add
Espresso. Fill with Cold
Milk.

 **SAINT PATRICK'S
DAY MOCHA JAVA**
Pour ¾ oz Thick
Chocolate Syrup, ½ oz
Irish Cream Syrup.
Add Espresso. Stir. Fill
with Foamed/Steamed
Milk. Top with
Whipped Cream and
Splash with Irish
Cream Syrup.

SAMBUCA COFFEE COOLER

Over Ice, Pour ¾ oz each Syrup: Coffee, Sambuca. Fill with Soda Water. Top with Whipped Cream and 3 Dark Roasted Coffee Beans.

 SAN JUAN SLING

Over Ice, Pour ¾ oz each Syrup: Rum, Cherry. Add ½ oz Lime Syrup. Fill with Soda Water. Splash with Lime Syrup.

 SANGRIA SPRITZER

Over Ice, Pour ¾ oz each Syrup: Orange, Creme de Cassis. Add ½ oz Lime Syrup. Fill with Soda Water.

 SARATOGA COOLER

Over Ice, Pour 1 oz Lemon Syrup. Fill with Ginger Ale.

 SAVORY LIME COOLER

Over Ice, Pour 2 oz Lime Syrup. Fill with Soda Water. Splash with Lime Syrup.

 SCREAMING ORGASM

Pour ¼ oz Kahlua Syrup, ¼ oz Irish Cream Syrup, ¼ oz Amaretto Syrup. Add 2 shots, Espresso and 6 oz Hot Water.

 SCORPION

Over Ice, Pour 1 oz Orange Syrup, ¾ oz Lemon Syrup, ¼ oz Pineapple Syrup. Fill with Soda Water.

 SEA BREEZE

Over Ice, Pour 4 oz Grapefruit Juice. Add Soda Water to ¼" from top of cup. Top with ½ oz of Cranberry Syrup.

 SHADY LADY

Over Ice, Fill with Grapefruit Juice to ½" from top of cup. Top with ½ oz Melon Syrup. Splash with Soda Water.

S

 SHANGHAI COOLER

Over Ice, Pour ⅔ oz each Syrup: Anisette, Lemon, Rum. Fill with Soda Water.

 SHIRLEY TEMPLE

Over Ice, Pour 1 oz Grenadine Syrup. Fill with Ginger Ale. Stir.

 SHORT "A" WITH ROOM

An 8 oz Americano with room for cream.

 SHORT SINGLE

A latte or an Americano in a short cup.

 SIESTA SLING

Over Ice, Pour ⅔ oz each Syrup: Apricot, Banana, Coconut. Fill with Soda Water. Splash with Lime Syrup.

 SILK BREVÉ

Pour ½ oz Honey, ¼ oz Anisette Syrup. Add Espresso. Stir. Fill with Foamed/Steamed Half-and-Half.

 SINGAPORE SLING COOLER

Over Ice, Pour ⅔ oz each Syrup: Almond, Grenadine, Orange. Fill with Soda Water. Stir.

SINGLE

A single shot of Espresso.

SKINNY SLEEPER

A latte made with decaf coffee and nonfat milk.

SKINNY TALLMOND

An almond latte, made with a double shot of espresso, nonfat steamed milk, no foam, in a tall cup.

 SMITH & KERNS

Over Ice, Pour 1⅓ oz Coffee Syrup, ⅔ oz Creme de Cacao Syrup, 1½ oz Half-and-Half, 2 oz Soda Water. Stir gently.

S

 SMITH & WESSON

Over Ice, Pour 1⅓ oz Coffee Syrup, ⅔ oz Creme de Cacao Syrup, 1½ oz Half-and-Half, 2 oz Cola. Stir gently.

 SNICKERS

Pour ⅓ oz each Thick Syrup: Chocolate, Caramel. Add ⅓ oz Hazelnut Syrup. Add Espresso. Stir. Fill with Foamed/Steamed Milk. Top with Whipped Cream and garnish with threads of Thick Caramel Syrup.

SNOW CAP

Pour 1 oz Vanilla Syrup. Fill with Foamed/Steamed Milk. Top with Whipped Cream and dust with Vanilla Powder and/or White Chocolate Powder.

SOLO

A single shot of Espresso.

SOLOMON'S SODA

Over Ice, Pour 1 oz each Syrup: Apricot, Creme de Cassis. Fill with Soda Water.

 SOUTH OF THE BORDER

Over Ice, Pour 1¼ oz Coffee Syrup, ¾ oz Orange Syrup. Fill with Soda Water.

 SOUTH SEAS COFFEE

Pour ½ oz Crème de Banana Syrup, ½ oz Rum Syrup. Add ½ tsp Brown Sugar, 2 shots, Espresso, 6 oz Hot Water. Top with 3 tbs Half-and-Half poured over a spoon. Dust with Grated Chocolate.

 SOUTH SEAS COOLER

Over Ice, Pour 2/3 oz each Syrup: Orange, Lemon. Add ½ oz Rum Syrup and splash of Almond Syrup. Fill with Soda Water. Top with Whipped Cream and Maraschino Cherry.

S

SOUTHWEST PRALINE PECAN LATTE

Pour ½ oz each Syrup: Praline, Pecan. Add Espresso. Fill with Foamed/Steamed Milk. Top with Whipped Cream.

SCRAP IRON

To cup of Brewed Coffee, add Espresso.

SNOW CAP

Pour 1 oz French Vanilla Syrup. Fill with Foamed/Steamed Milk. Top with Whipped Cream, Vanilla Powder and White Chocolate.

SOY MILK LATTE

Pour Espresso. Fill with Foamed/Steamed Soy Milk.

SPANISH COFFEE

Pour ½ oz Coffee Syrup, ½ oz Almond Syrup. Add Espresso and 6 oz Hot Water. Top with Whipped Cream.

SPANISH COFFEE II

Pour ½ oz Brandy Syrup, ½ oz Coffee Syrup. Add Espresso and 6 oz Hot Water. Top with Whipped Cream.

SPANISH EYES

Pour ⅓ oz each Syrup: Creme de Cacao, Rum. Fill with Hot Water to 1" from top of cup. Add a double shot of Espresso. Top with Whipped Cream. Splash with Creme de Cacao Syrup.

SPARKLING CITRUS COOLER

Over Ice, Pour 1 oz Lime Syrup. Add 4 oz Grapefruit Juice. Fill with Soda Water.

SPARKLING ROSY SODA

Over Ice, Pour 1¼ oz Apple Syrup, ¾ oz Strawberry Syrup. Fill with Soda Water.

S

 SPICE ISLAND SPECIAL

Pour ¾ oz Chocolate Syrup, ¼ oz Orange Syrup, and 1/8 oz Cinnamon Syrup. Fill with Foamed/Steamed Milk.

 SPICED & ICED COFFEE

Pour ½ oz Simple Syrup. Add Espresso. Add a Pinch of Cinnamon and Nutmeg Powder. Stir. Add Ice. Fill with Cold Water.

 SPICED RUM COFFEE

Pour ⅓ oz each Syrup: Rum, Cinnamon. Fill with Hot Water to 1" from top of cup. Add Espresso.

SPICED TEA SODA

Over Ice, Pour 1 oz each Syrup: Cinnamon, Lemon. Add ½ oz Orange Syrup. Fill with Soda Water.

 SPICY BANANA CREAM SODA

Over Ice, Pour 1½ oz Banana Syrup, ½ oz Cinnamon Syrup. Add Soda Water to ½" from top of cup. Fill with Half-and-Half.

SPICY CINNAMON MOCHA

Pour 1 oz Thick Chocolate Syrup, ⅓ oz Cinnamon Syrup. Add Espresso. Stir. Fill with Foamed/Steamed Milk. Top with Whipped Cream and Chocolate Sprinkles.

 **SPICY CRANBERRY LEMON SODA**

Over Ice, Pour ⅔ oz each Syrup: Cranberry, Lemon. Add ½ oz Cinnamon Syrup. Fill with Soda Water.

 SPICY ICED ESPRESSO

Pour 1 oz Cinnamon Syrup. Add Espresso. Fill with Ice. Add Cold Water to top of cup. Splash with Lemon Syrup.

S

SPICY LICORICE LATTE
Pour ⅓ oz each Syrup: Licorice, Orange, Cinnamon. Add Espresso. Fill with Foamed/Steamed Milk. Dust with Cinnamon Powder.

SPICY PEACH LATTE
Pour ½ oz Peach Syrup, ¼ oz Cinnamon Syrup. Add Espresso. Fill with Foamed/Steamed Milk.

SPIKE
Pour 6 oz Hot Water. Top with Decaf Espresso.

SPUMONI COFFEE
Pour ¼ oz each Syrup: Cinnamon, Creme de Cacao, Orange, Almond. Fill with Hot Water to 1" from top of cup. Top with Espresso and Whipped Cream.

ST. NICK'S NOGGIN
Pour ½ oz Irish Cream Syrup. Pour Espresso. Fill with Foamed/ Steamed Egg Nog. Top with Whipped Cream. Dust with Nutmeg.

STEAMBOAT SPRINGS CREAM SODA
Over Ice, Pour 1 oz each Syrup: Licorice, Blueberry. Add 2 oz Soda Water. Fill with Half-and-Half. Top with Whipped Cream.

STEAMER
Pour 1 oz any Flavored Syrup. Fill with Foamed/Steamed Milk. Top with Whipped Cream.

STRAWBERRY ANGEL
Over Ice, Pour 1½ oz Strawberry Syrup, ½ oz Coconut Syrup. Add Soda Water to ½" from top of cup. Fill with Half-and-Half. Top with Whipped Cream.

S

 STRAWBERRY APPLE LATTE

Pour ½ oz each Syrup: Strawberry, Apple. Add Espresso. Fill with Foamed/Steamed Milk.

 STRAWBERRY COLADA

Over Ice, Pour ⅔ oz each Syrup: Coconut, Pineapple, Strawberry. Fill with Soda Water.

 STRAWBERRY BANANA COOLER

Over Ice, Pour 1 oz each Syrup: Strawberry, Banana. Fill with Soda Water.

 STRAWBERRY BANANA MILK

Over Ice, Pour ¾ oz each Syrup: Strawberry, Banana. Fill with Cold Milk. Splash with Vanilla Syrup.

 STRAWBERRY BLOND

Over Ice, Pour 1⅓ oz Strawberry Syrup. Fill with Soda Water to ¼" from top. Top with ⅔ oz Lemon Syrup.

 STRAWBERRY CRANBERRY FROST

Over Ice, Pour 1 oz each Syrup: Strawberry, Cranberry. Fill with Soda Water. Splash with Strawberry Syrup.

 STRAWBERRY CREAM SODA

Over Ice, Pour 1 oz each Syrup: Strawberry, Vanilla. Add Soda Water to ½" from top of cup. Top with Half-and-Half.

 STRAWBERRY CRUSH

Over Ice, Pour 1½ oz Strawberry Syrup. Fill with Soda Water to ¼" from top of cup. Top with ½ oz Orange Syrup.

 STRAWBERRY DAWN

Over Ice, Pour 1¼ oz Strawberry Syrup, ¾ oz Coconut Syrup. Add Soda Water to ½" from top of cup. Fill with Half-and-Half. Splash with Strawberry Syrup.

STRAWBERRY LICORICE LATTE

Pour ½ oz Strawberry Syrup, ¼ oz Licorice Syrup. Add Espresso. Fill with Foamed/ Steamed Milk.

 STRAWBERRY LUAU

Over Ice, Pour 1 oz each Syrup: Strawberry, Banana. Add Soda Water to ½" from top of cup. Fill with Half-and-Half and top with Whipped Cream.

 STRAWBERRY MARGARITA

Over Ice, Pour 1⅓ oz Strawberry Syrup, ⅓ oz each Syrup: Orange, Lime. Fill with Soda Water.

 STRAWBERRY NEWTON CREAM SODA

Over Ice, Pour ⅔ oz each Syrup: Strawberry, Apple, Pineapple. Add Soda Water to ½" from top of cup. Fill with Half-and-Half.

 STRAWBERRY PINEAPPLE CREAM SODA

Over Ice, Pour ¾ oz each Syrup: Strawberry, Pineapple. Add ½ oz Vanilla Syrup. Add Soda Water to ½" from top of cup. Top with Half-and-Half.

 STRAWBERRY SHORTCAKE CREAM SODA

Over Ice, Pour 1¼ oz Strawberry Syrup, ½ oz Almond Syrup, ¼ oz Creme de Cacao Syrup. Add Soda Water to ½" from top of cup. Fill with Half-and-Half and top with Whipped Cream.

 STRAWBERRY SLIM

Over Ice, Pour 2 oz Strawberry Syrup. Add Soda Water to ½" from top of cup. Top with Nonfat Milk.

S

 STRAWBERRY SUNRISE

Over Ice, Pour 1 oz Strawberry Syrup. Add Orange Juice to ½" from top of cup. Fill with Soda Water.

 STRAWBERRY VANILLA CREAM SODA

Over Ice, Pour 1 oz each Syrup: Strawberry, Vanilla. Add Soda Water to ½" from top of cup. Fill with Half-and-Half. Splash with Strawberry Syrup.

 STRAWBERRIES AND CREAM

Over Ice, Pour 1½ oz Strawberry Syrup. Fill with Cold Milk or Half-and-Half. Splash with Strawberry Syrup.

 SUGAR DADDY LATTE

Pour ⅔ oz Thick Caramel Syrup, ½ oz Hazelnut Syrup. Add Espresso. Stir. Fill with Foamed/Steamed Milk.

 SUMMER CYCLIST

Over Ice, Pour ½ oz each Syrup: Strawberry, Lime, Orange, and Grape. Fill with Soda Water.

 SUN SODA

Over Ice, Pour 2 oz Orange Syrup. Add Half-and-Half to ½" from top of cup. Top with Ginger Ale or Soda Water.

 SUNBURST

Pour ½ oz each Syrup: Chocolate, Orange. Add Espresso. Fill with Foamed/Steamed Milk.

 SUNRISE SODA 1

Over Ice, Pour 1 oz each Syrup: Orange, Pineapple. Fill with Soda Water. Splash with Grenadine Syrup.

 SUNRISE SODA 2

Over Ice, Pour 1¾ oz Orange Syrup, ¼ oz Grenadine Syrup. Fill with Soda Water.

S

 SUNSET COOLER
Over Ice, Pour ½ oz
Grenadine Syrup, 1 oz
Orange Syrup, ½ oz
Pineapple Syrup. Fill
with Soda Water.

 SUNSET SODA
Over Ice, Pour ⅔ oz
each Syrup: Peach,
Raspberry, Pineapple.
Fill with Soda Water.

 **SUNSET STRIP
SODA**
Over Ice, Pour 1 oz
Mandarino Syrup. Fill
with equal parts of
Ginger Ale and Soda
Water. Splash with
Grenadine Syrup.

 SWAMP WATER
Over Ice, Pour 1 oz
each Syrup: Orange,
Root Beer. Fill with
Soda Water.

 SWEDISH COFFEE
Pour ½ oz Chocolate
Syrup. Add 1 tbs
Brown Sugar. Add
Espresso and 6 oz Hot
Water. Top with
Whipped Cream.

 **SWEET & SOUR
SODA**
Over Ice, Pour 1 oz
Apple Syrup. Add Soda
Water to 1" from top of
cup. Fill with
Grapefruit Juice. Splash
with Cherry Syrup.

 **TAHITI CLUB
COOLER**
Over Ice, Pour 1 oz
Rum Syrup, ⅓ oz each
Syrup: Lemon, Lime,
Pineapple. Fill with
Soda Water. Splash
with Maraschino
Syrup.

 **TAHITIAN
CARAMEL CREAM
SODA**
Over Ice, Pour ½ oz
each Syrup: Coconut,
Praline, Pineapple,
Caramel. Fill with Soda
Water to ½" from top
of cup. Fill with Half-
and-Half.

T

TAHITIAN COFFEE

Pour ¾ oz Coconut Syrup. Add 4 oz Hot Water. Add Espresso. Top with Whipped Cream. Dust with Chocolate Powder.

TALL "A" BLACK

Tall Americano with no cream.

TALL SKINNY LATTE

A tall latte made with nonfat milk.

TALL TOO

A tall latte made with 2% milk.

TALL WHIPLESS FOAMLESS

A tall mocha with all steamed milk and no foamed milk or whipped cream.

TANGELO COOLER

Over Ice, Pour 1 oz each Syrup: Mandarino, Pink Grapefruit. Fill with Soda Water.

TANGERINE AND LIME SODA

Over Ice, Pour 1 oz each Syrup: Tangerine, Lime. Fill with Soda Water. Splash with Lime Syrup.

TANGERINE CHERRY SODA

Over Ice, Pour 1¼ oz Mandarino Syrup, ¾ oz Cherry Syrup. Fill with Soda Water.

TEQUILA SUNSET

Over Ice, Fill to ¼" from top of cup with Orange Juice. Top with ¼ oz Grenadine Syrup.

TERESA'S TROPICAL COOLER

Over Ice, Pour ½ oz each Syrup: Pineapple, Mango, Orange, Coconut. Fill with Soda Water. Splash with Lemon Syrup.

T

 THAI ICED COFFEE

Pour a double shot of Espresso. Add Ice. Fill with Sweetened Condensed Milk.

 THRILLER

Over Ice, Pour ⅓ oz each Syrup: Grenadine, Orange, Pineapple. Add 1 oz Strawberry Syrup. Add Soda Water to ½" from top of cup. Top with 2 oz Half-and-Half.

 THAI ICED COFFEE II

Pour ½ oz Anisette Syrup. Add double shot, Espresso and Ice. Add Cold Water to ½" from top of cup. Top with Half-and-Half.

 THUNDER THIGHS

A double tall mocha made with whole milk and topped with extra whipped cream.

 **TOASTED ALMOND**

Pour ⅔ oz Amaretto Syrup, ¼ oz Almond Syrup. Add Espresso. Fill with Foamed/Steamed Milk. Top with Whipped Cream.

 **TOASTED COCONUT CREAM BREVÉ**

Pour ⅔ oz Coconut Syrup, ¼ oz Hazelnut Syrup. Add Espresso. Fill with Foamed/Steamed Half-and-Half and top with Whipped Cream.

TOASTED JOE

Pour 1 tbs Coffee Syrup. Foam and steam Milk with 1 tbs Toasted Walnut Syrup. Set pitcher aside. Pour 2 shots, Espresso. Stir. Allow Steamed Milk to Pour under Foam to ½" from top of cup. Top with 2" "cap" of Dense Foam.

T

TOASTED WALNUT BREVE

Pour 1 oz Toasted Walnut Syrup, 1 oz Vanilla Syrup. Add Espresso. Fill with Foamed/Steamed Half-and-Half. (Special Note: Pour Espresso first for this recipe, then add flavorings and steamed milk.)

TREE TOP CREAM SODA

Over Ice, Pour 1 oz each Syrup: Apple, Apricot. Add Soda Water to ½" from top of cup. Fill with Half-and-Half.

TRIPLE BERRY CREAM SODA

Over Ice, Pour ⅔ oz each Syrup: Blackberry, Cranberry, Raspberry. Add Soda Water to ½" from top of cup. Fill with Half-and-Half.

TRIPLE SQUEEZE SODA

Over Ice, Pour ⅔ oz each Syrup: Lime, Mandarino, Orange. Fill with Soda Water.

TRIPLE TALL ICED SKINNY WITH VANILLA

A nonfat milk iced latte with 3 shots of espresso and vanilla syrup.

TRIPLE TALL WHIPLESS

A mocha with a triple shot of espresso and no whipped cream, in a tall cup.

TRIPLE TALL WHIPLESS BILLIARD BALL

A mocha with a triple shot of espresso, no foam, no whipped cream, in a tall cup.

T

TROPICAL COFFEE
Pour 1 oz Rum Syrup, ½ oz Coconut Syrup. Add Espresso and 6 oz Hot Water. Top with Whipped Cream and Grated Coconut.

TROPICAL COFFEE COOLER
Pour Espresso. Add Ice. Add ½ oz each Syrup: Mango, Pineapple. Fill with Milk.

TROPICAL HEART
Pour ⅓ oz Passion Fruit Syrup into a steaming pitcher, add Apple Cider. Steam and serve.

TROPICAL COCONUT SODA
Over Ice, Pour 1½ oz Coconut Syrup, ½ oz Mango Syrup. Fill with Soda Water. Splash with Lime Syrup.

TROPICAL GRAPEFRUIT NOG
Over Ice, Pour 1 oz Mango Syrup, 3 oz Grapefruit Juice. Fill with Egg Nog. Dust with Nutmeg.

TROPICAL LATTE
Pour ½ oz each Syrup: Coconut, Pineapple. Add Espresso. Fill with Foamed/Steamed Milk.

TROPICAL PINEAPPLE SODA
Over Ice, Pour 1¼ oz Pineapple Syrup, ½ oz Amaretto Syrup, ¼ oz Rum Syrup. Fill with Soda Water.

TROPICAL TEASE
Over Ice, Pour ⅔ oz each Syrup: Passion Fruit, Banana, Coconut. Fill with Soda Water.

TROPIRITA
Over Ice, Pour ½ oz each Syrup: Coconut, Green Banana, Lime, Pineapple. Fill with Soda Water.

TURKISH COFFEE
Pour 3 oz Hot Water. Add 1 tablespoon Equal. Stir. Add a double shot Espresso. Splash a few drops of Rose Water (optional).

T

 TURKISH COFFEE COLA SODA

Pour a double shot of Espresso. Add Ice. Fill with Cola to ½" from top of cup. Top with Half-and-Half.

 TURTLE SUNDAE

Pour ¾ oz Thick Chocolate Syrup, ⅓ oz each Syrup: Caramel, Praline. Add Espresso. Stir. Fill with Foamed/Steamed Half-and-Half. Top with Whipped Cream.

TUTTI FRUTTI

Over Ice, Pour ½ oz each Syrup: Maraschino, Amaretto, Apple, Peach. Fill with Soda Water. Splash with Maraschino Syrup.

 TUSCANY

Pour ¾ oz Thick Chocolate Syrup, ⅓ oz Orange Syrup. Add Espresso. Stir. Fill with Foamed/Steamed Milk. Top with Whipped Cream and Chocolate Sprinkles.

 UNFUZZY NAVEL

Over Ice, Pour 1¼ oz Orange Syrup, ½ oz Peach Syrup, ¼ oz Lemon Syrup. Fill with Soda Water. Splash with Grenadine Syrup.

 VANILLA FUN CAPPUCCINO

Pour ¾ oz Vanilla Syrup into steaming pitcher. Fill pitcher ⅓ full with Cold Milk. Foam and steam Milk-Syrup mixture. Set pitcher aside. Pour Espresso. Allow flavored Steamed Milk to pour under Foam to ½" from top of cup. Top with 2" "cap" of dense, flavored Foam.

VANILLA COFFEE LATTE

Pour ½ oz each Syrup: Vanilla, Coffee. Add Espresso. Fill with Foamed/Steamed Milk.

V

 VANILLA ICED COFFEE

Pour ⅔ oz Vanilla Syrup. Add Espresso. Fill with Ice and Cold Water.

 VANILLA IRISH CREAM LATTE

Pour ½ oz Vanilla Syrup, ½ oz Irish Cream Syrup. Add 2 shots, Espresso. Fill with Foamed/Steamed Milk. Top with Chocolate and Vanilla Sprinkles.

 VANILLA MOCHA LATTE

Pour ½ oz Thick Chocolate Syrup, ½ oz Vanilla Syrup. Add Espresso. Stir. Fill with Foamed/Steamed Milk.

 VENETIAN COFFEE

Pour 1 oz Brandy Syrup. Add ¾ tsp Sugar. Add Espresso and 6 oz Hot Water. Top with Whipped Cream.

 VERY BERRY ITALIAN SODA

Over Ice, Pour 1 oz each Syrup: Raspberry, Boysenberry. Fill with Soda Water.

 VERY BERRY ROYAL SODA

Over Ice, Pour ⅔ oz each Syrup: Blackberry, Raspberry, Strawberry. Add Soda Water to ½" from top of cup. Fill with Half-and-Half. Top with Whipped Cream.

VIENNA MELANGE

In an 8 oz cup, Pour ½ oz Irish Cream Syrup, ¼ oz Orange Syrup. Add Espresso. Top with Whipped Cream.

VIENNESE CAFE MOCHA

A mocha with ½ oz of cinnamon syrup added.

V

VIENNESE COFFEE

Pour ½ oz Vanilla Syrup. Add 3 oz Hot Water and a double shot of Espresso. Top with Whipped Cream. Dust with Cinnamon or Nutmeg.

VIENNESE MOCHA

Pour ⅔ oz Thick Chocolate Syrup, ¼ oz each Syrup: Cinnamon, Almond. Add Espresso. Stir. Fill with Foamed/Steamed Milk. Top with Whipped Cream. Garnish with threads of thick Chocolate Syrup over Whipped Cream.

VIETNAMESE COFFEE

Pour Espresso. Add Ice. Fill with Sweetened Condensed Milk.

VINNY'S CAPPUCCINO

Pour ¾ oz Chocolate Mint Syrup, ¼ oz Cinnamon Syrup. Foam and Steam Milk. Set pitcher aside. Pour Espresso. Allow Steamed Milk to pour under Foam to ½" from top of cup. Top with 2" "cap" of dense Foam. Dust with Chocolate Powder.

WAKE-UP CALL

Top Brewed Coffee with 2 shots, Espresso.

WATERMELON LEMON SODA

Over Ice, Pour 1¼ oz Watermelon Syrup, ¾ oz Lemon Syrup. Fill with Soda Water.

WERTHER'S ORIGINAL COFFEE

Pour ½ oz each Syrup: Butterscotch, Irish Cream. Add Espresso. Fill with Hot Water.

W

 ### WEST INDIAN COOLER

Over Ice, Pour ½ oz each Syrup: Orange, Pineapple, Banana, Rum. Fill with Soda Water. Splash with Lime Syrup. Dust with Nutmeg Powder.

WET CAPPUCCINO

First Foam and Steam Milk. Set pitcher aside. Pour Espresso. Allow Steamed Milk to pour under Foam to ¼" from top of cup. Top with a short "cap" of dense Foam. Dust with Chocolate Powder or Nutmeg.

 ### WETZLAR COFFEE

Pour a double shot of Espresso. Add Ice. Pour ¾ oz each Syrup: Cherry, Creme de Cacao. Fill with Cold Milk or Half-and-Half.

WHITE CHOCOLATE MOCHA

Pour 1 oz White Chocolate Syrup. Add Espresso. Fill with Foamed/Steamed Milk. Top with Whipped Cream.

WHITE CLOUD

Over Ice, Pour 2 oz Anisette Syrup. Fill with Soda Water. Splash with Vanilla Syrup.

WHITE COW

Pour ¾ oz Thick Chocolate Syrup, ½ oz Vanilla Syrup. Add Espresso. Stir. Fill with Foamed/Steamed Milk. Top with Whipped Cream and Chocolate Sprinkles.

WHY BOTHER?

A latte made with decaf coffee and nonfat milk.

Z

WOO WOO

Over Ice, Pour 1 oz
each Syrup: Peach,
Cranberry. Fill with
Soda Water.

YANKEE DOG
WITH A WHITE
HAT ON A LEASH

Fill to ½" from top
with Hot Water. Add
Espresso. Top with Hot
Milk Foam. To Go.

YELLOWBIRD

Over Ice, Pour ½ oz
each Syrup: Pineapple,
Banana, Lemon, Rum.
Fill with Soda Water.

ZOMBIE

Over Ice, Pour ½ oz
Creme de Cacao Syrup.
Add ¼ oz each Syrup:
Strawberry, Vanilla,
Pineapple, Orange,
Lime. Fill with Soda
Water.

Chapter 3

Coffee & Espresso: Past to Present

The Evolution of Coffee:

1. It was first eaten as food: the berries were mixed with fat and rolled into balls to carry on long journeys.

2. It was also drunk as a fermented wine.

3. It was then taken as a medicine.

4. Finally, it was roasted and brewed as a beverage.

 Nomadic tribes preserved the coffee cherries to transport them long distances.

 Coffee has been in existence at least as long as man.

 The first coffee tree was discovered growing wild in Ethiopia, Africa. It was a species of the Arabica plant.

The most widely accepted legend associated with the discovery of coffee concerns a goatherder named Kaldi of Ethiopia. Around the year 600 A.D., Kaldi was amazed as he noticed his goats behaving in a frisky manner after eating the leaves and berries of a coffee shrub. Of course, he had to try them.

The coffee plant was first cultivated in Yemen in the seventh century.

The Arabs are generally believed to be the first to brew coffee.

The word *coffee* likely derives from the root meaning of the Arabic word *gahwa*, a word which may be translated as "wine" or as "excitement."

Coffee was first known in Europe as Arabian Wine.

Around the year 950 A.D., Arabs soaked green coffee beans in cold water to make the first coffee beverage.

Shortly before the year 1000 A.D., coffee frequently was administered as a medicine.

Roasted coffee goes back to the 13th century when people began roasting the beans before brewing them. Beans were generally roasted in a heavy pan over a charcoal fire before whole beans were boiled.

After the Arabs learned to boil water, they used green coffee beans to make their brew.

Turkey began to roast the coffee bean in the 13th century, and some 300 years later in the 1500s the country had become the chief distributor of coffee with markets established in Egypt, Syria, Persia, and Venice, Italy.

Late in the 1300s Arabs discovered the process of roasting coffee.

In the 14th century Arabs started to cultivate coffee plants. The first commercially grown and harvested coffee originated on the Arabian Peninsula near the port of Mocha.

In the early 1400s alcohol was forbidden by the Koran, and coffee soon became the replacement beverage. It was drunk both at home and at coffeehouses.

A four-verse poem to coffee, one of the first, was written in Mecca in 1511.

It is thought that the first roasted, *ground* coffee was probably brewed in Syria in the 1520s. Roasted beans were pounded to a powder with a mortar and pestle before being thrown into boiling water. The brew was consumed grounds and all.

Finely ground coffee beans boiled in water is still known as "Turkish coffee." Coffee is still made this way today in Turkey and Greece or anywhere else Turkish coffee is served.

In 1554 in Constantinople, two coffeehouses opened. They did very well. Soon there were many.

In 1586 Sassafras tea was about as popular as espresso is now. Sassafras stands could be found throughout London. The first large shipments from North America were Sassafras roots to quench the ever increasing demand. The tea stands vanished virtually overnight, however, when rumor spread that the New World Indians drank Sassafras broth to treat syphilis.

Coffee's first pitch man? In 1587 Sheik Abd-Al Kadir, theologian-lawyer and follower of Muhammed, was so captivated by the charm of coffee that he decided to convince his suspicious peers coffee wasn't incompatible with the prophet's law. His famous and successful argument in favor of the magic brew contained an Arabic quotation: "No one can understand the truth until he drinks of coffee's frothy goodness."

By 1600 A.D. coffee drinking had come to the Orient and soon became very popular.

The Venetians first introduced coffee to Europe in 1615.

Some experts believe that sugar as a coffee sweetener stimulated the rapid growth of coffee in Europe. As coffee was introduced into each European country, sugar was introduced with it.

The year was 1632: early European coffeehouses quickly became centers of social activities and culture.

In the mid-1600s, much British money flowed out of the empire to buy coffee. Its price rose to the equivalent of $48 per pound "Enough!" cried the powers. They replaced coffee with colony-grown tea and ordered a change in national taste. Profit precedes preference, does it not?

The first Turkish coffeehouse opened in London in 1650.

Coffeehouses of the late 1600s frequently hired live entertainment: singers, flute and violin players to amuse the clientele.

Many of these early day coffeehouses were known as "penny universities." They charged a penny for admission and a cup of coffee. You could then participate in the intellectual discussions of the time, all stimulated by the fresh-brewed coffee.

Coffeehouses not only served as "Penny Universities," but as "Penny Post Offices." In 1863 several coffeehouses in London collected mail and provided private boxes—before the government got involved. The king laid claim as a royal prerogative, and taxes were collected. Soon there were no longer "Penny Post Offices."

Lloyd's of London began as Edward Lloyd's coffeehouse.

It was during the 1600s that the first coffee mill made its debut in London.

Coffee was first introduced in America as a consumer good in 1660. It was sold to the affluent Dutch of New Amsterdam. The English soon conquered New Amsterdam and renamed it New York.

In 1645 a cafe in Venice began serving beverages made from water and ice as well as roasted coffee. By 1761 Venice had become the coffee capital of Italy with one coffee shop for every 500 inhabitants.

Coffee as a medicine reached its highest and lowest point in the 1600s in England. Wild medical contraptions were used to treat the sick by administering a mixture of coffee and an assortment of heated butter, honey, and oil.

In 1670 Dorothy Jones of Boston was granted a license to sell coffee and so became the first American coffee trader.

 William Penn purchased a pound of coffee in New York in 1683 for $4.68.

 One pound of coffee in New York was worth as much as four acres of land. The year was 1683.

 Coffee continues to play an important role in Turkish custom and social life. It is part of traditional courtship for a prospective bride to demonstrate her coffee-making skills to the parents of a suitor.

 Everything with either nicotine or caffeine in it—sometime, somewhere—has faced fierce attack. In 1674, the Women's Petition Against Coffee contained this line: "Trifle away their time, scald their chops, and spend their money, all for a little base, black, thick, nasty, bitter, stinking, nauseous puddle water."

 Milk as an additive to coffee became popular in the 1680s when a French physician recommended that cafe au lait be used for medicinal purposes.

 The first Parisian cafe opened in 1689 to serve coffee.

In 1711 coffee sold at an Amsterdam auction for 47¢ a pound. The commodity price on the world exchanges in 1993 dipped as low as 40¢ a pound. So much for inflation ....

Adding sugar to coffee is believed to have started in 1715 in the court of King Louis XIV, the French monarch.

Why did Frederick the Great of Prussia hate coffee so much? He thought it drained Prussian money out of state, money that could be spent locally. "My people must drink beer!" he cried.

About 250 years ago, England jacked up its import taxes mightily. Students of trade history will tell you two thirds of all the tea in England thereafter was smuggled into the country.

After the Boston Tea Party of 1773, Boston's "Bean Town" moniker took on a whole new meaning.

In the book, *Trip Through Happy Arabia,* (1716) a Frenchman included one of the first documentations of the history of coffee.

Wealthy Turkish homes of the 16th century employed full time coffee stewards.

By the 1720s coffee shops in Venice offered a wide range of goods and services including iced beverages and newspapers.

Coffee plants were introduced to the Americas for cultivation in 1723 when a French ship captain persuaded the crown to allow him to take a few small coffee plants back to Martinique.

The year was 1716: Venetian coffee shop merchants began distributing leaflets exalting their new product, coffee. This may be the first example of advertising for coffee shops.

In 1727 seedlings smuggled from Paris became the first coffee plants to be cultivated in Brazil. Brazil is presently by far the world's largest producer of coffee.

Bach wrote a coffee cantata in 1732.

Filtering coffee with metal, paper, and cloth filters began during the 1700s.

Before the first French cafe appeared in the late 1700s, coffee was sold by street vendors in Europe in the Arab fashion. Arabs were the forerunners of today's sidewalk espresso vendors.

In the year 1763 there were over 200 coffee shops in Venice, yet the world's first public restaurant in Paris would not open until 1770.

The heavy tea tax imposed on the colonies in 1773, which caused the "Boston Tea Party," resulted in America switching from tea to coffee. Drinking coffee was an expression of freedom.

During the revolution, the founding fathers of the U.S. formed their national strategies in coffeehouses.

In early America coffee was usually taken between meals and after dinner.

By 1777 almost 20 million coffee plants were being cultivated on Martinique. That number was sufficient to satisfy three-quarters of Europe's demand.

In the year 1790 there were two firsts in the United States: the first wholesale coffee roasting company; and the first newspaper advertisement featuring coffee.

By 1843 coffee had become ingrained in French society, with over 3,000 cafes serving it.

A Frenchman, Lebrun, invented the first working espresso machine in 1838.

Frontier lore suggests that Native Americans traded their buffalo hides and other furs to trappers and traders for precious coffee beans.

The authors of the book *Coffee and Tea* suggest that the site of Fort Laramie "… was swapped for tools, rifles, and a few bags of Java beans."

The Enterprise Manufacturing Co. of Philadelphia started manufacturing old general store coffee mills in the mid 1800s. Today the large two-wheel counter models are a popular item at antique auctions.

By 1850 the manual coffee grinder had found its way to most upper middle class kitchens of the U.S.

In 1864 Jabez Burns invented a coffee roaster that did not have to be removed from the fire to discharge the beans. Within ten years, home roasting was virtually obsolete.

The Civil War in the United States elevated the popularity of coffee to new heights. Soldiers went to war with coffee beans as a primary ration.

Abraham Lincoln never had anything more than a cup of coffee for breakfast.

The first espresso coffee machine with steam and water control was invented by Kessel in 1878.

Caleb Chase and James Sanborn first packaged ground coffee in a sealed tin can. The year was 1878.

That little turnkey that your parents used for opening coffee cans was patented in 1886. The whoosh sound of air and the seductive aroma of preground coffee beans was a great marketing ploy that sold millions of pounds of product over the next hundred years.

The year was 1885; the city was Turin, Italy. The first commercial bulk brewing espresso machine was patented.

 The ice cream soda was concocted in 1874.

 Hills Brothers' trademark Arabian, in his flowing robe and colorful turban, was designed by a moonlighting San Francisco *Examiner* cartoonist in 1897. The Arabian's symbol has endured hundreds of packaging changes over almost a century of advertising. He has become the patron saint of coffee advertising. The trademark Arabian is arguably the first occasion when an advertisement linked the coffee drinker to exotic cultures.

 "Candle auctions" of coffee lots took place on the Coffee and Tea Exchange in London during the late 1880s. A candle was lit, and bids were called. The last bid taken before the candle flickered out was the winner.

 The process of roasting coffee using hot air as the only medium was developed about 1885 when the beans were first placed in a chamber heated by natural gas. This method remains today the best and most popular method for roasting coffee.

 The vacuum pack, invented in 1898, made it possible to preserve roasted coffee. Preserved coffee, though, not fresh coffee. Ten years later, Hills Brothers Coffee began using this packaging method.

The first electric gear-driven coffee grinder made its appearance in 1900.

 By the early 1900s electricity had been merged with the coffee maker. Heating elements were attached to existing stove-top models. However, the very first electric coffeemaker was developed in London in 1881. This crude device featured electric coils encased in an urn. Electric coffeemakers would not achieve popularity for another 20 years.

 In 1900 coffee was often delivered door-to-door in the United States by horse-pulled wagons.

 Sans caffeine is a French phrase meaning "without caffeine." Sanka, the decaffeinated coffee, was packaged in 1903.

 The first commercial espresso machine was manufactured in Italy in 1906.

 While dining at the famous Hermitage, the old home of Andrew Jackson in Nashville, Tennessee, Teddy Roosevelt was asked if he wanted more coffee. "Deelighted!" responded Teddy. "It's good to the last drop!" Maxwell House® Coffee's advertising slogan was coined.

 Espresso is to Italy what champagne is to France.

 The average age of an Italian barista is 48. A barista is a respected job title in Italy.

In Italy coffee and espresso are synonymous.

Italians do not drink espresso during meals. Espresso is considered to be a separate event and is given its own time.

At a Walgreen's soda fountain during the 1920s, "Pop" Caulson invented the milk shake. Today the Moka shake is a popular request. Simply add a short shot of espresso before blending.

Around 1920 the Coffee table replaced the tea table in American living rooms. From the 17th century until the 1920s most people placed full height (at least 26 inches tall) tea tables in front of their sofas.

The "coffee break" in the American workplace came about during World War II. Employers found that their employees would work longer and harder if they were supplied with a coffee break during their shifts. U.S. studies shortly thereafter reported that 10,000 marriages a year were directly traceable to romances which began during these coffee breaks.

The year was 1928: Brazil's economy collapsed owing to the over-production of coffee. By 1931 the National Coffee Department in Brazil had ordered the destruction of surplus stocks.

Hill Brothers Coffee was the first commercial company to sell vacuum-packed coffee in 1900.

"[My] husband came home in great glee, giving me a recipe for fixing bran in such a manner that when we cooked it would taste very much like coffee," one pioneer woman said in a Work Projects Administration study from Washington State in the 1930s. Others parched peas, rye or barley as stand-ins for the genuine article.

 The year was 1929 when coffee was first served in a paper cup. Ray Kroc (before he introduced hamburgers "to go" by the billion) was responsible for the "to go" phenomenon of America's favorite hot beverage, back when he sold cups for Lily Tulip. Over 60 years later, millions of aficionados are lining up daily at busy espresso carts to maintain the tradition pioneered by this guru of take-out.

 The roots of live music in the coffeehouse may be traced to prewar Berlin. Cafes there developed the singing tradition of cabarets.

 The stovetop Moka Express coffee maker popular in Europe was designed in 1933. It took several years to achieve popularity. More than 20 million units have been sold since World War II.

 In 1936, Charlie McCarthy became the wooden pitch man for Chase and Sanborn Coffee on radio's *Chase and Sanborn Hour.* Edgar Bergen, of course, was Charlie's voice.

The coffee break was a common practice in the Middle East and Europe for centuries before it became standard operating procedure in the United States during World War II.

Stephanie Foster, director of public relations at the Buffalo and Erie County Historical Society in New York State, claims the very first coffee break in the U.S. was taken in 1902 at "the nation's oldest manufacturer of reclining chairs," the Barcalo and Boll Manufacturing Company in Buffalo. A one-time company vice president was quoted in a 1965 news article recalling the details of how it all came about.

In the early 1950s the Moka Bar opened in London. It was England's first "Espresso Bar." Many followed. Popular with both teens and adults, these espresso bars served up espresso, cappuccino, poetry, acoustical music, and socializing.

U.S. troops got used to instant coffee while fighting World War II. Nestlé turned out 25 million pounds of it for the GIs, and other companies also shipped "soluble coffee" to the front. After the war, instant continued to enjoy considerable popularity.

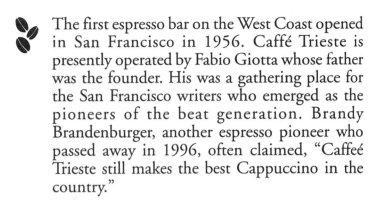

The first espresso bar on the West Coast opened in San Francisco in 1956. Caffé Trieste is presently operated by Fabio Giotta whose father was the founder. His was a gathering place for the San Francisco writers who emerged as the pioneers of the beat generation. Brandy Brandenburger, another espresso pioneer who passed away in 1996, often claimed, "Caffeé Trieste still makes the best Cappuccino in the country."

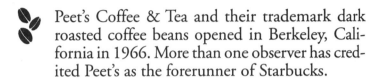

Peet's Coffee & Tea and their trademark dark roasted coffee beans opened in Berkeley, California in 1966. More than one observer has credited Peet's as the forerunner of Starbucks.

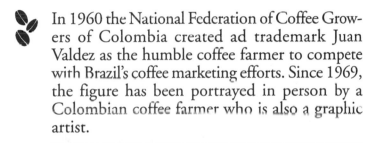

In 1960 the National Federation of Coffee Growers of Colombia created ad trademark Juan Valdez as the humble coffee farmer to compete with Brazil's coffee marketing efforts. Since 1969, the figure has been portrayed in person by a Colombian coffee farmer who is also a graphic artist.

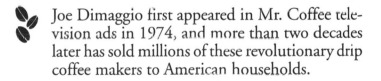

Joe Dimaggio first appeared in Mr. Coffee television ads in 1974, and more than two decades later has sold millions of these revolutionary drip coffee makers to American households.

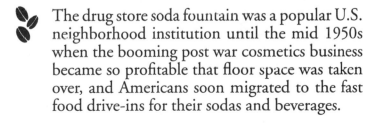

The drug store soda fountain was a popular U.S. neighborhood institution until the mid 1950s when the booming post war cosmetics business became so profitable that floor space was taken over, and Americans soon migrated to the fast food drive-ins for their sodas and beverages.

By the 1960s coffeehouses and folk musicians had appeared on the U.S. scene. Usually adjoining university districts in large cities, they seemed to focus their appeal and marketing efforts towards the counter-culture, a far cry from the polished coffee bars of the 1990s.

Germany began marketing the Melitta® drip coffeemaker in 1960. Later this vastly improved coffee making method spread to the U.S. and Canada. Drinking recirculated coffee from percolators became a thing of the past.

Irish coffee was first served up in the U.S. at the Buena Vista Cafe in San Francisco in 1953. An immediate hit, the drink continues to draw throngs of tourists to the San Francisco waterfront to this day.

Through trial and error, the then-owner of San Francisco's Buena Vista and the former mayor of that city (a prominent dairy owner) discovered how to make whipped cream float over a hot Irish coffee. The bottom-bent cream was aged 48 hours before being whipped to a precise consistency. It would now float on the hot nectar.

The "Killer Frost" of 1975 in the coffee growing regions of Brazil created a serious shortage of coffee on the international market. Prices skyrocketed to three to four times their previous costs.

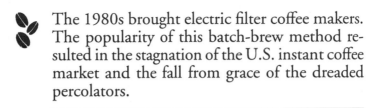 The 1980s brought electric filter coffee makers. The popularity of this batch-brew method resulted in the stagnation of the U.S. instant coffee market and the fall from grace of the dreaded percolators.

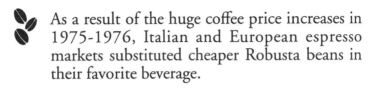 As a result of the huge coffee price increases in 1975-1976, Italian and European espresso markets substituted cheaper Robusta beans in their favorite beverage.

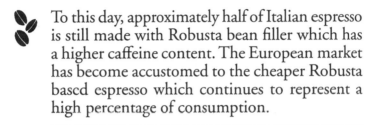 To this day, approximately half of Italian espresso is still made with Robusta bean filler which has a higher caffeine content. The European market has become accustomed to the cheaper Robusta based espresso which continues to represent a high percentage of consumption.

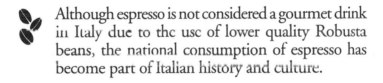 Although espresso is not considered a gourmet drink in Italy due to the use of lower quality Robusta beans, the national consumption of espresso has become part of Italian history and culture.

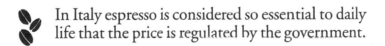 Italy now has over 200,000 coffee bars.

 In Italy espresso is considered so essential to daily life that the price is regulated by the government.

Dr. Ernesto Illy of Italy's Illy Caffe is considered one of the world's foremost experts in coffee and espresso research. He holds a degree in chemistry. His work ranges from the study of physiological effects of coffee on the body to his current project—genetic engineering techniques applied to coffee plants.

Dr. Illy has been in charge of Illycaffe s.p.a. in Trieste, Italy, since 1963. His father, Francisco, started Illycaffe. Francisco developed the pressurization packaging of coffee to hold in the volatile oils and gasses in beans and grounds.

As late as the year 1976 people drank horrible coffee. At least 86% of the American people claimed they drank their home coffee from percolators (electric and stove-top). *Coffee,* written by Charles and Violet Schafer and published in 1976, pictures various coffeemaker types of the day, including the new filter drip cone maker. The drip cone would revolutionize traditional coffee brewing.

The new moderation evident in attitudes throughout the world in the 1980s inspired the popularity of mocktails and gourmet coffee beverages.

By the mid 1980s, upscale coffee bars featuring espresso beverages, an array of fresh roasted gourmet coffees, and coffee accessories, had appeared on the U.S. landscape.

The French philosopher, Voltaire, reportedly drank fifty cups of coffee a day.

Drinking coffee is considered to be a religious or social ritual in many countries.

In Greece and Turkey the oldest person is always served his coffee first.

In the ancient Arab world coffee became such a staple in family life that one of the causes allowed by laws for marital separation was a husband's refusal to produce coffee for his wife.

Raw coffee beans soaked in water and spices are chewed like candy in many parts of Africa.

How do you stop an asthma attack? Drink a cup of coffee ... so states *The Doctor's Book of Home Remedies.*

Regular coffee drinkers have about one-third fewer asthma symptoms than noncoffee drinkers according to a Harvard researcher who studied 20,000 people.

A 1993 medical report states that drinking up to three cups of coffee a day during pregnancy is probably safe.

In the last three centuries 90% of all people living in the Western world have switched from tea to coffee.

A ten-year follow-up study of 128,000 patients in a medical research program found that the chance of suicide fell as people drank more coffee. The same study found no overall difference in the death rates between those who drank coffee and those who didn't.

Coffee represents 75% of all the caffeine consumed in the United States.

Retail espresso vendors report an increase in decaffeinated sales in the month of January due to New Year's resolutions to decrease caffeine intake.

Coffee consumption throughout the world is dictated by the quality of the coffee available. If only low quality coffee is available, coffee consumption is low. If high quality coffee is available, then consumption is high.

The British are sophisticated people in almost everything except their choice of coffee. They still drink instant ten-to-one over fresh brewed coffee.

Japan ranks number three in the world for coffee consumption.

Over 15,000 coffee cafes and several thousand vending machines dispensing both hot and cold coffee serve the needs of Tokyo alone.

In Japan coffee shops are called Kissaten.

 Japanese companies have not only bought up virtually all the Jamaican Blue Mountain coffee crop, but the highest grades of many other coffee crops also. Their passion for the finest coffee and coffee related technology abounds.

 For reducing wrinkles and improving their skin, the Japanese have been known to bathe in coffee grounds fermented with pineapple pulp.

Espresso businesses generally fall into these categories:

Espresso Cafe: features espresso by the drink but serves at least two meals (usually breakfast and lunch).

Espresso Bar: features espresso and gourmet coffees by the drink and whole bean. Serves no meals, only pastries and gifts.

Espresso Vending Carts: sidewalk or indoor carts that feature espresso beverages, Italian sodas, and pastries.

Drive-thru Espresso: a small stationary building serving espresso beverages, Italian sodas, and pastries to customers in their cars through serving windows.

Drive-up Espresso: normally an espresso cart positioned so that customers can pull up and order in their cars.

by Rich Abker

Australians consume 60% more coffee than tea, a sixfold increase since 1940.

 What made Sao Paulo the biggest city in South America? The coffee trade.

 The world can be divided into nations of coffee drinkers and nations of tea drinkers.

 Scandinavia has the world's highest per capita annual coffee consumption at 26.4 pounds. Italy has an annual coffee consumption per capita of only ten pounds.

 Finland has excellent quality coffee and high coffee consumption. Conversely, there are Italy and Great Britain, with poor quality coffee and the lowest coffee consumption of the European countries.

 The Brazilian plantation frosts of 1975-76 raised coffee prices worldwide and resulted in smaller price gaps between standard and gourmet coffee. Customers were willing to spend the small premium for gourmet coffee and the gourmet specialty coffee market was born.

 Full-bodied coffee has become more popular in recent years, among the trends of the gourmet coffee revolution.

 U.S. coffee consumption peaked in the early 1960s when 75% of the population drank more than four cups of coffee a day.

The average annual coffee consumption of the American adult is 26.7 gallons, or over 400 cups.

The United States consumes over one-third of the world's coffee, while Brazil produces about one-quarter to one-third of the world's coffee; each is a world leader in consumption and production.

Worldwide, there are over 400 billion cups of coffee consumed each year.

The 26 million acres on this globe devoted to the cultivation of coffee generate employment for over 30 million people: One of every 177 inhabitants on the planet is employed in the coffee industry. The fruit of this labor is consumed by more than one-third of the world's population.

Coffee as a world commodity is second only to oil.

The modern day espresso street vending cart evolved from a Boeing Company shuttle cart purchased from surplus. The first cart was initially utilized to serve espresso at an arts and crafts fair in Edmonds, Washington, before being moved to downtown Seattle.

After traveling the fair circuit, the first espresso cart found a semi-permanent home under Seattle's Monorail in 1978. An explosion of self-contained espresso carts followed. By 1994 over 450 such carts operated in the Seattle area alone.

Popularity of espresso grew quickly, and Seattleites, enamored with the brew, have made espresso a necessity for coffee consumers.

Nordstrom, a Seattle-based, prestige department store chain, opened its first espresso cart in 1982 in downtown Seattle. It is estimated that each of its carts averages over 1,000 customers per day.

Espresso street cart vending is the biggest food and beverage marketing trend to happen in the United States since fast food drive-ins. Elsewhere, street cart vendors have marketed soft pretzels, hot dogs, ice cream, fresh produce, shrimp, cold pop, lemonade, and sassafras tea.

A "Coffee Community" movement is gaining momentum whereby Seattle's espresso cart licensing rules would become a national model.

When espresso carts must rent outside space from an anchor retail business, the cost usually totals 5% to 12% of total sales.

Over a hundred different varieties of coffee are imported into the United States each year.

Economic downturns have little effect on retail sales of espresso beverages. A cup of gourmet coffee or espresso is one of the "affordable luxuries," according to the CEO of a major U.S. coffee retailer.

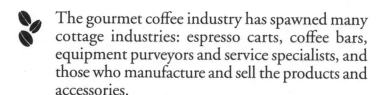

The gourmet coffee industry has spawned many cottage industries: espresso carts, coffee bars, equipment purveyors and service specialists, and those who manufacture and sell the products and accessories.

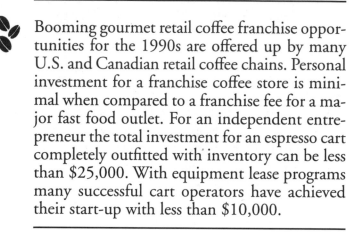

Booming gourmet retail coffee franchise opportunities for the 1990s are offered up by many U.S. and Canadian retail coffee chains. Personal investment for a franchise coffee store is minimal when compared to a franchise fee for a major fast food outlet. For an independent entrepreneur the total investment for an espresso cart completely outfitted with inventory can be less than $25,000. With equipment lease programs many successful cart operators have achieved their start-up with less than $10,000.

Retail espresso and coffee stores are finding an ever increasing number of local cash-and-carry wholesale stores where they may purchase their syrups, supplies, and accessories.

National wholesale distributors such as the ten-year-old RSVP International in Seattle offer espresso products, supplies, and accessories to the fast growing retail coffee market.

Health regulations and city ordinances vary widely from state to state in governing operations of espresso vending carts.

Stateside espresso cart entrepreneurs are having great difficulty penetrating the Japanese market. The Japanese customarily take coffee sitting down and find it an awkward sensation to sip while walking.

A barista is said to be "slammed" when he is bombarded with business (usually five or more people waiting to be served).

In 1991 Japanese inventor Enomoto created a fully automatic roaster/grinder/drip brewer, all-in-one. The unit is controlled by an electronic chip and from roasting through brewing, requires 17 minutes to produce six cups of coffee.

One forecaster claims that by the year 2000, 50% of coffee consumed at home will be brewed in home espresso machines.

According to a 1995 A.C. Nielsen survey commissioned by Maxwell House, the citizens of Syracuse, New York each consume 5.3 cups of coffee per day, placing them first in coffee consumption—even above the consumption of Seattleites. Among larger U.S. cities, the highest per capita consumption occurs in Seattle, New Orleans and Minneapolis.

Milk is one of the best items sold in the supermarket. That's why it's usually at the back of the store—so you'll see other desirables on your way to it.

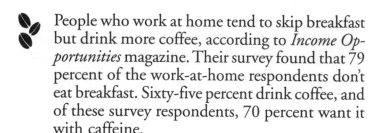 People who work at home tend to skip breakfast but drink more coffee, according to *Income Opportunities* magazine. Their survey found that 79 percent of the work-at-home respondents don't eat breakfast. Sixty-five percent drink coffee, and of these survey respondents, 70 percent want it with caffeine.

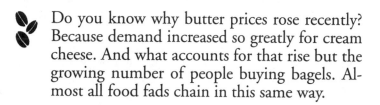 Do you know why butter prices rose recently? Because demand increased so greatly for cream cheese. And what accounts for that rise but the growing number of people buying bagels. Almost all food fads chain in this same way.

Supermarkets have begun increasing their shelf space to accommodate a plethora of flavored milks and milk-based drinks with flavor titles often preceded by "smooth" or a derivation thereof. These low fat fruit-based packaged concoctions contain a high percentage of real milk.

Ten years ago the average supermarket had about 15,000 items. Today, the same store offers 40,000. Ten years ago there were five or six milk varieties displayed in the supermarket at most. Today the dairy section is a milk-lover's heaven. Consider the offering: Whole milk, two percent, one percent, skim, fortified skim, lactose-reduced, lactose-free, farm fresh in bottles, goat's milk, organic milk, heavy cream, half-and-half, and the hundreds of new fruit-flavored "smooth" milk offerings.

The consumption of whole milk, which accounted for more than 70 percent of milk sales in 1974, was 19.5 gallons per capita. By 1995 the per capita consumption of whole milk had fallen to 8.1 gallons. During this same period, per capita consumption of low fat milk, the one percent and two percent varieties, more than doubled, from 5.2 gallons in 1974 to 10.5 gallons in 1995.

 Skim milk started its upward trend slightly over a decade ago from an annual consumption of 1.4 gallons per person in 1985 to 3.6 gallons per year in 1995. Today skim milk is the fastest growing category of non-flavored milk sales.

 An eight-ounce glass contains:

Whole Milk: 150 calories, 8.2 grams of fat,
33.2 milligrams of cholesterol;
Two Percent: 121 calories, 4.7 grams of fat,
18.3 milligrams of cholesterol;
One Percent: 102 calories, 2.6 grams of fat,
9.8 milligrams of cholesterol;
Skim Milk: 88.5 calories, 4 grams of fat, 4.4
milligrams of cholesterol.

 Eight O'clock Whole Bean Coffee, one of the most famous names in American coffee history, has been around since 1859.

The drugstore soda fountain which disappeared from the American landscape in the mid 1950s was a popular social institution. Cultural anthropologists have two theories for its demise: The post World War II cosmetics industry was booming, and this high profit cosmetic merchandise literally pushed the soda fountain out of its floor space; or the 50s also brought the affordable home freezer that allowed practically every household to store their own ice cream.

Water Joe, first introduced in the Midwest in October '95, is perhaps one of the strangest new age beverages yet—artesian well water mixed with a dollop of coffee.

The name Water Joe is a nod to World War II slang for coffee.

Which is more popular in the U.S.—hot or iced tea? Iced accounts for 80 percent. For that, credit Richard Blechynden. He was the hot tea vendor who almost went broke at the 1904 Louisiana Purchase Exposition when St. Louis temperatures soared. When he poured his tea over ice, buyers flocked.

Among beverages, coffee ranks second in popularity to soft drinks, followed by beer and milk.

Americans consumed 9.7 gallons of bottled water apiece in 1994. Per person consumption of bottled water more than tripled from 1983 to 1993.

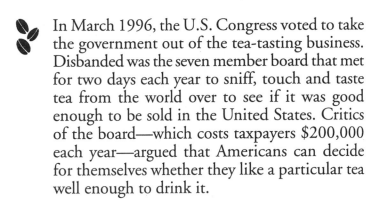

In March 1996, the U.S. Congress voted to take the government out of the tea-tasting business. Disbanded was the seven member board that met for two days each year to sniff, touch and taste tea from the world over to see if it was good enough to be sold in the United States. Critics of the board—which costs taxpayers $200,000 each year—argued that Americans can decide for themselves whether they like a particular tea well enough to drink it.

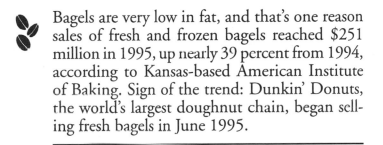

Bagels are very low in fat, and that's one reason sales of fresh and frozen bagels reached $251 million in 1995, up nearly 39 percent from 1994, according to Kansas-based American Institute of Baking. Sign of the trend: Dunkin' Donuts, the world's largest doughnut chain, began selling fresh bagels in June 1995.

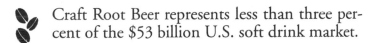

Craft Root Beer represents less than three percent of the $53 billion U.S. soft drink market.

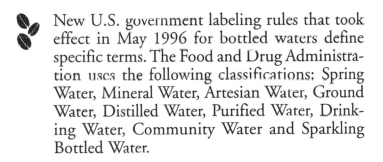

New U.S. government labeling rules that took effect in May 1996 for bottled waters define specific terms. The Food and Drug Administration uses the following classifications: Spring Water, Mineral Water, Artesian Water, Ground Water, Distilled Water, Purified Water, Drinking Water, Community Water and Sparkling Bottled Water.

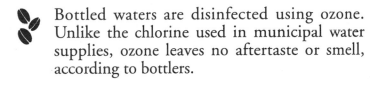

Bottled waters are disinfected using ozone. Unlike the chlorine used in municipal water supplies, ozone leaves no aftertaste or smell, according to bottlers.

Espresso Dental is not alone in combining the espresso bar with retail business. Others combinations include the espresso bar and pet wash, bookstore, church lobby, cyber cafe, bike rental shop, antique store, hospital, ballpark, ski lift.

 What Starbucks is doing:

+ Using earth, fire, water and air tones in décor, minimizing green colors
+ Setting up Brevé bars—165 square feet (average) lobby espresso sites
+ Lending the cachet of Starbucks espresso to other branded products
+ Testing Briazz gourmet prepackaged sandwiches
+ For the year ending September 29, 1996, some store sales are up 7%. In corporate terms, on sales of $696.5 million, earnings were $42.1 million for a 6% net profit.
+ Customizing new store décor to fit community architecture and client needs.

 In a January 1996 merger, Starbucks Coffee acquired a 20% share of Noah's New York Bagels. The $100 million acquisition teams up two of the hottest consumable commodities as side-by-side companion profit centers. Noah's, with its 37 stores (none of them in New York) is expected to expand in number as stores are located next door to Starbucks. The intent is to draw more foot traffic from bagel eaters.

 Starbucks has overtaken Folgers as the number one importer of coffee beans.

$8 billion in coffee is sold in U.S. supermarkets annually. It has been estimated by one expert that high grade gourmet varieties account for 10 percent of the total.

 Many stressed-out nine-to-fivers have turned to the espresso business, attracted by its simplified menu, high transaction count and cash-only sales, unheard of profit margins, and low initial cash investment.

 The Blauerts, as many other espresso cart owners, take advantage of mobile equipment and advertise and promote mobile espresso and coffee catering. Charity auctions, community festivals and many other functions find Greg loading his cart to truck it to these gala occasions. The vast majority of self-contained carts operate from a 220-volt power source with a 50-amp circuit breaker box built in. Most have as many as 10 110-volt outlets for the machine, coffee grinders (usually two—one for regular grind; one for decaf), the cash register and other electrical equipment. Should electrical power not be accessible, whisper quiet 220-volt power generators can be rented.

 How hot is tea? In 1990, sales in America totaled $1 billion. A leading forecaster predicts 1997 sales will top $4.6 billion.

 A study in Holland revealed that more than 800 men who were heavy tea drinkers had half the risk of fatal heart attacks of men who consumed less tea.

Chapter 4

The Coffee Bean: Growing, Harvesting, Processing, Roasting

Two species of coffee beans are of economic significance.

1. *Coffea arabica*—commonly called Arabica, grows best in altitudes beyond 3,000 feet above sea level. This species is considered a high quality bean and produces very flavorful and aromatic coffee. Arabica trees require more rigid growing requirements and are more expensive. The beans are low in caffeine, low in acidity, and high in flavor and aroma.

2. *Coffea robusta or canephora*—commonly called Robusta, grows best in altitudes that are below 2,000 feet above sea level. Robusta is less flavorful and less aromatic than Arabica. This species is normally purchased as a "filler" bean for canned coffees in order to reduce roasters' costs. Robusta is also widely used in instant coffees. This is not the bean that is normally used by gourmet coffee roasters. It has twice the caffeine of Arabica, is high in acidity, low in flavor and aroma, and is the least expensive.

Coffee trees are evergreen and grow to heights above 15 feet. Under cultivation they are normally pruned to around eight feet in order to facilitate harvesting.

The world's most valuable agricultural commodity is the coffee bean.

Coffee trees produce highly aromatic, short-lived white flowers producing a scent between jasmine and orange. These blossoms produce cranberry-sized coffee cherries. Four to five years are required to yield a commercial harvest.

Coffee cherries begin in a green stage then turn yellow, orange, red and dark crimson when ripe. Coffee cherries must be picked ripe to yield the best coffee. Each coffee cherry normally produces two green seeds that are flat on one side and concave on the other. These green seeds are the coffee beans. The green beans must have their silverskins and parchments removed before roasting.

Only 25% of the coffee plant's flowers produce mature beans.

Green coffee beans are nonvolatile until roasted. In fact, green beans that are stored while still maturing in their silverskins and parchments can be stored for years if cared for properly. These green beans are referred to as pergamino beans (parchment beans).

When green coffee seeds fail to divide into two seeds, they form one concave seed called a peaberry. Peaberries can be very flavorful due to their unique development and demand a high price.

Arabica constitutes 75% of the world's coffee production, but only the top 10% of Arabicas have fine enough characteristics to meet specialty coffee standards.

Arabica is the original coffee plant. It still grows wild in Ethiopia.

Coffee trees are planted in nurseries and later transplanted to the fields. When mature, they flower at the beginning of the wet season and are generally picked at the end of the dry season.

Coffee beans are similar to wine grapes in that they are affected by the temperature, soil conditions, altitude, rainfall, drainage, and degree of ripeness when picked.

A coffee plant requires more than 70 inches of water per year to thrive.

The red coffee cherries are known as drupes. Unlike such other drupes as cherries and peaches, coffee is consumed by throwing away the fruit, then roasting, grinding, brewing, and consuming the pits.

It takes about five years for an Arabica coffee plant to mature and produce its first crop (about two pounds).

 The Arabica coffee bean requires only six to eight weeks after flowering before the fruit fully ripens. The Robusta bean takes nine to eleven weeks to ripen.

 Coffees grown at higher elevations generally exhibit finer qualities than those grown at lower elevations.

 Organic coffee is grown without the use of insecticides, herbicides, growth regulators, or synthetic fertilizers.

 Coffee buyers separate the world's coffee production into three main categories: High-grown Mild Arabica, Brazilian Arabica, and Robusta.

 Of the several species of coffee trees, 99% are represented by either the Arabica or Robusta types.

 More than 100 kinds of coffee beans are grown commercially in 59 countries throughout the tropical regions of the world.

 The first historical blend of coffee was the mocha-java, still a popular blend today.

The rarest premium coffee on earth is Jamaican Blue Mountain: Only 100,000 pounds are produced each year. The Japanese buy up practically all of this green gold.

The Japanese tend to favor a lighter roast than North Americans.

Java led the world in coffee production until rust disease almost destroyed the coffee industry there.

Between 1740 and 1805, coffee cultivation achieved its widest expansion in Central and South America.

Coffee is grown more widely in South America than on any other continent.

Brazil and Colombia together produce approximately 45% of the world's coffee.

Brazil accounts for almost one-third of the world's coffee production, producing over 3⅓ billion pounds of coffee each year.

Brazil is the largest producer and exporter of coffee, and the United States is by far the greatest consuming country in the world.

Colombia is the world's second largest coffee producer.

The Indonesian islands are the world's third largest producer of coffee. Out of over 13,000 islands, only ten produce coffee, and of those, three produce 90% of the total crop: Java, Sumatra, and Sulawesi (formerly Celebes).

Arabica represents only 10% of Indonesia's production, and only a fraction of this amount is considered exceptional. This small portion of select gourmet coffee is highly coveted by the select roasters.

Although coffee is grown around the globe, along a narrow subtropical belt, Australia with its limited production is the clear exception located outside coffee's typical geographical range.

Kona coffee growers, like most coffee growers, start their Arabica trees from seed in nurseries. The best trees are hand-selected for planting in the growers' field estates.

Hawaii is the only state of the United States in which coffee is commercially grown.

In 1974 "The Coffee Store" opened in Honolulu as Hawaii's first specialty coffee store.

Hawaii features an annual Kona Festival which includes a coffee picking contest. Each year the winner becomes a state celebrity.

In the tropical and subtropical regions where they are grown, estate coffees are confined to a specific region with the farmer specializing in only the coffee crop.

 In Hawaii coffee is harvested between November and April.

 Over five million people in Brazil are employed by the coffee trade. Most of those are involved with the cultivation and harvesting of more than 3 billion coffee plants.

 The 2,000 Arabica coffee cherries it takes to make a roasted pound of coffee are normally picked by hand as they ripen. Since each cherry contains two beans, about 4,000 Arabica beans are required to make a pound bag of roasted coffee.

 The *Gourmet Retailer* magazine states that more hand labor goes into a pound of coffee than goes into a pound of any other food product.

 A plantation worker typically picks 150 pounds of ripe coffee cherries daily. This harvest equates to approximately 30 pounds of roasted product. A picker's daily pay is equivalent to just a few U.S. dollars.

 After the coffee cherries are picked, they are checked for impurities, washed, processed, dried, and then graded.

The removal of the three sets of skin and their attendant layers of pulp is accomplished by pressing and hulling machines.

 After the coffee bean is picked and the outer layers of skin have been removed, it is soaked. The pulp is then fermented off the beans, which are again soaked and washed, then dried on open air patios or in drying machines.

 During a drying-out period which lasts approximately twenty days, coffee beans are raked frequently to reduce any molding.

 An alternative method for processing coffee cherries is the Dutch (WIB) method. The coffee berries are stoned to separate the beans from skin and pulp. This approach accelerates the drying process.

 Rain and high humidity are harmful to the coffee berries during the drying-out period.

 The last two crumbly layers of skin remaining on the dry bean are removed by tumbling. Once the last bits of skin have been shaken free, the beans are polished to improve their appearance.

 After harvest, coffee beans are hulled and graded by size and weight. The largest beans are usually considered premium. Although the coffee industry generally considers the large beans a good grade, size has no relation to taste or aroma.

COFFEE BEAN
VARIOUS STAGES

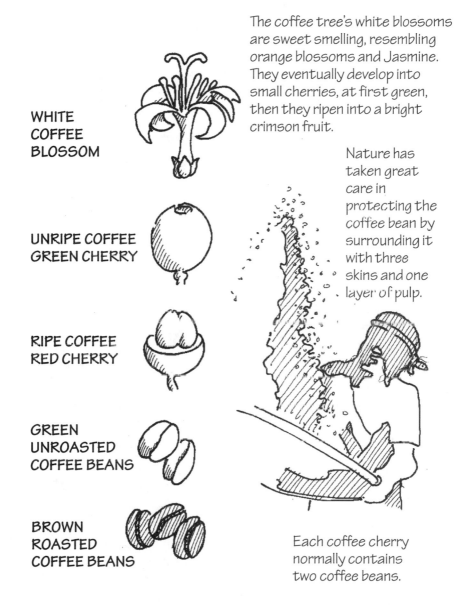

The coffee tree's white blossoms are sweet smelling, resembling orange blossoms and Jasmine. They eventually develop into small cherries, at first green, then they ripen into a bright crimson fruit.

Nature has taken great care in protecting the coffee bean by surrounding it with three skins and one layer of pulp.

WHITE COFFEE BLOSSOM

UNRIPE COFFEE GREEN CHERRY

RIPE COFFEE RED CHERRY

GREEN UNROASTED COFFEE BEANS

BROWN ROASTED COFFEE BEANS

Each coffee cherry normally contains two coffee beans.

COFFEE ROASTER

Depending on variety, coffee beans are generally roasted for 10 to 20 minutes at a temperature of 400 to 500°F.

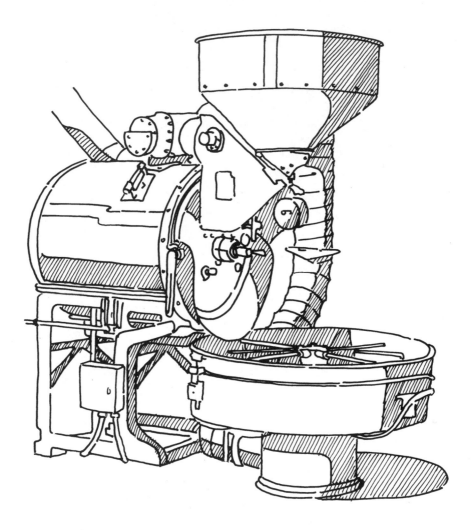

The roasted beans are unloaded into the cooling hopper and stirred mechanically while cool air is blown through them to prevent overcooking. Water is sometimes sprayed into the cooling air.

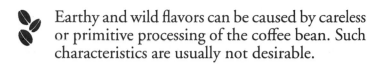 Earthy and wild flavors can be caused by careless or primitive processing of the coffee bean. Such characteristics are usually not desirable.

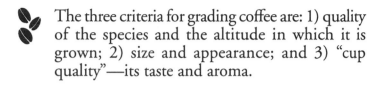 The three criteria for grading coffee are: 1) quality of the species and the altitude in which it is grown; 2) size and appearance; and 3) "cup quality"—its taste and aroma.

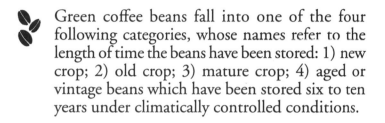 Green coffee beans fall into one of the four following categories, whose names refer to the length of time the beans have been stored: 1) new crop; 2) old crop; 3) mature crop; 4) aged or vintage beans which have been stored six to ten years under climatically controlled conditions.

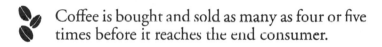 Coffee is bought and sold as many as four or five times before it reaches the end consumer.

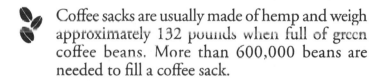 Coffee sacks are usually made of hemp and weigh approximately 132 pounds when full of green coffee beans. More than 600,000 beans are needed to fill a coffee sack.

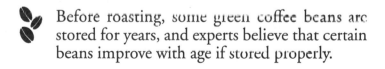 Before roasting, some green coffee beans are stored for years, and experts believe that certain beans improve with age if stored properly.

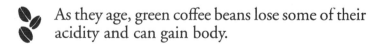 As they age, green coffee beans lose some of their acidity and can gain body.

Coffee is picked, sorted, cleaned, bagged, roasted, and then re-bagged.

 The most important factors that influence the taste and aroma of coffee are: the type and quality of coffee beans; freshness; degree of roast; size of grind and proper extraction method; and the cleanliness of the espresso machine.

 Until the late 1800s people roasted their coffee at home. Popcorn poppers and stove-top frying pans were favored.

 The vast majority of small specialty coffee roasters in the U.S. purchase their beans from importers in San Francisco or New York City.

 Roasters strive for two important elements when creating a blend: 1) flavor quality of the beans; and 2) consistency.

 When creating an espresso blend, roasters strive for a balanced flavor—a minimal amount of bitterness, the right acidity, and the maximum amount of sweetness.

 Blending varieties of coffee for the ultimate taste requires combining those beans that complement one another, with characteristics that enhance the final product.

No coffee can simply be blended by recipe. Too many variables subtly impact taste. Commercial roasters reassemble blends often to maintain desired flavors. Maintaining consistency is part of the formula.

 A quality espresso blend contains anywhere from two to ten separate Arabica bean varieties.

 Blends of different beans represent the vast majority of coffee available to consumers.

 In Italy most beans are blended before roasting. In the U.S. some roasters blend their beans after roasting because smaller beans would be burned if roasted with larger beans, and different beans reach their flavor peaks at different roasting times.

 Roasters try to achieve coffee blends which marry a strong and pleasant aroma with an enjoyable taste.

 Unripe, overripe, and diseased beans, all that when roasted would give the brew undesirable off-tastes, are detected by a scanner, and are blown away before they would be dumped in the roaster.

 Most roasters use a gas flame to roast beans in a rotating air drum.

Coffee is generally roasted between 400° and 425°F. The longer it is roasted, the darker the roast. Roasting time is usually from 10 to 20 minutes.

Roasting changes the chemical make-up of the coffee bean. The new substances developed represent about 30% of the weight of the roasted bean.

Beans cooling from the roaster release about 700 chemical substances that make up the vaporizing aromas.

Darker roasted beans contain less acid and slightly less caffeine than lighter roasted beans. Much of the caffeine and acid substance goes up the chimney during the roasting process.

In the roasting process, *coffeol* gathers in pockets throughout the bean. In dark roasts this substance is forced out to the surface as the moisture is lost, giving the bean an oily appearance.

The roasting process causes the bean to swell and the size to increase by about 60% in volume. However, this same roasting process that inflates the bean's size also takes away between 14% and 19% of its weight.

When roasted, the coffee bean doubles in size, and the caramelization of the sugar turns it from green to brown.

There is no single shade of roast that is ideal for all coffees, but if a coffee is roasted too dark, the oils, waxes, and other flavor elements are driven to the surface and are partially dissipated in roasting.

Oily beans lose flavor quicker than those with oils still inside the bean.

The darker the roast, the more weight is lost.

When the interior of the bean reaches 400°F in the roasting process, the bean develops oils in a process called *pyolysis*, and the outer part of the bean darkens.

At the point of pyolysis, beans are dumped from the roaster and cooled immediately, normally with cold air. Misting the beans with water is an option.

Darker beans are stronger, more bittersweet, and usually have a shorter shelf life.

The burnt taste nuance produced by dark roasting effectively masks the shortcomings in flavor that a light roast will reveal. In other words, dark roasts can mask beans that are low in flavor.

Over-roasted coffee beans are very flammable during the roasting process.

 Lightly roasted coffee beans have a sharper, more acidic taste than darker roasts, which are more bittersweet.

 The traditional term "full-city" roast is used to describe a dark roast with a slight amount of oil on the surface.

 Labels given roasted coffees in the retail stores, such as Italian, French, Continental, and Viennese, do not refer to the origin of the beans. Rather they refer to the length of time the bean is roasted, a characteristic manifested by the color.

 Since the espresso boom of the early 1980s in the United States, espresso roasts have come from the more expensive Arabica bean with its lower caffeine content. Thus the myth, "only the premium espresso roasts are from Italy," can be dispelled.

 In Italy, espresso contains approximately 40% of the higher caffeinated Robusta bean.

 Arabica coffee beans contain 1-1.7% caffeine, while Robusta beans contain 2-4.5% caffeine.

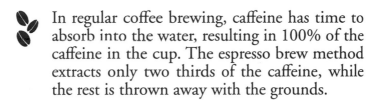 In regular coffee brewing, caffeine has time to absorb into the water, resulting in 100% of the caffeine in the cup. The espresso brew method extracts only two thirds of the caffeine, while the rest is thrown away with the grounds.

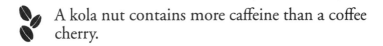 A kola nut contains more caffeine than a coffee cherry.

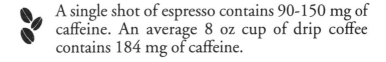 A single shot of espresso contains 90-150 mg of caffeine. An average 8 oz cup of drip coffee contains 184 mg of caffeine.

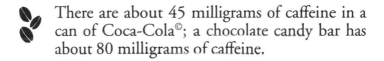 There are about 45 milligrams of caffeine in a can of Coca-Cola©; a chocolate candy bar has about 80 milligrams of caffeine.

Studies tell us the human body will absorb only 300 milligrams of caffeine at a given time. Additional amounts are cast off and will provide no additional stimulation. The human body dissipates 20% of the caffeine in the system each hour.

MIT research indicates a 30% increase in alertness after only 30 mg of caffeine is consumed.

Milk coats the stomach lining, slowing the absorption of caffeine.

Southern Europeans roast their beans darker than northern Europeans. Southern Californians roast their beans lighter than northern Californians.

 In general, the West Coast favors a darker roast than the East Coast, with the Midwest somewhere in between.

 In the late 1970s, the present method of flavoring coffee in its whole bean form was developed.

 Commercially flavored coffee beans are imbued with flavoring after they are roasted and partially cooled to around 100°F. At this temperature the coffee beans' pores are open and therefore more receptive to absorption. The flavoring agent is applied with spraying or tumbling with the beans in a kettle or a metal drum.

 Decaffeinated coffee is less popular in the Pacific Rim countries than it is in the U.S.

 "Flavored gourmet coffee initially served as a vehicle for introducing non-coffee drinkers to good coffee. It was an entry-level beverage in the beginning, but it has carved out its own niche now. Many people enjoy it for its own sake. It's like a dessert treat without the calories and without the fat." The preceding quote in the April, 1994 issue of *Tea & Coffee Trade Journal* was from Michael S. Abrams, vice president of sales and marketing (flavors and fragrances) for Melchers & Co., a San Francisco-based flavor producer.

The process by which coffee becomes decaffeinated was discovered in 1906.

 The three major methods of decaffeinating coffee are: 1) Swiss Water Process; 2) Natural Process—Ethyl Acetate; and 3) Natural Process—Coffee Oil Process. Other less used methods are the carbon dioxide (CO_2) super-critical process, and the methlene chloride method.

 The 40-year-old Swiss Water Process, an all-water method of decaffeinating coffee, is the trade name of Coffex, the Swiss company that patented this process. In 1988 this company moved from Switzerland to Vancouver, British Columbia, where all U.S. Swiss Water Process "decaf" coffees are treated.

 After the decaffeinating process, processing companies no longer throw the caffeine away; they sell it to pharmaceutical companies.

 When roasted coffee beans are exposed to air, they begin to release carbon dioxide which carries with it the beans' vaporizing aromas.

 Roasted coffee is a highly perishable product, vulnerable to moisture, light, and above all, oxygen. Oxygen can cause the coffee oil to become stale, decreasing the coffee's aroma and flavor.

Roasted coffee beans start to lose small amounts of flavor within two weeks. Ground coffee begins to lose its flavor in minutes. Brewed coffee and espresso begin to lose flavor within minutes.

A high percentage of the coffee in the United States is probably purchased stale due to improper handling and packaging.

There is no packaging technique that can remove all the air from the can. What air remains reacts with the aroma and flavor factors of ground coffee, although at a reduced rate.

Roasted coffee beans properly stored in an airtight container will stay reasonably fresh for only up to ten days.

With rare exceptions, coffee cans do not have vapor locks. After coffee is roasted it gives off carbon dioxide and cannot be vacuum-packed for several days. Otherwise the cans will explode. Perfect freshness will be lost. A vapor lock can be an important factor in reducing such losses.

Small one-way valves used in most of today's specialty packaging are known as "belly button valves." They allow carbon dioxide to escape the bag, relieving built-up pressure and thereby preserving freshness and adding to the shelf life of the roasted espresso beans. The valves were introduced in 1968.

Never freeze dark roasted espresso blends. The delicate oils on the surface of the beans jell, and the flavor is jeopardized.

It's best not to refrigerate your roasted coffee beans. Even if they are stored in airtight containers, the beans are very porous and will absorb even mild odors from the refrigerator.

A Tupperware® container or an airtight glass is best for the storage of coffee beans. Earl W. Tupper started Tupperware® in 1945, the same year the word *Espresso* first appeared in American print.

Store the airtight container in a slightly cool, dark place at a temperature between 50°-70°F.

Grinding accelerates the staling process by exposing more surface area of the bean to air, the number one staling agent. Each shot of espresso should be ground just prior to brewing for peak freshness.

Stale coffee becomes softer with age and therefore grinds differently from fresh coffee.

The freshness of brewed coffee normally expires after 20 minutes when the liquid has been heated in a pot on a warmer. Freshness can be preserved for up to two hours in a vacuum air pot or thermos bottle.

Coffee is a deciduous evergreen. Its leaves are never replaced.

 Over 90 percent of the coffee tree's roots lie in the upper one foot of soil.

 Fifty percent of the coffee tree's flowers set (produce blossoms), while only 25% produce mature beans.

 On/off year: Tree growth competes with the cherry growth nutrients, so a heavy crop year will not have much vegetative growth, all things being equal with outside stress factors. Interestingly, the largest number of berries grows on new branches, so the following year the crop will be smaller. Thus a cycle is created.

 While it takes perhaps 15 minutes to drink a cup of coffee, it takes seven years for a tree to start flowering with coffee "cherries," and it takes one tree to produce one pound's worth of green coffee beans.

 Coffee picked is paid per almud. Almud is a 28-pound measure for coffee cherries. Each almud will produce approximately 4 to 5 pounds of mature coffee beans.

All in all, coffee is handled approximately 150 times between plant and cup, estimates R.C. Beall, owner of Montana Coffee Traders, in an article published in September 1995 in a coffee trade journal.

Harvested Arabica consists roughly of:
39% pulp
17% mucilage
7% parchment and skin
37% bean

500-600 pounds of cherries are required to produce a 100-pound bag of coffee

Iowa-based Frontier Coffee is the largest supplier of organic coffee in the United States.

Genetic engineers at California-based Escagenetics Corporation were the first to produce genetically transformed coffee plants. Benefits claimed for this bio-engineered java include beans with lower caffeine content—without the expense of decaffeination or the chemical concerns—beans with improved flavor and aroma, plants with increased pest resistance, and vastly accelerated breeding of new coffee plants.

The FDA has cause to remove coffee beans from the retail store if 10 percent by count are insect-infested or insect-damaged or show evidence of mold.

One cup of black coffee contains 59 mg of sodium. One cup of juice contains 4 mg of sodium.

 Does evening coffee keep you awake? University of Chicago students were once divided into two test groups. Before bedtime, one drank coffee; the other, milk. In the morning, the coffee drinkers said they slept fitfully; the milk drinkers, soundly. Then they were told the milk had been spiked with more caffeine than had been in the coffee.

 Most food service packaging is done through flushing of the package with nitrogen just before sealing, providing an environment for extended shelf life.

 Most growers don't know much about coffee.

 Japan is now the world's third-largest importer of coffee, after the U.S. and Germany. Coffee has supplanted green tea as Japan's most popular beverage. According to the All Japan Coffee Association, coffee consumption has risen about sixfold since 1980, while tea consumption fell eight percent.

 Finca is a non-profit group which has created Community Banks for the poor in 12 different countries. These banks provide start-up capital to those who might otherwise not be given a chance. The banks make self employment loans averaging $150 per borrower. These loans have an astonishing payback of 99 percent.

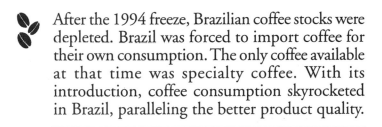 After the 1994 freeze, Brazilian coffee stocks were depleted. Brazil was forced to import coffee for their own consumption. The only coffee available at that time was specialty coffee. With its introduction, coffee consumption skyrocketed in Brazil, paralleling the better product quality.

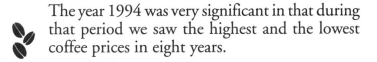 The year 1994 was very significant in that during that period we saw the highest and the lowest coffee prices in eight years.

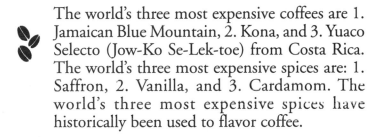 The world's three most expensive coffees are 1. Jamaican Blue Mountain, 2. Kona, and 3. Yuaco Selecto (Jow-Ko Se-Lek-toe) from Costa Rica. The world's three most expensive spices are: 1. Saffron, 2. Vanilla, and 3. Cardamom. The world's three most expensive spices have historically been used to flavor coffee.

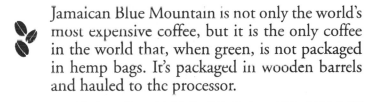 Jamaican Blue Mountain is not only the world's most expensive coffee, but it is the only coffee in the world that, when green, is not packaged in hemp bags. It's packaged in wooden barrels and hauled to the processor.

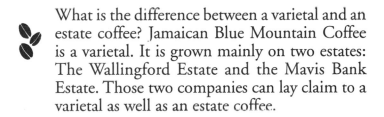 What is the difference between a varietal and an estate coffee? Jamaican Blue Mountain Coffee is a varietal. It is grown mainly on two estates: The Wallingford Estate and the Mavis Bank Estate. Those two companies can lay claim to a varietal as well as an estate coffee.

Of Indonesia's 13,000 islands, only 10 produce coffee, and three (Sulawesi, Sumatra, and Java) account for more than 90 percent of that harvest.

According to the book Stuff: *The Secret Lives of Everyday Things,* it takes 12 coffee trees to feed a two-cup-a-day habit.

Although most people associate India with tea, few know that India has been a producer and exporter of exceptional coffees for over 150 years. In recent years, India has consistently been one of the world's top 10 coffee producers.

Coffee plants were first introduced in India almost 400 years ago.

The Dutch, who occupied parts of India in the 17th century, shipped cuttings from these plants to establish coffee estates in the East Indies islands of Java and Sumatra. The first plantations started in 1696 were lost to natural disasters. The second shipment of seedlings in 1699 were successful and ultimately led to the coffee trade of Dutch East Indies.

India produces both Arabica and Robusta coffee beans in roughly equal amounts.

"Everyone thinks Turkish coffee must be a dark roast, but it's not true. Turkish coffee is pale-pale to medium, because if you use quality beans there's no need to roast darker. Turkish coffee is always Brazilian Arabica beans." Quotation from Mehmet Kurukaveci, "Coffee Man of Istanbul," *Tea & Coffee Trade Journal.*

"Turkish coffee refers to the method of preparation: Using a demitasse of fresh drinking water for each cup, pour the water, two spoonsful of coffee for each cup, and sugar according to taste into the pot and stir. Heat the mixture until it almost boils, pouring a little of the foam into each cup. Bring the coffee almost to a boil a second time and serve." Recipe of Mehmet Kurukaveci, "Coffee Man of Istanbul," *Tea & Coffee Trade Journal.*

Within 30 to 60 minutes of drinking coffee, caffeine levels peak in the bloodstream to produce the highest alertness and concentration.

Caffeine's ability to provide a rapid boost mentally and physically has promoted the National Academy of Sciences' Institute of Medicine to recommend ways to add caffeine to the rations of U.S. soldiers.

Caffeine can squelch headaches by constricting blood vessels in the head, which is why it's added to some pain relievers.

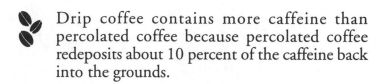 Drip coffee contains more caffeine than percolated coffee because percolated coffee redeposits about 10 percent of the caffeine back into the grounds.

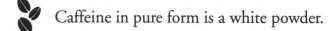 Caffeine in pure form is a white powder.

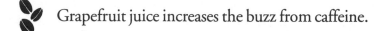 Grapefruit juice increases the buzz from caffeine.

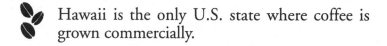 Hawaii is the only U.S. state where coffee is grown commercially.

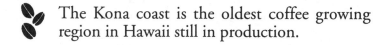 The Kona coast is the oldest coffee growing region in Hawaii still in production.

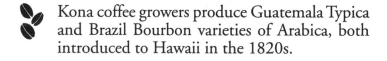 Kona coffee growers produce Guatemala Typica and Brazil Bourbon varieties of Arabica, both introduced to Hawaii in the 1820s.

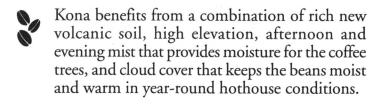 Kona benefits from a combination of rich new volcanic soil, high elevation, afternoon and evening mist that provides moisture for the coffee trees, and cloud cover that keeps the beans moist and warm in year-round hothouse conditions.

Kona benefits from a combination of rich new volcanic soil, high elevation, afternoon and evening mist that provides moisture for the coffee trees, and cloud cover that keeps the beans moist and warm in year-round hothouse conditions.

The Kona weather is unique in that it has rainy summers and drier winters. Depending on the rainfall, this typically means that in a good year the farmers can have five or more coffee flowerings in a season.

Virtually all Kona coffee is hand-picked, and about two million pounds are produced each year.

Because of the cooler temperatures at the farms' elevation, Kona coffee has a higher acidity level and is generally considered to be one of the highest quality coffees in the world.

In 1996 there were 570 farms raising coffee in Kona. They ranged in size from 1½ to 72 acres, with an average size of 2½ acres and a combined area of less than 1,800 acres.

Kona coffee farmers in 1996 averaged a gross annual income of $8,000-$10,000 per acre.

Some 65 growers in 1996 marketed themselves as "estate coffees," that is, coffees planted and processed in one contiguous area.

There is a controversy regarding the common practice of mixing a small proportion of Kona coffee with less expensive imported coffees and selling the result as Kona blend. Hawaii state law requires that Kona blend be at least 10 percent Kona coffee, but purity is difficult to monitor, and there has been little enforcement (especially once the coffee has left Hawaii).

Because of high international demand for, and limited supply of, Kona coffee, its prices are calculated on a different basis from other coffees. In 1996, green Kona coffee wholesaled at about $6.50 to $10 per pound. Kona coffee is currently the second most expensive coffee regularly sold in the world, after Jamaican Blue Mountain.

 MAUI:

There are two coffee regions on the island of Maui. The largest is the 400-acre Kaanapali Estate coffee farm, owned by AMFAC-JMB Corporation. The farm was first planted in 1989 and is drip irrigated. Because the coffee trees are newly planted, yields are expected to reach full production by the year 2000.

 OAHU:

Dole Food Company recently planted 45 acres of Guatemala Typica in Waialua on land that was formerly used for growing sugar cane. This follows seven years of trials on 20 acres planted with four varieties—Guatemala, Caturra, Catuai, and Jamaican Blue Mountain. Dole intends eventually to plant coffee on 100 more acres. All of the coffee will be marketed under the Dole Foods Waialua Coffee label.

 In a determined move to become the producer of one of Hawaii's foremost specialty coffees, Dole has decided that all of their coffee will be hand-picked, and only ripe red cherries will be selected.

KAUAI:

Island Coffee Company is the largest coffee producer in Hawaii and sells under the Kauai Coffee label. The 4,000 acre mechanized farm currently produces 43 percent of all the coffee grown in the U.S. and represents 60 percent of the total coffee acreage in Hawaii. More than $40 million has been spent on the venture since the coffee was first planted in 1987.

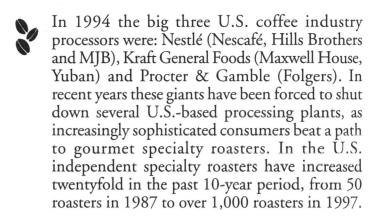

In 1994 the big three U.S. coffee industry processors were: Nestlé (Nescafé, Hills Brothers and MJB), Kraft General Foods (Maxwell House, Yuban) and Procter & Gamble (Folgers). In recent years these giants have been forced to shut down several U.S.-based processing plants, as increasingly sophisticated consumers beat a path to gourmet specialty roasters. In the U.S. independent specialty roasters have increased twentyfold in the past 10-year period, from 50 roasters in 1987 to over 1,000 roasters in 1997.

Governments have been known to rise and fall in Third World countries because of the prices set in the pit, on the floor of the Coffee, Sugar and Cocoa Exchange in Manhattan's World Trade Center.

New Orleans is the largest coffee importing port in the U.S.

ESPRESSO ACCESSORIES

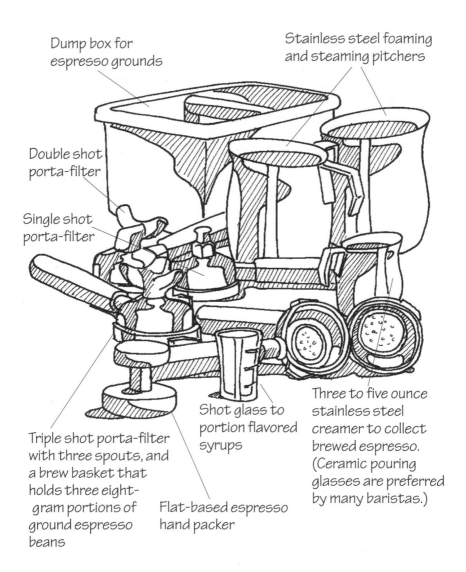

Dump box for espresso grounds

Stainless steel foaming and steaming pitchers

Double shot porta-filter

Single shot porta-filter

Triple shot porta-filter with three spouts, and a brew basket that holds three eight-gram portions of ground espresso beans

Shot glass to portion flavored syrups

Flat-based espresso hand packer

Three to five ounce stainless steel creamer to collect brewed espresso. (Ceramic pouring glasses are preferred by many baristas.)

Chapter 5

The Barista's Supplies

Some of the many barista tools used are: milk steaming pitchers, pouring glasses, grounds box, thermometer, spoons, spatulas, cleaning and scrubbing brushes, measuring shot glass, bar towels, and hand tamper.

 The first coffee drinkers, the Arabs, flavored their coffee with spices during the brewing process.

 Sugar first replaced honey as a sweetener in European kitchens in medieval times, although it was used in China and India more than 2,000 years ago.

 The explosion of espresso based beverages across North America has generated the demand for quality flavored "Italian Style" syrups.

Italian Style Syrup Flavors

Almond
Amaretto
Anisette
Apple
Apricot
B-52
Banana
Bavarian Bing Cherry
Black Cherry
Black Forest
Blackberry
Blue Curaçao
Blueberry
Boysenberry
Butter Rum
Butterscotch
ButterscotchToffee
Caliente Orange
Canadian Cream
Caramel
Cherry
Chocolate
Chocolate Fudge
Chocolate Malt
Chocolate Mint
Chocolate Peanut
 Butter
Chocolate Raspberry
Cinnamon
Coconut
Coffee
Cola
Cranberry

Creme de Cacao
Creme de Cassis
Creme de Menthe
Curaço Orange
Egg Nog
French Vanilla
German Chocolate
Ginger
Grape
Grapefruit
Green Banana
Grenadine
Hazelnut
Highlander Grog
Irish Cream
Jasmine
Kahlua Coffee
Kiwi
Lemon
Licorice
Lime
Macadamia Nut
Mandarino
Mango
Maple Nut
Maraschino
Melon
Mint
Mocha
Monte Cristo
Orange

Orange Brandy
Orange Mocha
Passion Fruit
Peach
Pear
Pecan
Peppermint
Peppermint
 Schnapps
Pina Colada
Pink Grapefruit
Pistachio
Praline
Raspberry
Rootbeer
Rose
Rum
Sambuca
Simple Syrup
Spanish Coffee
Strawberry
Swiss Chocolate
 Almond
Tamarindo
Toasted Walnut
Triple Sec
Tropical Fruit
Vanilla
Vanilla Nut
Watermelon
White Chocolate
White Creme de
 Menthe
Wild Cherry

Exotic Syrups—Flavor Descriptions

Amaretto	Comes from apricot pits and herbs; yields a pleasant almond flavor.
Anisette	An anise-based syrup, very sweet, similar to licorice.
B-52	A combination of Kahlua, Irish Cream, and Grand Marnier.
Blue Curaçao	Flavored with green peels of under-ripe oranges; pronounced CURE-A-SOW.
Creme de Cacao	Rich blend of cocoa and vanilla beans.
Creme de Cassis	Black currant flavored syrup.
Creme de Menthe	A peppermint-flavored syrup.
Grenadine	A pomegranate-flavored syrup.
Irish Cream	A slightly tangy coconut-vanilla cream-flavored syrup.
Kahlua	A Mexican coffee flavor.
Kiwi	An egg-sized fruit of subtropical origin possessing a sweet, green pulp having a strawberry-like flavor.
Mandarino	Has a tangerine flavor derived from peels of Mandarin oranges.
Mango	Similar to apricot taste, from a yellowish-red tropical fruit.
Maraschino	Derived from Dalmation Marasca cherries and their pits.
Orgeat	An almond-flavored syrup, pronounced OR-zhat.
Passion Fruit	A pleasant sweet tasting syrup from a pale-yellow small tropical fruit.
Praline	A syrup made from nut kernels boiled in sugar, with a slight hint of vanilla.
Sambuca	Flavored with anise and the witch elderberry bush, a licorice taste.
Tamarindo	A date-flavored syrup.

INVENTORY CHECKOFF

Milk & Milk Products
Nonfat (Skim Milk)
2% Milk
Whole Milk
Half-and-Half
Whipped Cream
Condensed Milk
Egg Nog
Soy Milk
Milk Substitute
Butter

Coffee
Espresso blend
Espresso decaf

Soft Drinks
Cola
Ginger Ale
Seltzers
Seven-Up
Soda water

Juices
Apple Juice
Grapefruit Juice
Orange Juice

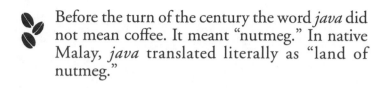 Before the turn of the century the word *java* did not mean coffee. It meant "nutmeg." In native Malay, *java* translated literally as "land of nutmeg."

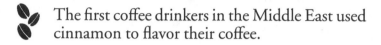 The first coffee drinkers in the Middle East used cinnamon to flavor their coffee.

Centuries ago on the Arabian peninsula coffee was commonly mixed with butter, molasses, and cardamom.

Citrus has been added to coffee for several hundred years.

The Europeans first added chocolate to their coffee in the 1600s.

Frederick the Great had his coffee made with champagne and a bit of mustard.

English scientist Joseph Priestley, discoverer of oxygen, invented carbonated soda water in 1767. By 1807 fruit flavors were added to the bubbly producing Nephite Julep—the world's first soda pop.

Dr. Pepper®, first sold in America in 1885, is the oldest commercial soft drink on the U.S. market.

GARNISHES

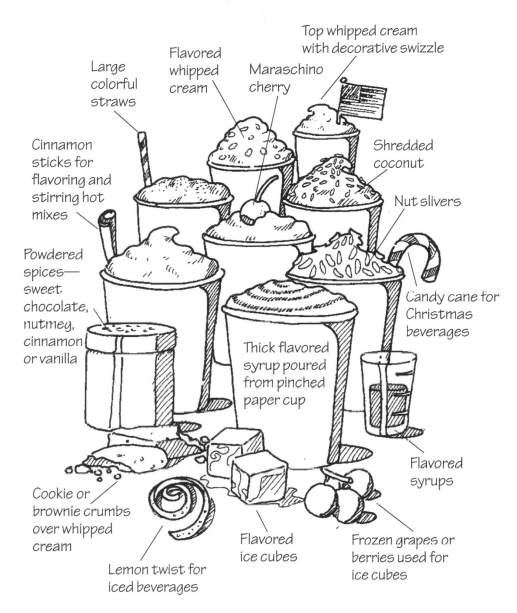

Top whipped cream with decorative swizzle

Flavored whipped cream

Maraschino cherry

Large colorful straws

Cinnamon sticks for flavoring and stirring hot mixes

Shredded coconut

Nut slivers

Powdered spices— sweet chocolate, nutmeg, cinnamon or vanilla

Candy cane for Christmas beverages

Thick flavored syrup poured from pinched paper cup

Flavored syrups

Cookie or brownie crumbs over whipped cream

Frozen grapes or berries used for ice cubes

Flavored ice cubes

Lemon twist for iced beverages

229

ITALIAN STYLE FLAVORED SYRUPS

With over 40 primary flavors now available, over 800 separate two-flavor combinations can be created.

PREPARING*

Easy rule for hot, flavored espresso beverages:
1. Pour the flavoring first.
2. Pour the espresso second.
3. Pour the milk last.

*Heat intensifies the sweetness of sugar. Thus ½ to ¾ ounce of Italian flavored syrup is recommended to sweeten and flavor a 12 ounce hot espresso based beverage. For a 16 ounce cold beverage, filled ⅔ full with ice, a 2 ounce portion of syrup combined with soda water would be the recommended portion.

*Flavored coffee lends its popularity to the fact that just about all flavors mix well with it when used proportionally.

In 1886 an Atlanta druggist made a great discovery. When he mixed the extract of the African kola nut with the coca extract (a derivative of coca leaves) Coca-Cola® was born.

In 1888 Marvin Stone patented the first wax-coated straw. Before that, hollow stalks of rye were used for sipping flavored beverages. Such straws often cracked.

The ice machine was invented in 1865 and first appeared in a restaurant in New Orleans in 1875. The technology was slow to reach soda fountains and bars, however, and ice cubes weren't much in evidence until after WW II.

The first drugstore soda fountain appeared in 1825. By 1891 fountains had become so popular that in New York City they outnumbered the saloons.

By the 1880s, such was the popularity of the ice cream sodas that many towns in the Midwest prohibited their sales on the Christian Sabbath. By removing the carbonated water from these creations, soda fountain owners found a way of pleasing their customers without breaking the law. The Sunday soda became the Sundae.

Iced Italian style beverages are visually appealing and should be served in clear glasses or clear plastic glasses.

 Confused about the difference between soda water and seltzer? Both are carbonated. They both add sparkle to Italian sodas. Soda water or club soda is man-made and contains various sodiums and salts. Seltzer can be man-made, but is often a naturally carbonated mineral water. Seltzer contains no sodium or salt.

 Soda water and seltzer are calorie free. However a typical 8 ounce serving of soda water will contain 70 mg of sodium.

 Seltzer is derived from the German city of Nieder Selters. The term denoted a popular sparkling water consumed years ago in that city.

 Italian syrups for flavoring espresso and soda beverages have been available in Europe for many years, but their actual popularity in the U.S. is fairly recent.

 Aside from espresso and soda-water beverages, Italian flavored syrups are merchandised for ice cream toppings, milk shake flavorings, and desserts.

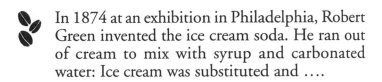 In 1874 at an exhibition in Philadelphia, Robert Green invented the ice cream soda. He ran out of cream to mix with syrup and carbonated water: Ice cream was substituted and ....

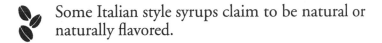 Some Italian style syrups claim to be natural or naturally flavored.

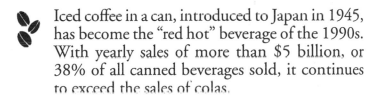 Citric and malic acids are often used as additives in Italian style syrups. They are used as stabilizers and flavor enhancers. Careful—when the acid content is too high, the syrup will curdle when blended with milk if the mixture is too hot.

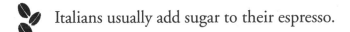 Italians usually add sugar to their espresso.

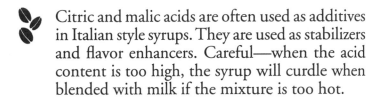 Iced coffee in a can, introduced to Japan in 1945, has become the "red hot" beverage of the 1990s. With yearly sales of more than $5 billion, or 38% of all canned beverages sold, it continues to exceed the sales of colas.

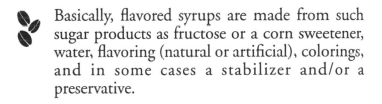 Basically, flavored syrups are made from such sugar products as fructose or a corn sweetener, water, flavoring (natural or artificial), colorings, and in some cases a stabilizer and/or a preservative.

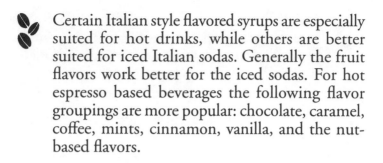 Certain Italian style flavored syrups are especially suited for hot drinks, while others are better suited for iced Italian sodas. Generally the fruit flavors work better for the iced sodas. For hot espresso based beverages the following flavor groupings are more popular: chocolate, caramel, coffee, mints, cinnamon, vanilla, and the nut-based flavors.

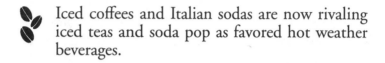 Iced coffees and Italian sodas are now rivaling iced teas and soda pop as favored hot weather beverages.

Flavor chemists say the overwhelming use of artificial flavors has resulted in the public's preference for them over natural flavors.

A maraschino cherry is a cherry that has simply been dyed.

Among the various natural fruit juices, orange is the flavor choice of 65% of people in the United States.

Here's a creative way to sweeten your coffee: try individually wrapped swizzle sticks made from crystallized sugar. Stir, and they dissolve. Chocolate spoons that dissolve are another option.

Rhode Islanders and *only* Rhode Islanders drink a whole lot of milk mixed with coffee syrup.

Flavored syrup preferences vary from city to city and region to region. In Seattle, caramel and chocolate are preferred; in Portland, vanilla. Californians favor the taste of berries, and Easterners choose almond, amaretto, and coffee flavors.

Carob or other natural chocolates can be substituted for the artificial product in mochas.

Coffee shop owners report higher cookie sales when they keep display jars full.

Just over 30 years ago a flightless New Zealand bird gave its name to a fuzzy fruit known as the Chinese gooseberry. This Kiwi soon succeeded in the export market and has subsequently become a popular flavored syrup for Italian style sodas.

Gail Borden invented condensed milk in 1856. Evaporated milk was invented in 1884 by John Meyenberg.

Of all the additives used over the centuries to enhance coffee's flavor, from sugar and honey to spirits and spices, hot frothy steamed milk has become its most popular condiment.

Some brands of milk have a shelf life of nine months and don't require refrigeration. They're made by using an ultra-high temperature to kill disease-causing bacteria. Nutritional elements are unaffected. These brands can be used for steaming lattes.

To make powdered milk, the dairies simply remove the cream from whole milk and use heat to extract water. Only dry powder remains.

Lactase is an enzyme which allows our bodies to digest the milk sugar lactose. An estimated 70% of the world's population suffers from lactase deficiency. Asian, Mediterranean, Arab and southern Italian peoples are especially prone to this deficiency.

Intolerance to milk in these regions has caused cappuccinos to be smaller or to be made with nondairy substitutes. Such substitutes are especially popular in Asia.

For those who love lattes but suffer from milk allergies, there are soybean, rice, almond, and potato milk "alternatives." They are all either high in calories or sodium and some carry a strong flavor. The proponents of the dairy-based whey "alternative" claim it tastes like milk and is no more expensive.

The USDA provides the following nutritional data for an 8 ounce (1 cup) serving of milk for each of the four milk varieties.

Variety	Fat Grams	Calories	% Calories from Fat
Whole milk	7.7	150	46
2% milk	4.9	121	37
1% milk	2.4	102	22
Nonfat milk	0	86	0

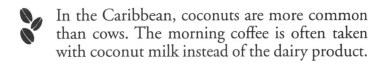 The whey-based product, low in calories, and with no cholesterol, is also now being offered as a milk alternative for espresso based beverages.

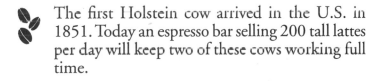 The dairies have certainly become beneficiaries of the espresso boom. One large retail coffee chain sold over 2½ million gallons of milk in 1993 in Washington State alone. A 12 ounce single latte requires 7 ounces of milk to a single shot of espresso.

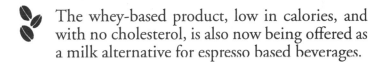 The first Holstein cow arrived in the U.S. in 1851. Today an espresso bar selling 200 tall lattes per day will keep two of these cows working full time.

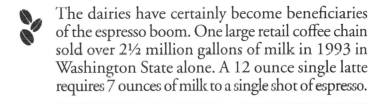 In the Caribbean, coconuts are more common than cows. The morning coffee is often taken with coconut milk instead of the dairy product.

An experienced practitioner recommends the following nondairy substitute for best tasting and steaming characteristics: one-third light soy milk to two-thirds rice milk. The soy milk has sufficient protein for foaming and texture, and the rice milk provides the flavor.

Preheating the ceramic espresso cups will help to slow the coffee's flavor loss.

Tip on foaming/steaming eggnog: mix one third 2% milk with two-thirds eggnog for better results.

Lavazza is Italy's largest coffee retailer, serving three-quarters of Italian households. The company introduced its products to American markets in the late 1980s.

Maxim®, the first freeze-dried coffee, was introduced in 1965. Two years later, Taster's Choice® (Nestlé) appeared on store shelves.

At its Turin plant, Lavazza produces about 300 tons of coffee per day. Panels of consumers periodically check the roasted and packaged coffee to insure the product's consistency.

The dried and ground root of the chicory plant is often used as an additive or substitute for coffee in Creole brewing.

 During the Civil War food and coffee were scarce in New Orleans, and bitter chicory root was widely substituted for coffee. The brew's bitterness was often moderated with milk. Chicory/coffee blends continue to enjoy regional popularity.

 Coffee purists claim that syrup bastardizes specialty coffee. Others would counter that syrup removes specialty coffee's snob appeal. New customers leery of trying an espresso beverage they expect to be harsh or bitter can often be enticed with their favorite flavoring. Flavoring can initially serve as a vehicle for introducing non-espresso drinkers to latte and cappuccinos. According to Derek Chasan, vice president of Starbucks, "The appeal of flavored coffees is analogous to a wine drinker's initiation with fruity wines. Gradually, the wine drinker makes the move to drier wines, to Chardonnay and finally to cabernets. Coffee enthusiasts often begin with flavored coffees, which soften coffee's strong flavor. They're both on the path to a premium varietal."

Flavor chemists are continually at work creating new flavors. It can take anywhere form fifteen minutes to over 50 days to develop a flavor. Once the chemists are satisfied, the flavor and the aroma are "fingerprinted" utilizing scientific analyzers. The new product is then stored in a Retained Sample Room, a sort of library vault of past flavors.

Flavor chemists say the overwhelming use of artificial flavors has resulted in the public's preference for them over natural flavors. This preference also makes economic sense, especially when artificial vanilla costs $6 per pound, and natural vanillin costs a whopping $2,000 per pound.

Coffee consumers should actually disregard commodity prices. Why? The commodity is a small part of the cost of producing a cup of coffee. At a typical Starbucks or Coffee Connection outlet, the coated paper cup costs the company more than the coffee inside it.

Not all who drink their coffee black know this: You put cream in coffee to keep it hot. Cream first cools coffee just enough, then forms an insulating layer of fat molecules across the surface to hold in the heat that's left.

Most non-dairy creamers are made from coconut oil, a substance very high in fats. Mocha Mix is the best choice.

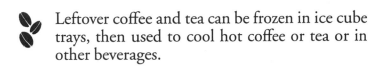 Leftover coffee and tea can be frozen in ice cube trays, then used to cool hot coffee or tea or in other beverages.

Silver polish will remove coffee stains from plastic cups.

Coffee, juice, and tea stains may be removed by scrubbing them vigorously with a paste made of baking soda and water.

To repair a nail hole on woodwork, mix a small amount of instant coffee with a spackling paste of starch and water.

Genghis Khan carried powdered mare's milk.

Heavy cream is lighter than light milk.

Philadelphian Henry R. Heyl invented the paper milk container. Dairymen told him it was worthless.

Why do cans of diet cola float while cans of regular cola sink? Sugar and corn syrup weigh more than artificial sweeteners.

Bartenders in Italy never put ice in any drink.

The claim has been made that the fat in chocolate doesn't raise blood cholesterol.

Pure chocolate is too bitter to eat.

 Listed atop the roster of world-class chocolate eaters are the people of the Netherlands.

 Americans consumed a record 23.4 pounds of confections last year, between 11 and 12 pounds of chocolate.

 Coffee grounds kept in an open jar will help absorb odors.

 The eggshell your great-grandmother threw into the coffee pot was intended to settle the grounds and had nothing to do with your daily calcium requirement.

 For visually appealing ice cubes, freeze red and green maraschino cherries in the ice cube tray. Lemon peel may also be frozen in ice cubes for use in the water glasses.

The bagel, a bread with a three-step cooking procedure, has been around for 400 years. The first mention of a bagel in print was recorded in 1610 in Krakow, Poland, where it was cited as a gift for women at childbirth. The first mention of the bagel in print in the U.S. didn't occur until 1932.

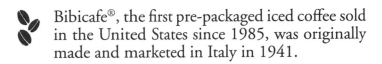

Bibicafe®, the first pre-packaged iced coffee sold in the United States since 1985, was originally made and marketed in Italy in 1941.

Scientists tell us a beverage's thirst-quench-quotient depends on high water content. Coffee ranks fourth behind plain water (first), club soda (second), and iced tea (third). Other beverages in descending order are: diet cola, presweetened Kool-Aid®, beer, ginger ale, and milk.

Tiramisu (tear-a-MEE-su), one of the latest Italian dessert rages, is basically layers of ladyfingers soaked with espresso and sandwiched with fluffy clouds of eggs and Mascarpone cheese. The assembly is topped with shaved chocolate or cocoa powder.

Biscotti (bee-SKOAT-tee), a traditional Italian cookie, has become popular at espresso bars. Often flavored with almond and poppy seeds, biscotti are twice baked. The cookie's crunchy texture is specifically designed to be dipped.

Proper tea etiquette dictates first tea, then in order: cream, sugar, cookies, and mints. Such a formal service order has not yet been established for coffee. However, a popular ordering procedure for espresso based beverages has emerged and appears on the following page.

Order Etiquette
For Espresso Based Beverages

Example:
A mocha with two shots of espresso, nonfat milk, and no whipped cream, in a 12 ounce cup.

Double Tall Skinny Whipless Mocha

Double	Number of shots of espresso (2)
Tall	12 ounce cup
Skinny	Milk type (nonfat)
Whipless	No whipped cream
Mocha	Name of beverage (mocha)

Order Procedure:

1. Number shots of espresso *if* more than one.

2. Size of cup *if* other than a regular 8 ounce cup.

3. Type of milk *if* other than 2%.

4. If foam is to be withheld, state "foamless."

5. If whipping cream is to be withheld, state "whipless."

6. If beverage is to be other than latte, state name of beverage (i.e. mocha).

Espresso Slang

"A"	Americano
Brevé	Latte with half-and-half substituted for milk
Double	Two shots of espresso
Dry	More foamed milk—less steamed milk. (i.e. dry cappuccino).
Foamless	No foam
Grandé	16 ounce cup
Harmless	Made with decaf espresso
Lungo	(Long pour) 1½ ounces water through a single measure of espresso
Nofun	Made with decaf espresso.
Quad	Four shots of espresso.
Ristretto	(Short pour) ¾-1 ounces water through a single measure of espresso.
Short	8 ounce cup
Single	One shot of espresso
Skinny	Made with nonfat milk
Sleeper	Made with decaf espresso
Solo	Single shot of espresso
Tall	12 ounce cup
Triple	Three shots of espresso.
Wet	More steamed milk—less foamed milk (i.e. wet cappuccino).
Whipless	No whipping cream.
With Room	Cup not completely filled with coffee, so there is room for cream.

COMMERCIAL
ESPRESSO MACHINES

Manually operated
by lever action

On/off button control;
continuous pour until
off is pushed

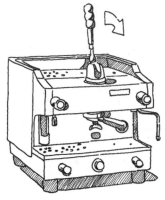

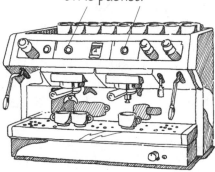

**PISTON TYPE OR MANUAL
STYLE ESPRESSO MACHINE**

**SEMI AUTOMATIC
ESPRESSO MACHINE**

Push button with water dosage
control and automatic shut-off

Push button and computerized
to serve complete drinks such as
lattes and cappuccinos

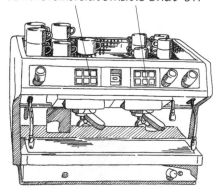

**AUTOMATIC ESPRESSO
MACHINE**

**FULLY AUTOMATIC
ESPRESSO MACHINE**

Chapter 6

The Equipment

The first roasted coffee beans were boiled whole in water. Later, man ground the roasted beans with a mortar and pestle, then boiled them, which added flavor and aroma.

In 1908 Melitta Bentz, a housewife from Dresden, Germany, took blotting paper from her son's notebook and used it as a coffee filter, thus creating the world's first drip coffeemaker.

Today, nearly three-quarters of the U.S. ground roast coffee drinkers enjoy the drip method invented by this entrepreneurial woman. Succeeding generations of the Bentz family have continued the company and tradition of its founder.

The infusion method makes coffee with boiling water poured over ground coffee, the method used to make tea.

In the percolation method of brewing coffee the boiling water passes through coffee grounds by only the force of gravity.

In 1935 Italian Francisco Illy substituted compressed air for steam and produced the first automatic espresso machine.

 In 1947 Achilles Gaggia introduced a hand lever mechanical piston to replace steam pressure. His refinement produced a fast, high pressure extraction, characterized by a thick layer of foam or crema, the signature of good espresso. Gaggia's piston could produce 130 pounds per square inch of pressure.

 Gaggia's new method of high pressure extraction is hailed by many as perhaps the greatest development of all time in coffee brewing.

 Crema, the heart and soul of espresso, was now achievable with Gaggia's new machine. This light-colored foam covering each shot was baffling to the Italian "experts" as Gaggia attempted to market his invention. Most prospective customers declined. By 1950 a total of only 30 of his machines were sold.

 Prior to the emergence of the pump drive machine in 1947, steam-pressure machines could only exert 22 pounds per square inch of pressure to extract the espresso. This amount was not nearly enough pressure to produce "crema."

 The manual or lever espresso machine was sold widely in Italy during the 1950s. This type of machine drives a piston which compresses the water into the ground beans.

In 1961 Ernesto Valente replaced the spring of the lever machine with a rotating pump driven by a small electric motor.

Since the pump would not work with hot water, Valente decided to compress the water while it was still cold, before it passed into the heat exchanger in the boiler of his machine. Previously the water had been first heated and then compressed.

In 1961 the first model of the "continuous delivery" machines was created in Italy. This is the most common machine in commercial use today.

The first automatic espresso machine that portioned the amount of water for a preset shot of espresso appeared in 1965.

The espresso machine provides energy to the water which passes through the pressed coffee grounds capturing only the best flavor essences. The two sources of this energy are pressure and heat.

Domestic (household) espresso machines added rotative and later vibrating pumps by the 1960s. Pressurized extraction could finally be accomplished without the cumbersome manual lever. These household units were capable of frothing the milk as well.

An Italian, Sr. Paoletti, invented a spring-loaded brew basket (porta-filter) in 1984. This basket compressed the ground coffee when the basket was twisted into the espresso machine's brew chamber. The spring-loaded device insured separation of the crema by automatically packing the grounds correctly. This type of porta-filter is a very popular feature of high-end home espresso makers.

Pre-infusion is a feature option available on a few commercial espresso machines. The brew basket is wet with hot water prior to the brew pressure being applied. This option provides the optimum extraction.

There are over 80 separate home and commercial espresso machine brands. The vast majority of these machines are manufactured in Italy.

The world's largest espresso station is owned by Chateau Miel in California, makers of ICE CAP® frosty cappuccino. The station measures 14 feet high by 12 feet long.

In the past five years, the number of espresso makers sold in the U.S. has grown from 500,000 in 1989 to 1.2 million last year, according to *Appliance* magazine.

Commercial espresso machines can be powered by one of two types of pumps: 1) compact vibrator pump; or 2) heavy duty rotary pump. Either can create 130 PSI, the optimum pressure for extracting perfect espresso.

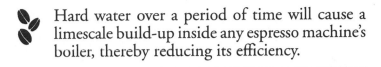 Hard water over a period of time will cause a limescale build-up inside any espresso machine's boiler, thereby reducing its efficiency.

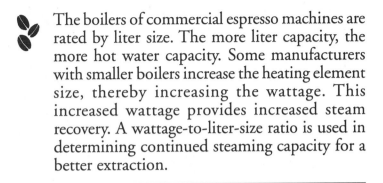 The boilers of commercial espresso machines are rated by liter size. The more liter capacity, the more hot water capacity. Some manufacturers with smaller boilers increase the heating element size, thereby increasing the wattage. This increased wattage provides increased steam recovery. A wattage-to-liter-size ratio is used in determining continued steaming capacity for a better extraction.

It can be argued that a larger boiler, providing more hot water capacity, would be useful when a high portion of Americanos are served. But in the U.S. only about 3% of the total drinks are Americanos. The vast majority of espresso beverages require steamed milk; thus the wattage-to-liter-size ratio is critical when rating a commercial machine.

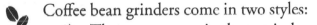 Coffee bean grinders come in two styles:
  1) The more expensive burr grinder.
  2) The blade grinder, similar to a miniature electric blender.

Burr grinders are greatly preferred, as the rough metal plates flake the beans apart and don't heat and burn the bean granules as blade grinders often do. Also, blade grinders have no grind settings and must be regulated manually.

The burr grinder's wheels turn slowly, keeping the heat to a minimum, flaking the coffee beans, and exposing maximum surface area for extracting the flavor oils.

Much flavor is destroyed by blade grinders through heat from the violent pounding. Such grinders offer you no precise way to adjust the fineness of grind.

The electric blade grinder was introduced in the 1950s. It has only recently become popular in U.S. households.

Although the vast majority of commercial espresso machines are manufactured in Italy, a handful of brands are manufactured in the United States.

The Caffé Acorto, a completely automated commercial espresso machine, can make a latte in 32 seconds. The average two-group automatic espresso machine can make four lattes in slightly more time.

Ian Bersten's majestic tome, *Coffee Floats—Tea Sinks* (1993), states that, "The commercial espresso machine of the first half of the twentieth century was the greatest and most exciting development in the history of coffee."

ESPRESSO CONCEPTS

Espresso is extracted by hot water under pressure, that
is forced through a bed of finely ground coffee.

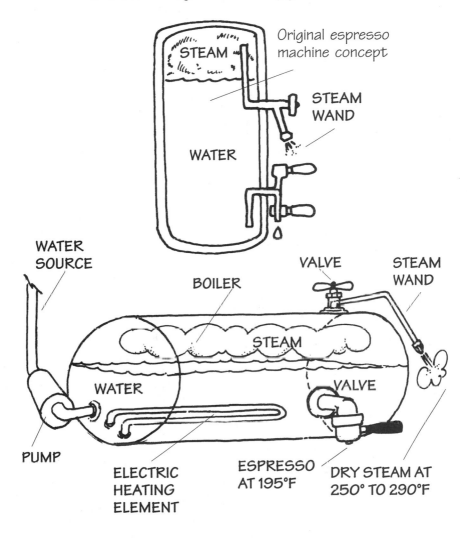

Early espresso machine concept after pump and heating
element were added

HOME TYPE PUMP BOILER SYSTEM ESPRESSO MACHINE

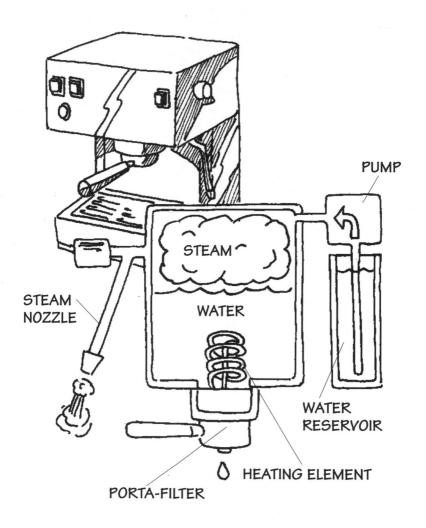

PUMP

STEAM

WATER

STEAM NOZZLE

WATER RESERVOIR

HEATING ELEMENT

PORTA-FILTER

THE FOUR TYPES OF HOME MACHINES

1. Stove Top (Moka Maker)

Price Range—$20 up

 a. ***Does not make true espresso with crema.***
 b. Water heated to boiling in bottom of three chambers is forced up through the middle chamber containing coarse ground coffee (reverse drip), and is deposited in the top chamber.
 c. No milk steaming capability.
 d. Scalded coffee—boiling water at 212°F scalds the coffee. Correct water temperature for quality espresso is 195°F.
 e. Easy to use.

 More than 20 million Moka Makers have been sold, most in Europe since WWII.

2. Electric Steam Machines (Non Pump Boiler)

Price Range—$60 to $130

    a.   ***Does not make true espresso with crema.***

    b.   Heating element in boiler, heats water close to boiling, forcing low pressure extraction through brew chamber.

    c.   Batch brewed, low pressure extraction, one to four cups at a time.

    d.   Steaming attachment is tricky to use. Very poor steam capability.

    e.   Caution—machine must be cooled down before removing pressure cap to refill the boiler.

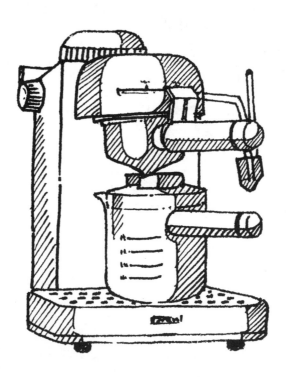

3. Electric Piston Lever (Manual)

Price Range—$350 to $1,000

a. ***Makes excellent true espresso with crema.***
b. Exotic antique appearance.
c. A hand lever attached to a piston forces water heated by an electric element in boiler through finely ground coffee.
d. Good milk steaming capability.
e. Temperature gauge for thermostatic control over both brewing (195°F) and steaming temperature (260°F).
f. Takes practice to master manual (leverized) control of extraction.
g. Water whistling like a tea kettle during warm-up can be annoying.

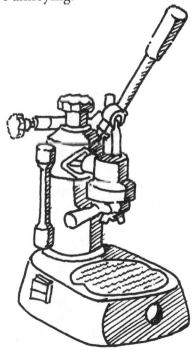

4. Electric Pump—Pump Boiler/Pump Thermal Block

Price Range $175—$550 and up

a. ***Better machines make excellent espresso with crema and foamed/steamed milk beverages.***

b. These machines represent **90%** of total home machine sales.

c. **Pump Boiler**—Most similar to commercial machines, in that water is pumped from water source (reservoir) into boiler heated by electric element. High pressure espresso extraction (aided by pump). Two separate thermostats control both extraction temperature (195°F) and the steaming temperature (260°F). Warm-up takes up to ten minutes.

d. **Pump Thermal Block Machine**—Water is pumped through radiator type heating coils and is instantly heated to correct brewing temperature, which is controlled by one of two thermostats. Mid to high pressure extraction dependent upon pump and machine type. Separate steaming temperature thermostat. Warm-up as fast as 30 seconds.

e. Better machines have both high pressure espresso extraction and high volume steam pressure.

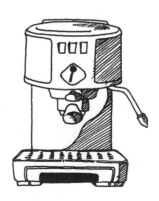

ELECTRIC PUMP ESPRESSO MACHINES

What to look for when purchasing a home machine:

❏ Heavy duty over-all construction and weight of machine.

❏ Wattage of 750 or more.

❏ Two thermostats for separate control over:
- Brewing temperature 195°F
- Steaming temperature 260°F

❏ Extraction pressure of 6-9 atmospheres (90-130 P.S.I.); 130 P.S.I. is the optimum.

❏ Enough steam volume to foam/steam 6 oz of cold milk to a temperature of 130°F within 1½ minutes. Ask your salesperson.

❏ Does the steam wand swivel? Can a ½ liter steaming pitcher be placed under the tip of the steam wand with ease?

❏ Is porta-filter of commercial size—7 gram (Single) 14 gram (Double)—and is it of heavy duty commercial weight?

❏ Does it come with user-friendly instruction manual, a 1-800 customer assistance number, or a "how to video"?

❏ How knowledgeable is the salesperson in demonstrating the machine and answering questions?

❏ Warranty and local service considerations.

Other considerations:

Price? Size of water reservoir? Does the pump require priming before each use? Does porta-filter handle adjust for variation in the coffee grind? Capacity of drip tray, and its ease of use? Are there status indicator lights for: (1) Power; (2) When the water has reached brewing temperature; and (3) When steam has reached steam temperature?

FOAMING ATTACHMENTS FOR HOME ESPRESSO MACHINES

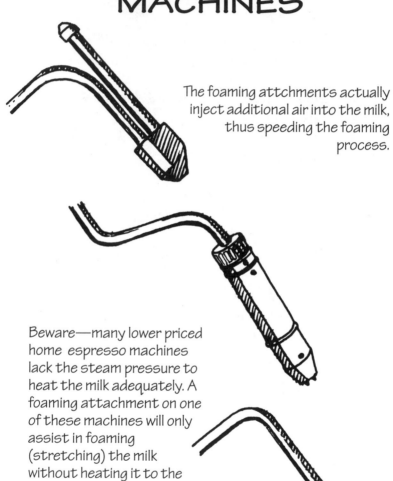

The foaming atttchments actually inject additional air into the milk, thus speeding the foaming process.

Beware—many lower priced home espresso machines lack the steam pressure to heat the milk adequately. A foaming attachment on one of these machines will only assist in foaming (stretching) the milk without heating it to the recommended temperature of 140°F.

GRINDERS

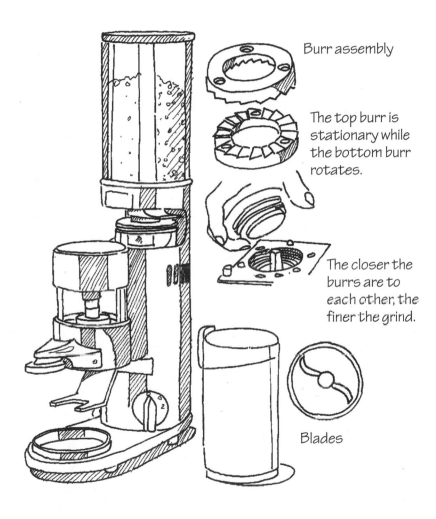

Burr assembly

The top burr is stationary while the bottom burr rotates.

The closer the burrs are to each other, the finer the grind.

Blades

Commercial electric burr grinder and doser

Home-type electric blade grinder

THE TWO TYPES OF HOME COFFEE GRINDERS

The exact fineness of the grind is much more critical with espresso than with drip coffee.

1. Electric Blade Grinders

Price Range—$15 to $30

  a. The electric blade grinder introduced in the 1950s has only recently become popular in U.S. households. It is similar to a miniature electric blender.
  b. Blade grinders destroy much of the coffee's flavor through heat from the violent pounding.
  c. Inexpensive blade grinders are quick and can be used for flavored coffees.
  d. These units have no grind settings for the precise, uniform grind necessary for quality espresso. Just *On* and *Off.*

> **Appropriate Time for Grinding Coffee Beans with Electric Blade Grinder:**
>
> Drip Grind   20-30 seconds
>
> Espresso Grind   40-50 seconds

2. Burr-Wheel Grinders

Price Range—$150 to $400 Home Type
$500 to $1,000 Commercial Type

a. The burr grinder's wheels turn slowly, keeping the heat to a minimum, flaking the coffee beans, and exposing maximum surface area for extracting the flavor oils.

b. Be warned that flavored coffees may flavor the coffee grinder burrs, which can in turn flavor high quality coffee beans ground later. It is nearly impossible to clean the burr-wheels completely.

c. Most units have an adjustable dosing mechanism that measures the amount of ground coffee dispensed into the porta-filter (brew basket).

d. Burr grinders are greatly preferred because the rough metal plates flake the beans apart and don't heat and burn the bean granules as blade grinders often do.

e. The grind settings are tricky and must be constantly fine tuned to compensate for the many variables: humidity, degree of roast, and the bean density.

f. A burr-wheel grinder-doser is required for the optimum espresso grind.

Antique Burr-wheel Grinder

ESPRESSO MACHINE COMPARISON

Home Machines	Commercial Machines
Must refill water manually. Waste water drains into drip tray that must be emptied.	Plumbed into an in-line water supply and a direct drain.
Unable to extract espresso and foam/steam milk simultaneously. **Two separate operations are required** because espresso is extracted at 195°F and milk is foamed/steamed at 260°F. After the espresso extraction (195°F), the heating element inside the boiler must switch to a high-heat setting. A typical waiting period of **30 seconds** is required before the boiler is super-heated to 260°F and steaming can proceed.	Can extract espresso and foam/steam milk simultaneously. Both processes completed within **20-25 seconds total time.**
Many home machines must be primed before each use (a separate operation).	Priming not required.
Only the better machines have high pressure extraction, 130 P.S.I., required to separate, (emulsify) the oils and colloids from the coffee and produce crema.	High pressurized espresso extraction resulting in crema with each shot of espresso.

MACHINE COMPARISON, cont.

Home Machines	Commercial Machines
Low steam volume requiring additional time to foam/steam the milk.	High steam volume allows fast foaming/steaming of the milk. (15 seconds)
Only better home machines include commercial-size porta-filters and brew chamber assemblies.	Heavy duty construction.
Manual control over the amount of espresso extracted (must switch pour button *On* and *Off*).	Most commercial machines have an automatic extraction portion control for singles and doubles, and will shut off after the desired portion is extracted.

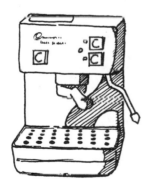
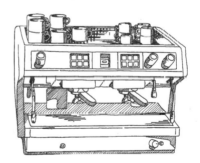

ELAPSED TIME COMPARISON
Preparing a Latte

Home Machines	Commercial Machines
Espresso extraction at 195°F **30 seconds** Wait period for boiler to super-heat to 260°F **30 seconds** Milk foaming/ steaming time, 45 seconds to 2½ minutes **90 seconds average**	Espresso extraction and foaming/steaming milk **20-30 seconds**
Total time to make a Latte with a home machine— **2½ minutes**	**Total time to make a Latte with a commercial machine—** **30 seconds**

Places to purchase your home espresso machine: houseware departments of better department stores, kitchen specialty stores, and retail coffee stores.

 Warranty centers for home espresso machines are located in most large U.S. cities.

 One major difference between home and commercial espresso machines is the elapsed time it takes to foam/steam milk to 140°F. Six ounces of milk foamed/steamed to this temperature can vary, dependent upon the steam volume of the home machine, from 45 seconds to 2½ minutes. A commercial machine will perform this task in 15 seconds.

 To speed the milk foaming process, many home espresso machines include a frothing attachment to the steam wand. These attachments inject additional air into the milk to speed the foaming. Trouble is, they often foam (stretch) the milk without providing enough heat to bring the temperature to the recommended 140°F.

 Many people making espressos at home solve the milk-heating problem by pre-heating the milk to 90°-110°F in the microwave before foaming it with the frothing attachment. Unlike the steam wand without the frothing attachment, the frothing attachment will permit the user to foam heated milk.

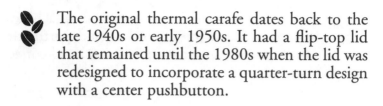 The original thermal carafe dates back to the late 1940s or early 1950s. It had a flip-top lid that remained until the 1980s when the lid was redesigned to incorporate a quarter-turn design with a center pushbutton.

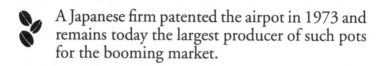 A Japanese firm patented the airpot in 1973 and remains today the largest producer of such pots for the booming market.

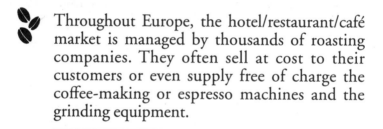 Insulated airpot coffee servers will hold coffee at a serving temperature for a few hours. Such pots maintain coffee quality by keeping the coffee from excess heat and exposure to air, both factors that break down coffee and destroy its flavors. One company offering these pots reported a 40 percent sales increase between 1994 and 1995.

Throughout Europe, the hotel/restaurant/café market is managed by thousands of roasting companies. They often sell at cost to their customers or even supply free of charge the coffee-making or espresso machines and the grinding equipment.

Coffee grounds sink; tea leaves rise. Pot shapes reflect as much.

The only cowboy who always ordered milk at the bar was Hopalong Cassidy.

Two espresso machines in the Milan, Italy airport brew 15,000 shots of espresso each day. Each is a six-group (six brew-head) machine. Still, amazing!

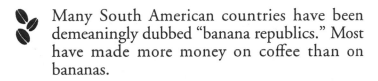 Many South American countries have been demeaningly dubbed "banana republics." Most have made more money on coffee than on bananas.

Visually appealing take out coffee packages sell product. Your grandparents used to buy both garden seeds and coffee by the scoopful. When the Shakers started selling garden seeds in little packets, Americans everywhere took up home gardening. Just as the garden seed packets propelled home gardening's boom, fresh roasted coffee in demi-sized packages is fueling specialty coffee growth.

There are 80,000 convenience stores in the U.S..

One survey company projected that in 1995 there was still room for 13,390 additional espresso outlets nationwide.

According to one Italian manufacturing organization, in 1994 there were only 5,000 commercial espresso machines exported to the U.S. from Italy.

75 million people in the U.S. drink coffee. Of these people, 20 to 25 percent are specialty coffee drinkers, which means that *15-18.75 million people in the U.S. drink specialty coffee.*

Retail dollar sales volume of specialty coffee:

1969	$ 44 million	1970	$ 763 million
1971	1.5 billion	1972	3.0 billion (projected)

LAYERING A LATTE

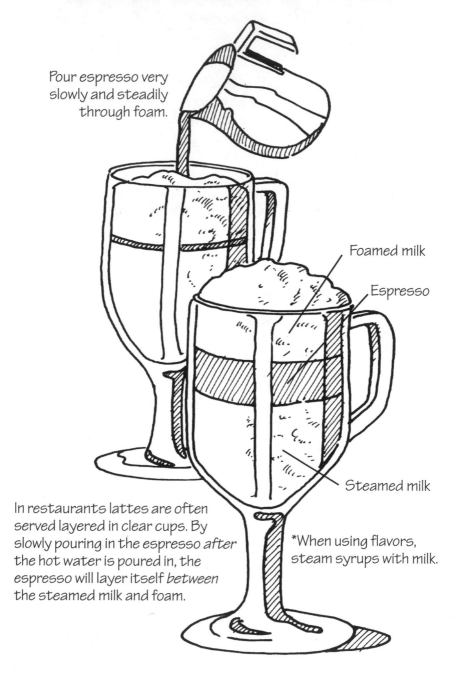

Pour espresso very
slowly and steadily
through foam.

Foamed milk

Espresso

Steamed milk

In restaurants lattes are often
served layered in clear cups. By
slowly pouring in the espresso *after*
the hot water is poured in, the
espresso will layer itself *between*
the steamed milk and foam.

*When using flavors,
steam syrups with milk.

Chapter 7

How to Make the Perfect Cup

ESPRESSO: THE PERFECT SHOT *by Rich Abker*
If you take the time and use a few steadfast rules, you can perfect the art of making the very best espresso. After all, this is the first step to creating perfect lattes, cappuccinos, mochas, Americanos and their many varieties.

Step 1:   Use only freshly roasted coffee especially blended for espresso (whole bean).

Step 2:   Check your grind daily and adjust burr settings to maintain the correct grind size (coarseness/fineness). The grind should feel slightly smaller than sugar granules when rubbed between thumb and index finger.

Step 3:   Use the correct amount of coffee in your porta-filter, about 7 grams for a single shot and 14 grams for a double shot.

Step 4:   When loading the porta-filter, use a firm pack and level your coffee to create a smooth rich crema with optimum extraction. Rule of thumb is to exert a firm push of your hand packer while applying a slight twisting motion to the coffee.

Step 5:   The water temperature at the point of extraction (for both group and porta-filter) is crucial to proper extraction. This should be close to 195°F for best results.

Step 6:   Water pressure of approximately 130 PSI. is needed from your espresso machine in order to extract only the best in coffee flavor in a speedy and efficient manner.

Step 7:   The amount of hot water used for your shot needs to be proportionally correct for the type of pour required. (The amount of coffee remains the same.)

The Perfect Latte

1. Use a fresh roasted espresso blend, finely ground just prior to brewing.
2. Measure 7 grams, (or the amount your coffee roaster or machine manufacturer recommends, 6-8 grams).
3. Your porta-filter and container for collecting the extracted espresso should be preheated.
4. Pack the measured grounds into the brew basket; insert into the machine and begin extraction of 18-23 seconds.
5. Pour very cold milk into steam pitcher until it is ⅓ full.
6. Turn on the steam wand for about three seconds, to bleed out any excess moisture that will otherwise dilute your milk.
7. Insert the steam wand in the middle of the pitcher with the tip approximately ½" below the milk's surface. *Turn on the steam wand fully.*
8. Stretch (foam) milk for three to four seconds by lowering the pitcher slightly while listening for a hissing (*sssst-sssst*) sound as the milk takes in air and expands. Keep the tip of the wand ½" below the milk's surface.

9. Now tilt your pitcher about 45°F until a whirlpool action is created. Keep the whirlpool going as you *slowly* lower the pitcher, keeping the tip of the wand ½" below the milk's surface.

10. You will hear a hissing sound *(sssst-sssst)* as the milk takes in air while foaming. **Do not break the milk's surface with the tip of the steam wand.** If you do, large bubbles will sud-denly appear, and you will lose your dense foam.

11. When the milk stretches (expands) and reaches the top of the pitcher, tilt the pitcher back to the upright position and *lift* the pitcher so that the tip of the wand is at the bottom of the pitcher. Leave in this position until the milk heats to 140°F.

12. Turn off the steam valve while the wand is still in the pitcher.

13. Remove the pitcher and collapse any large foam bubbles by slapping the pitcher on the counter a few times or by tapping the side of the pitcher several times with a large spoon.

14. Immediately after removing the pitcher, turn the steam valve on again to bleed any milk that might have back-siphoned into the wand. Wipe the wand clean with a damp rag.

15. Pour the espresso into the serving cup.

16. Tilt the serving cup slightly toward you and begin pouring the milk down the front of the cup, moving the pour from one side to the other side in a back-and-forth motion.

17. As the cup fills with this marbleization of foamed/steamed milk and espresso, tilt the cup upright and continue the pour until the mixture rises slightly above the cup's rim.

18. With a typical home espresso machine the foaming/steaming process will take anywhere

from 45 seconds to 2½ minutes, depending on the volume of steam. Commercial machines extract the espresso and foam/steam the milk simultaneously, all within 25 seconds.

The Perfect Cappuccino

1. It is crucial to prepare the milk before pulling the espresso.
2. Pour fresh, cold milk into steaming pitcher until about ⅓ full.
3. Turn on steam wand for about three seconds to bleed out any excess moisture that may otherwise dilute the milk.
4. Position the steam wand just below the milk's surface, in the middle of the pitcher. Turn on the steam fully.
5. Increase the volume of the milk foam rapidly while maintaining tiny bubbles that will create very dense foam. A slow, gentle lowering of the pitcher should produce a continuous (sssst-sssst) hissing sound.
6. Keep adding air into the steamed milk until the foam rises to the top of the pitcher. When the milk stretches (expands) and reaches the top of the pitcher, tilt the pitcher back to the upright position, and *lift* the pitcher so that the tip of the wand is at the bottom of the pitcher. Leave in this position until the milk heats to 140°F.
7. Now turn off the steam and remove wand from milk.
8. Bang the bottom of the pitcher firmly on the counter several times. This will help to collapse the bubbles and thicken the milk foam. Set the pitcher aside to allow separation of milk and foam.

9. Wipe the steam wand with a clean damp towel. Then clean out any excess milk by bleeding the steam wand for a few seconds.
10. Now prepare your espresso and pour into serving cup.
11. Quickly add only the hot steamed milk until the cup is ¾ full. The milk should pour out easily from *under* the denser foam.
12. Spoon out the dense milk foam to fill the cup about two inches above the cup rim. Shape foam to form a peak (cap) on the cappuccino.
13. Dust the "cap" with either powdered chocolate, cinnamon, or nutmeg.

This style cappuccino is known as a "wet" cappuccino because steamed milk is used along with the foam.

A "dry" cappuccino is prepared with straight espresso and dense milk foam but no steamed milk.

The Perfect Mocha

A mocha is a chocolate latte and is usually topped with whipped cream.

To prepare, first add one ounce thick chocolate syrup to the serving cup, add espresso and stir. Then follow instructions for the perfect latte.

There are two standardized methods of pour:
1. **Ristretto** (short pour): ¾-1 ounce for a single espresso with pour time of 17 to 20 seconds. This is a very strong, highly concentrated form of true espresso coffee.

Ristrettos are most often used to prepare:
   a. European style (especially Italian) espresso: It has a thick body, taste, and aroma and is served straight or with sugar.
   b. Espresso using milk: lattes, cappuccinos, mochas, and brevés.
   c. Americanos (full strength).
   d. Cold espresso beverages.
2. **Lungo** (long pour): 1½ to 2 ounces of single espresso with pour time of 25 to 30 seconds. This medium strength form of true espresso is used to prepare:
   a. American style straight espresso.
   b. Americanos (mild in strength and taste).

Step 8: The amount of rich golden crema is an indication of how well you did. The crema must be dense with a golden-brown color. Light brown or white foam indicates the beginning of overextraction.

Step 9: Serve it hot, and serve it quickly. You've served the perfect shot.

The espresso brew method extracts all that is best from the coffee and nothing more.

High concentration of flavor and aroma is the greatest distinction between espresso and regular coffee.

Each cup of espresso is individually made to order from gourmet coffee that is ground just prior to brewing.

The four components of brewing flavorful espresso are the machine, the grinder, the blend of coffee, and the hand of the operator.

Because 98% of a straight shot of espresso is water, good water quality is fundamental to a good tasting brew.

The Northwest, Northeast, and parts of the South generally have the best water quality for brewing espresso.

Hard water works best for brewing tea and batch-brewed coffee. Soft water is best for brewing espresso.

Distilled water makes bad coffee.

Chlorination, excessive hardness, brackishness, alkalinity, and mineral content all can have a negative effect on quality espresso beverages.

If excessive chlorination is a problem, simply let the water stand in a large container for 12 to 24 hours. The chlorination will dissipate—resulting in a much improved espresso brew.

In making espresso, water heated to 195°F (just below boiling) is forced through finely ground coffee under pressure. This captures the greatest amount of flavor.

Lighter roasted coffees generally benefit from a slightly lower brewing temperature, while darker roasted beans require a higher extraction temperature.

Water temperature of less than 192°F produces a distinct sourness in the finished espresso, and the color may be a bit lighter than it should be.

A temperature of over 198°F will burn the coffee oils, creating dark flecks in the crema and producing sharp tasting product (overextraction).

As a rule the amount of soluble solids expressed as a percentage of the total weight of the coffee extracted into the water in the brewing process is: 19% for coffee; 25% for espresso; and 30% for Turkish coffee.

Fruit flavored syrups are best for Italian style sodas and for steamers, while nut flavored Italian style syrups generally taste best in espresso blend beverages.

Darker roasting swells the beans and allows the water more completely to penetrate the finely ground particles during the espresso brewing process. It also reduces the acidity. Filtered coffee can be made from either dark or light roasts, but for the espresso brewing method light roasts are not recommended.

A single shot, or "pull" of espresso in commercial operations, varies from 1 to 1½ ounces. Espresso purists prefer 1 ounce for a most flavorful and aromatic extraction.

After 1¼ ounces of water is extracted through a 7 gram portion of grind, the subsequent extraction starts to turn bitter.

Overextraction occurs when you continue to force hot water through the grind that has already surrendered all its flavor oils.

In brewing coffee or espresso, the longer the bean granules are in contact with the water, the larger the granules should be (the coarser the grind). Due to pressurized extraction in the espresso brew process (18-23 seconds), the granules should be ground finer until they are roughly the consistency of sugar.

30 seconds is perfect extraction time for one shot.

The optimum machine pressure for extracting espresso is 130 PSI or 9 atmospheres.

Grinding your beans just prior to brewing is the single most important thing you can do to improve the quality of your espresso.

 When not in use, porta-filters should be stored attached to the espresso machine to keep them warm. Coffee grounds placed in a cold porta-filter produce a flat tasting espresso.

 Always preheat the shot glass or small stainless steel container that collects the espresso from the machine. Ceramic collection cups should also be preheated. A cold container will "shock" the espresso, and the flavor will be jeopardized.

 A 7 gram portion, roughly equivalent to ¼ ounce, is recommended for a single shot ("pull") of espresso.

 A tamping tool with a flat base should be used to hand pack the coffee in the brew basket with firm downward pressure and a slight twisting motion.

 A mathematician at the University of Florence has written a 30-page mathematical description of coffee extraction.

 Many espresso coffee grinders have an attached tamper. Italian baristas will never use this device. They will always use the hand tamper as they press downward with a twisting motion to level the grounds in the basket.

TAMPING TOOLS & TECHNIQUES

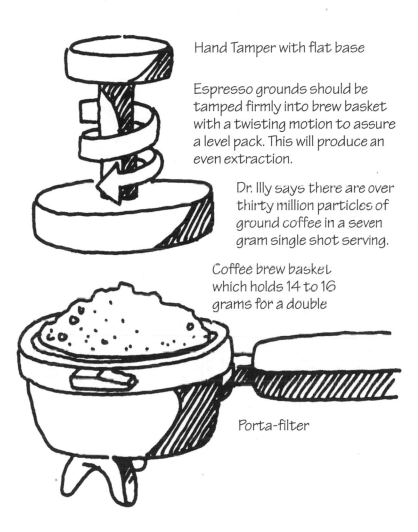

Hand Tamper with flat base

Espresso grounds should be tamped firmly into brew basket with a twisting motion to assure a level pack. This will produce an even extraction.

Dr. Illy says there are over thirty million particles of ground coffee in a seven gram single shot serving.

Coffee brew basket which holds 14 to 16 grams for a double

Porta-filter

BREW HEAD ASSEMBLY

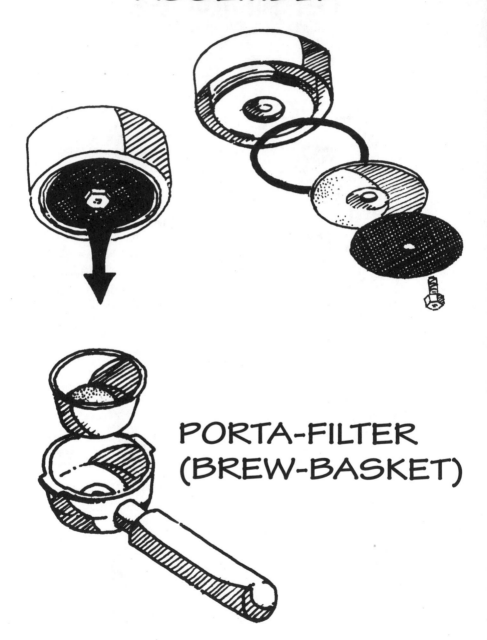

PORTA-FILTER (BREW-BASKET)

Baristas always wipe the edge of the porta-filter with the flat of their hands to remove excess grinds before attaching the unit to the machine. Loose grinds would be abrasive to the rubber gasket in the brew chamber.

Once the porta-filter is firmly packed, insert it firmly into the machine.

A single "pull" of espresso should take from 18 to 23 seconds. As the liquid extracts, it should appear thick and creamy and a little bit lazy.

During the brewing process about 10% of the oils in the ground coffee will separate to form the crema.

The crema, a golden-brown foam that covers a perfectly brewed shot of espresso, can only be achieved by a high pressured method of extraction.

A thick, rich layer of crema impedes the loss of heat and aroma from the espresso before it is consumed.

Women (if they are not pregnant) metabolize caffeine in an hour and a half, men in three hours.

The crema is formed from microscopic bubbles of coffee gas, oils, and gelatinous colloids. These substances are vectors of the wonderful aroma.

Caution: If you notice a dime-size white area in the midst of your golden brown crema, stop the pour. This area represents caffeine and bitter oils from overextraction.

More water passing through coffee grounds does not make the brew stronger. Excess water weakens the finished beverage, and the last flavors extracted are bitter.

The aroma from crema and espresso is made up of more than 700 chemical components.

Foaming and steaming milk with a steam wand is unique to the espresso business.

The steam wand releases a hot-dry steam at a temperature between 250° and 290°F. This steam method actually alters the proteins of the milk and creates a pleasantly different taste that blends well with espresso.

Soft water steams much better than hard water.

The best shot of espresso extracts 25% of coffee bean solids.

Espresso professionals realized early in the history of the technology that steam collected atop the tank could be used to heat milk as well as to provide pressure for extracting the brew. Soon a valve with a long nozzle was placed into the upper part of the tank for this purpose.

Clip-on dial thermometers that attach to the steaming pitcher are a must for the home espresso maker as well as the professional. Only a few seasoned professional baristas are able to steam the milk to the proper temperature by feeling the heat from the pitcher's surface.

Before steaming milk, open the steam valve to clear the condensed water from the nozzle. After the steaming process, open the line once again to force out any milk that might have been siphoned back into the nozzle when the steam nozzle was last turned off.

To steam and foam the milk, use very cold milk. Also, use a cold stainless steel pitcher for the best results. Warm milk will not foam well.

In the steaming process milk proteins are coagulated, resulting in a thick foam.

The lower the butterfat content of the milk, the better it will foam. Thus when using nonfat milk, stop the foaming (stretching) at 60 F and begin steaming, (heating) to 140°F. When using whole milk, stop the foaming at 100°F and begin steaming.

Coffee has 750 components.

Hard water and coffee go together.
The two phases of foaming and steaming milk are stretching (foaming) and heating (steaming to the correct temperature of 140°F).

FOAMING AND STEAMING MILK

1. Begin by filling cold stainless steel pitcher slightly more than ⅓ full of very cold milk.

3. After tip of nozzle is ½" below surface of milk, open steam valve completely and tilt pitcher to one side to create a whirlpool.

4. As milk takes in air, you will hear an intermittent ssst-ssst-ssst sound. Keep lowering pitcher as milk stretches and dense foam is created.

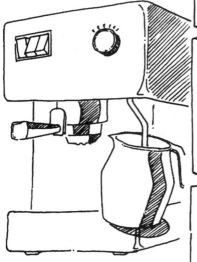

5. After the dense foam has formed, heat the milk mixture to the desired temperature. Turn the steam valve off before removing the wand.

2. When tip of nozzle is ½" below surface of milk, open valve rapidly to completely open position; do not open valve partially.

It is difficult to foam (stretch) whole milk after it reaches 100°F unless a frothing attachment is used. These frothing attachments are generally only available with home-type espresso machines.

Steaming milk is easy, but foaming the milk requires an understanding of the technique and its application.

When preparing to foam and steam the milk, place the nozzle of the steam wand into the center of the pitcher, with the tip of the nozzle ½" below the surface of the milk. Open the steam valve fully.

As the tip of the steam wand takes in air from the surface of the liquid, the milk will expand (stretch), forming dense foam.

Slowly lower the pitcher, keeping the tip of the wand just below the surface of the milk as it continues to expand with foam.

Crunch up the shell of a boiled egg and throw it in the pot. Cowboys claimed this technique not only settled the grounds but provided them with their daily calcium requirement.

In the foaming and steaming process, you are continuously listening for the intermittent hissing sound "ssst-ssst-ssst." This sound is created from taking in air at the milk's surface. This hissing sound is so important for the skilled barista that the phrase, "A blind person can steam milk, but a deaf person cannot," has been coined.

With a commercial espresso machine the foaming and steaming process should only take from 10 to 15 seconds. Once the foam has stretched to the top of the pitcher, it may be necessary to heat the milk to 140°F. Do this by lifting the pitcher so the tip of the wand goes to the bottom of the pitcher for only a few seconds or until the bottom of the pitcher is too hot to touch.

White milk is best steamed to a temperature of 140°F, while chocolate milk is best steamed to a temperature of 150°F.

If you hear a jet-like howling sound during the foaming and steaming process, the steam wand is too far below the surface of the milk. This sound lets you know you are scalding the milk.

Over-steaming or boiling the milk will result in the lactose, or milk sugar, caramelizing. Many can relate this taste to hot milk that has been scorched atop the stove.

Many commercial espresso operations suffer the effects of high employee turnover and inexperienced or poorly trained baristas. Inept operators routinely burn and scorch milk by leaving the steam nozzle in the pitcher too long.

Leftover milk can be re-steamed if it is immediately refrigerated and if new milk is added to regenerate the protein content that creates the foam.

After steaming the milk, always wipe the steam wand immediately with a damp cloth. Forgetting to do this results in caked-on milk, which can be removed by immersing the wand in a pitcher of water, turning on the steam wand, and allowing the hot water to dissolve and loosen the caked-on milk.

Straight espresso flavor begins to fade rapidly as it cools. The beverage should be mixed and served quickly.

The hot foamed and steamed milk (140°F), when combined with hot espresso (195°F), will hold its temperature even in a paper cup, especially if a domed lid is snapped on. This traveling lid with sipping hole has greatly helped popularize espresso beverages for early morning commuters who enjoy their beverages hot.

There are more than 1,200 chemical components in a single roasted coffee bean. Many of the components give coffee the flavor and aroma we enjoy.

The oils and gasses from the fatty substances in freshly ground coffee, along with the gelatinous colloids, cannot dissolve in water. After a high temperature pressurized extraction, they float to the surface, forming the crema and giving the espresso its incomparable aroma.

The coffeol substances within the coffee bean that flavor the brew constitute only ½ of 1% of the weight of the bean.

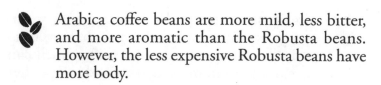 Arabica coffee beans are more mild, less bitter, and more aromatic than the Robusta beans. However, the less expensive Robusta beans have more body.

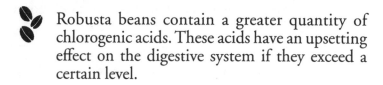 Robusta beans contain a greater quantity of chlorogenic acids. These acids have an upsetting effect on the digestive system if they exceed a certain level.

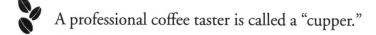 A professional coffee taster is called a "cupper."

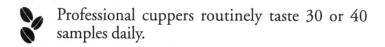 Professional cuppers routinely taste 30 or 40 samples daily.

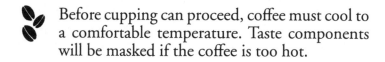 Before cupping can proceed, coffee must cool to a comfortable temperature. Taste components will be masked if the coffee is too hot.

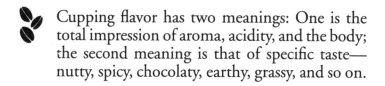 Cupping flavor has two meanings: One is the total impression of aroma, acidity, and the body; the second meaning is that of specific taste—nutty, spicy, chocolaty, earthy, grassy, and so on.

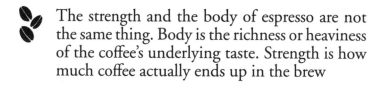 The strength and the body of espresso are not the same thing. Body is the richness or heaviness of the coffee's underlying taste. Strength is how much coffee actually ends up in the brew

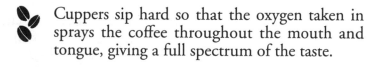 Cuppers sip hard so that the oxygen taken in sprays the coffee throughout the mouth and tongue, giving a full spectrum of the taste.

Cupping or sampling is a daily ritual at most coffee companies. Seven and one-quarter grams of coarsely ground coffee are combined with five ounces of boiling water and stirred. After the water cools to a drinkable temperature, a spoon is pushed through the grounds at the top, "breaking the crust," and the coffee is smelled, slurped, and then spat out.

Professional "cuppers" use a cuspidor to expectorate, thus avoiding the effects of a high caffeine intake and bloating.

The "slurp and spit" method of "cupping" (tasting) coffee was developed in the early 1900s by the Folger's® Coffee Company.

The taste buds on the surface of your tongue will immediately detect the three basic flavors: 1) sweetness; 2) acidity, which should be a snappy quality rather than a heavy sourness; and 3) bitterness, which should be faint unless the beans were over roasted or the brew overextracted.

The human tongue includes over 9,000 taste buds. The life span of a human taste bud is said to be ten days.

During hot weather, coffee in the grinder goes stale more rapidly.

The receptors on the tongue that identify the three taste characteristics are located on the tip for sweet, on the sides for acid, and on the back or root of the tongue for bitter taste.

Sweetness is the taste most desired by the general public in regard to the taste of coffee.

 Because the tip of the tongue is continually being washed by saliva, sweet taste disappears first.

 Human taste buds are reportedly more sensitive at sea level than at higher altitudes.

 Most experts agree that the electric recirculating percolator popular into the 1970s made the worst coffee ever. Such percolators continually recirculated and rebrewed the coffee.

 Bitter tastes linger in the mouth longest because the receptors that identify this taste at the back of the tongue are less frequently washed with saliva.

According to the coffee cupping guidelines of the SCAA the sensory evaluation includes the six basic coffee characteristics:

Fragrance	Nose
Aroma	Aftertaste
Taste	Body

Both green and roasted beans are visually examined during the cupping. Samples are continually compared one against the other using these guidelines.

A CUPPER AT WORK

Two tablespoons of ground coffee are placed in 6 oz of hot water.

Examine the aroma of the grounds.

Break the crust and scoop floating grounds out of a cup. Let remaining grounds settle before tasting.

Take a forceful sip, letting the coffee spray over the tongue, toward the rear of the mouth.

Examine the taste sensations:
-Sweetness
-Faint saltiness
-Acidity
-Bitterness

Expectorate into cup or a spittoon.

Rinse mouth with water.

Begin with another bean type.

A rotating professional cupper's table

*Sweetness is the taste most desired by the general public.

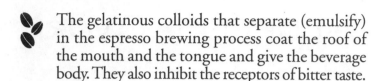 The gelatinous colloids that separate (emulsify) in the espresso brewing process coat the roof of the mouth and the tongue and give the beverage body. They also inhibit the receptors of bitter taste.

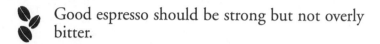 Good espresso should be strong but not overly bitter.

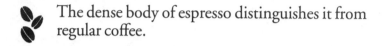 The dense body of espresso distinguishes it from regular coffee.

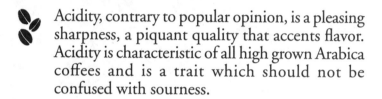 Acidity, contrary to popular opinion, is a pleasing sharpness, a piquant quality that accents flavor. Acidity is characteristic of all high grown Arabica coffees and is a trait which should not be confused with sourness.

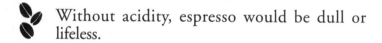 Without acidity, espresso would be dull or lifeless.

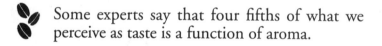 Some experts say that four fifths of what we perceive as taste is a function of aroma.

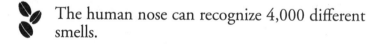 The human nose can recognize 4,000 different smells.

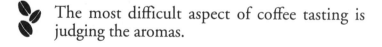 The most difficult aspect of coffee tasting is judging the aromas.

Our olfactory system, which gives us our sense of smell, continues to perceive the aromas up to ten minutes after drinking an espresso.

Our sense of smell more than any of our other senses makes our final judgment on coffee.

Coffee—along with beer and peanut butter—is on the national list of the "ten most recognizable odors."

Medical experts state that it is the sense of smell, not taste, that greatly diminishes as we age.

A double-blind taste test is one in which the identity of the product being tested is not disclosed to either the tester or the person being tested to avoid slanting the results.

Even expert tasters have great difficulty telling the difference between regular and decaffeinated coffee.

Coffee served in many restaurants has cooled to 160°F by the time it reaches the table. The addition of milk or cream makes the beverage instantly tepid, devoid of many of its flavor essences.

In many upscale restaurants, lattes are often layered (parfait style) in clear cups. By slowly pouring in the espresso after the foamed and steamed milk is poured in, the espresso will layer itself between the steamed milk and foam. When lattes are served in paper cups at espresso carts and stands, the espresso is almost always poured first.

The entire brewing, foaming, and steaming process is very theatrical, and this personal touch helps the barista merchandise his product.

Manhattan and Miami are two cities where espresso is generally consumed straight, as in Italy, without adding steamed milk.

Prior to the mid-17th century, no coffee drinker would have dreamed of flavoring his beverage with a dairy product. His preference would have been liquor, sugar, candy, honey, or such spices as cloves, cinnamon, ground cardamom seeds and—in some cases—even mustard.

For their lattes, Southern Europeans combine milk and espresso simultaneously into a bowl as a favorite breakfast drink.

As people age, many lose their ability to digest milk sugar—all but the northern Europeans. Research shows that most people in this region can go on drinking milk into old age.

Italians drink their espresso with sugar; the Germans and the Swiss drink their coffee with equal parts of hot chocolate. The Mexicans like their coffee with cinnamon, the Belgians with chocolate, the French with equal parts of hot milk. Ethiopians add a pinch of salt to their coffee. In the Middle East and Africa, cardamom and spices are added, while Austrians add whipped cream. The Moroccans add peppercorns to their coffee.

Chapter 8

Troubleshooting & Equipment Maintenance

Follow the procedures below to achieve the freshest taste in espresso and to save on replacement parts:

Home espresso machines should be cleaned after each use, and commercial machines should be cleaned daily.

- Use a clean moist towel to clean steam wands, hot water spout and glass gauges. Soak steam wand nozzle.
- Use another towel to wipe down espresso machine, counter area, and grinder.

Home Espresso Machines—Cleaning Procedures:
1) Wipe down counter area.
2) Wipe down espresso machine.
3) Wipe down espresso grinder.
4) Remove drip tray and clean well.

Note: Each manufacturer has unique cleaning requirements. Refer to your owner's manual for instructions. The cleaning and maintenance procedures are relatively simple when compared to commercial machines.

Commercial Machines—Daily Cleaning Procedures:

1) Wipe down counter area.

2) Wipe down espresso machine.

3) Wipe down espresso grinder.

4) Remove drip tray and clean well.

5) Place ½ teaspoon coffee oil remover, such as PuroCaf® into drain tray and backflush with hot water.

6) Check for water leaks around drain hose and drain tray.

7) Remove showerhead screen, screw, and any other parts from group. Place loose items in a metal basket and soak in sink filled with hot water and two tablespoons of coffee detergent. Soak overnight. Scrub with firm brush. Rinse in hot water then cold water.

8) Remove metal filter baskets from hand filters. Use one hand filter with the blank filter (no holes) and place ½ to 1 teaspoon of coffee detergent in filter. Place hand filter into group and back flush by triggering hot water through the group. Back flush should take about 30 seconds. Repeat four or five times until water becomes clear. Do each group.

9) Clean and rinse dump box.

10) Clean plastic hopper and grinder with soft and moist bar towel. Clean doser with a soft brush.

One of the most common reasons for bitter espresso is the failure of the operator to clean the espresso machine properly. Coffee oils will become bitter with age and need to be completely removed by cleaning.

The number of wear-and-tear parts can be reduced and the life expectancy of your espresso machine increased by many years if a daily maintenance program is followed.

For optimum performance and grind, the burr-wheels of burr-grinders should be replaced after 600 pounds of coffee is ground. Six hundred × 50 servings equals 30,000 single shot servings before burr-wheels should be replaced.

Hand filters should be mounted in groups (clean) when not being used. This approach provides a better tasting shot because porta-filters remain hot, and a cold surface tends to shock the espresso and flatten the taste.

How do you remove a coffee stain? Rinse in cool water, rub with liquid laundry detergent or paste of laundry detergent and water, then launder.

Water impurities and rancid coffee will play havoc with espresso equipment in the absence of routine cleaning and water filtration. One maintenance expert claims that 60% of all the problems with espresso machines are water-related.

Hard water is best for tea and batch-brewed coffee. Soft water is best for espresso.

 The build-up of limescale is a very common problem without a water filtration system. The more water circulated, the greater the limescale build-up. Commercial espresso machines are more prone to this problem.

 Limescale results from mineral deposits in hard water that collect and form on the interior of the brew tank and tubing. Water flow, temperature, and taste are all affected.

 Never attach a packed porta-filter to the brew chamber unless the shot will be extracted immediately. Heat radiated from the chamber will burn the fresh grounds, producing a very off taste in the finished drink.

 Home espresso machines generally come with user-friendly cleaning instructions. Cleaning and maintenance procedures for these units are relatively simple when compared to commercial machines.

 Espresso needs to be extracted under pressure. The pump should provide required pressure of about nine atmospheres (130 PSI). This means the pressure is nine times normal atmospheric pressure.

Troubleshooting Guide for Good Espresso

1. Espresso is flat with very little or no crema:
   + Grind may be too coarse.
   + Use coffee that has been ground just prior to brewing.
   + Let machine warm up a little longer. (Proper temperature needed.)
   + Pack coffee with more pressure.
   + Preheat pouring glasses.
2. Espresso is muddy, watery, and bitter:
   + Select a coarser grind.
   + Place more coffee in porta-filter. Fill to rim before packing.
3. Steam lacks adequate volume:
   + Wand is clogged with milk or sugar crystals. Soak wand nozzle and bleed wand.
4. The porta-filter keeps popping out of the group when extracting:
   + Too much coffee is being placed in filter baskets. Keep coffee just under basket rim before packing.
5. Espresso takes too long to extract and produces dark brown specks:
   + Begin extraction as soon as coffee is placed in the group. Coffee oils will burn if held in the group before extracting.
6. Water leaks from porta-filter or group:
   + Rubber group gasket is worn and needs replacement.
7. Coffee pours out too quickly:
   + Grind is too coarse. Correct fineness to a 20-25 second pour.
8. Coffee pours out too slowly:
   + Grind is too fine. Correct coarseness to a 20-25 second pour.

GRANITA MACHINE

Liquid mix is poured in top of machine and then frozen into a smooth substance consisting of thousands of tiny ice crystals.

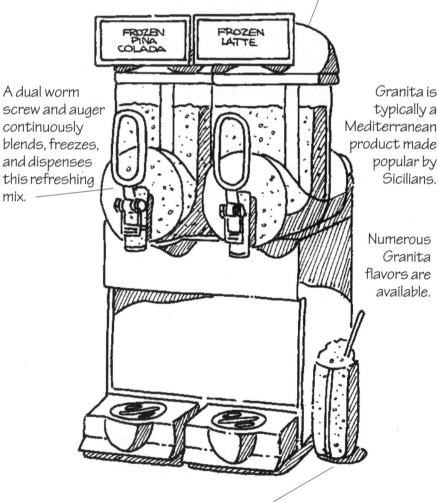

A dual worm screw and auger continuously blends, freezes, and dispenses this refreshing mix.

Granita is typically a Mediterranean product made popular by Sicilians.

Numerous Granita flavors are available.

FROZEN PINA COLADA

FROZEN LATTE

To form a smooth consistent slush base, the mixes should contain about 19% sugar in the recipe.

Chapter 9

Pronunciation Guide & Glossary

Pronunciation Guide

Americano	Ameri-CAH-no
Brevé	BREV-ay
Cappuccino	Cap-oo-CHEE-no
Crema	CREM-uh
Creme de Cacao	KREHM-de-Ko-KO
Creme de Cassis	KREHM-deh-kah-SEES
Doppio	DOPE-eo
Espresso	Ess-PRESS-o
Espresso con Panna	Ess-PRESS-o CONE PA-na
Espresso Macchiato	Ess-PRESS-o MOCK-e-AH-toe
Grandé	GRAWN-day
Granita	Gran-E-ta
Latte	LA-tay
Latte Macchiato	LA-tay MOCK-e-AH-toe
Latteccino	La-ta-CHEE-no
Maraschino	MAH-rah-SKEE-no
	or MAH-rah-SHEE-no
Mocha	MO-kah
Orgeat	OR-zhat
Ristretto	Ris-TRETTO

Glossary

Acidity

A gentle pucker found in the body of a good cup of coffee or espresso. A moderate amount of acidity—but not too much—adds balance to the flavor of coffee.

Aftertaste

The lingering taste that clings to your palate after swallowing coffee or espresso.

Aged Coffees

This term normally applies to green coffee beans that have been aged for several years in proper storage conditions. These green beans do not deteriorate but may improve in flavor.

Americano

A gourmet cup of coffee, made by pouring one or two shots of espresso over a 6-ounce cup of hot water. The crema from the espresso will float on top.

Arabica

Coffea arabica is the original species of the coffee plant found growing wild in Ethiopia, Africa. Arabica coffee beans are the most sought after in the world due to their intense aromatic flavors. These quality beans are used exclusively by specialty or gourmet coffee roasters.

Aroma

The delightful bouquet of aromatic gasses released by freshly ground coffee.

Balance

Refers to coffees that offer just the right balance in flavor, aroma, and body after extraction. Balance is also used to describe a nicely blended coffee.

Barista

An uncommonly good espresso bartender who understands coffee and the espresso machine's purpose. A barista is an expert at making espresso and a master of a variety of espresso beverages.

Bitter

This taste is perceived toward the rear of your tongue. A slight bittersweet flavor in dark roasts is appealing to some people.

Blend

A marriage of two or more coffee bean varieties (Colombia, Panama, Cuba, Kenya, etc.) that when mixed together improves the qualities of taste and aroma.

Body

The strength and viscosity of the coffee extraction.

Boiler

The hot water and steam source of an espresso machine. Its purpose is to offer hot water at about 195°F for espresso extraction and steam for heating and frothing milk.

Brevé

Any milk based espresso beverage where half-and-half is substituted for milk. Brevés can be flavored.

Brew (Porta-filter) Basket

The filter basket inside your hand filter that allows the espresso to be extracted, while holding back the spent grounds.

Burnt

Carbonized flavor in coffee beans when they have been over-roasted or very darkly roasted. The taste will be burnt or charcoal like.

Caffeine

One of the most noticeable compounds present in coffee. Caffeine is known for its abilities to alert the mind, stimulate the body's nervous system, and reduce fatigue or sleepiness. Moderation is the key.

Cappuccino

An espresso based beverage, topped with equal parts of steamed and foamed milk (wet cappuccino). A dry cappuccino is topped with all foamed milk. The milk is foamed/steamed prior to the espresso extraction, allowing the foam to set, or jell. The foam topping is shaped to form a peak (cap) on the cappuccino. Cappuccinos are usually dusted with nutmeg, cinnamon, or chocolate powder.

Caramelly

The caramel-like body noted in good espresso crema or a flavor found in some coffee beans.

Coffeol

The oils in coffee that are both soluble and nonsoluble. The nonsoluble oils are emulsified and become rich crema.

Crema

In good espresso, crema is considered to be the heart of the espresso extraction. Crema is a dense golden brown foam that covers straight shots of espresso. It is thick with aroma and flavor and is a sign of proper extraction.

Cupping

A tasting procedure used to determine the qualities of taste and aroma in coffees or a specific coffee. The procedure uses freshly ground coffee or coffees placed in a cup. First aroma is examined. Then hot water—just off the boil—is poured over the coffee. Aroma is checked again. The coffee grounds that remain floating are stirred to the bottom of the cup. Tasting is done next by slurping the coffee toward the rear of the mouth then spitting the coffee out instead of swallowing it. This test is performed often by those in the specialty coffee industry as a means of controlling consistency in coffee blends.

Decaffeinate

Describes a method used to remove about 97% of the caffeine from whole bean coffees. The Swiss Water Process and the methylchloride solvent process are the two most used methods.

Demitasse

A small porcelain or stoneware cup that holds two to three ounces of straight espresso.

Doppio

Double shot of espresso with one measure (shot) of water.

Doser

A holding chamber for freshly ground coffee used to measure and dispense the correct amount of coffee into your porta-filter. The doser can be a separate piece of equipment but is normally connected to the front of your espresso grinder.

Double

Describes the amount of freshly ground espresso coffee which is dispensed into a double porta-filter. A double contains 14 grams, and a single uses seven grams in a single porta-filter. There are two popular styles of making a double: 1) American Style (double)—Double the amount of hot water is used to extract double the amount of coffee. 2) Italian or European Style (doppio)—This method for a double uses a single amount of hot water over a double amount of coffee.

Earthiness

This is a term that normally describes the flavor found in coffees processed in the dry or natural way. *Muddy* is another word for earthiness.

Espresso

Proper espresso is made from a special blend of Arabica coffees chosen for intense aromatic flavors and quality of performance during extraction. Espresso uses freshly roasted beans that are finely ground in the correct amount, firmly packed and then extracted under pressure. The end result will be a rich concentration of coffee taste and aroma, topped with a dense golden-brown foam called crema.

Espresso con Panna

An espresso topped with a dollop of whipped cream.

Espresso Romano

A serving of straight espresso with a twist of lemon added.

Estate Coffees

Normally quality Arabica coffees that are grown by a single owner or company on individual farms. Estate coffees are not mixed with coffees from other plantations.

Flavor

Describes the tastes and aromas given by the coffee in the mouth. Flavor descriptions can be winey, earthy, chocolaty, fruity, etc.

Fresh

Freshly roasted coffee maintains its freshness for two to three weeks. It is best stored in whole bean form at room temperature with oxygen and moisture excluded. Coffees preserved for long periods in special packaging are not the equivalent of freshly roasted coffees.

Grandé

Espresso-milk beverages are usually served in an 8-ounce to-go cup called a short; a 12-ounce cup called a tall; or a grandé 16-ounce cup. A grandé normally uses a minimum of 14 grams of coffee (a double).

Green Coffee

The processed seeds of the coffee cherry are greenish in appearance and are referred to as green coffee. Unripe coffee cherries are sometimes called green coffee as well.

Grinder

There are basically three types of grinders used for whole bean coffee: 1) hand mill grinder; 2) electric blade grinder; and 3) burr grinder. The adjustable burr grinder is normally the only style grinder that is used for finely ground espresso.

Group

The metal brewing chamber on your espresso machine where espresso is extracted from the coffee in the porta-filter.

Hard bean

A term used to describe Arabica beans. These beans develop denseness due to high altitude pressures during growth.

High grown

Another term that refers to the Arabica coffee species, normally grown at altitudes greater than 2,000 feet above sea level. In fact, most quality Arabicas are grown beyond 3,000 feet.

Iced espresso based beverages

Serve in clear plastic or clear glassware. If flavored, the flavoring is added first followed by espresso. When thick syrup is used, stir beverage before adding ice. Fill cup with **cold milk**. Top with whipped cream, if desired.

Italian cream soda (Cremosa)

Similar to Italian soda except soda water is poured to ½" from the top of the cup. Cup is then filled with approximately two ounces of half-and-half. Italian cream sodas may be topped with whipped cream.

Italian soda

An iced beverage usually served in a 14- to 16-ounce clear plastic cup. The drink is flavored with two ounces of Italian style syrup or syrups (usually fruit-based) and filled to the top with soda water. The recommended mix ratio is one part syrup to four parts soda water. Italian sodas may be topped with whipped cream.

Latte

An espresso based beverage created by pouring foamed/steamed milk at 140°F down the side of a cup containing a serving of espresso. The pour allows the milk and espresso to marbleize, forming a very dense mixture and allowing the espresso taste to be experienced with the first sip.

Latteccino

An espresso based beverage with two parts steamed milk and one part foamed milk—a cross between a cappuccino and a latte.

Lungo

This is the Italian word for *long* and refers to a long pour of espresso. This extraction usually takes 25 to 30 seconds and is primarily used for straight shots.

Macchiato

The Italian word for *marked*. There are two types of macchiatos: 1) straight espresso marked with a dollop of warm milk froth; and 2) a steamed milk macchiato (latte or cappuccino) where the steamed milk is marked with an espresso poured slowly over the milk foam at the side of a clear glass. This technique will display a layered effect and is used in restaurants.

Milds

An industry name for quality Arabica beans processed by the wet method. The wet method is a quality process to remove the pulp and skin from the seeds.

Mocha

A chocolate flavored latte with an option of whipped cream for garnish and enjoyment.

Moka

Stove top espresso pot. This appliance is used widely in Europe, especially in Italy. Steam pressure created from hot water in the bottom chamber pushes hot water up a metal tube to extract the espresso in the top chamber.

Mouth feel

The sensation of coffee clinging to the inside of your mouth. Determination of body and degree of aromatics are experienced during mouth feel.

Nutty

Nuttiness is a flavor perceived in freshly roasted coffee similar to that experienced in eating roasted sunflower seeds. Nuttiness is normally considered a good flavor if it is in balance with other aromatic qualities of the coffee.

Overextraction

Caused by the continuous flow of hot water over ground coffee (espresso) even after all of the good qualities have been released. Overextraction is also caused by too fine a grind or hot water temperatures above 197°F, which cause bitterness.

Peaberry

This is a single elongated coffee bean (seed) that can develop in a coffee cherry due to poor pollination during the flower stage. This process happens in only about 2% of the harvested cherries. Peaberries tend to be more flavorful than normal coffee beans.

Porta-filter (brew-basket)

A portable hand filter used to hold coffee during the espresso extraction process. The actual filter basket is removable and is held in place by a single circular spring. Generally there are two types of porta-filters: a single, which has a single spout for the pour and holds between seven and eight grams of finely ground espresso to be extracted in the group brewing chamber; and a double, which has two spouts below the filter basket for the pour. A double basket will hold 14 to 16 grams of coffee. The output can be used to serve one double or two single espressos.

Pyrolysis
> The chemical changes occurring during the roasting process. Compounds are developed that will become aroma, taste, and body upon completion.

Rancidity
> The tainting and spoiling of the coffee oils, which produce bitterness and a rancid flavor.

Recovery time
> A term that refers to the amount of time an espresso machine may need to recover either the proper hot water temperature for extraction or the proper temperature to produce steam. Today recovery time is either reduced or eliminated by a) adequate boiler size; b) configuration and size of heating element (proper wattage-to-water ratio); and c) fresh water heat exchangers.

Richness
> The intensity of aromatic flavors in the body of a good coffee blend, especially prevalent in espresso blends.

Ristretto
> Ristretto means *restricted* in Italian. It is a short pour of espresso (highly concentrated) using three-quarters to one ounce of hot water to extract the correct amount of coffee in a double or single portion.

Robusta

Commercially, the second largest selling species of coffee. *Coffea canephora* was first discovered growing wild in the Congo in Africa. Because Robusta lacks intensity in flavor as compared to the Arabica coffees, it is usually sold as filler coffee for canned blends sold in supermarkets or as instant style coffees. Robustas have twice the caffeine of Arabicas.

Short

The size of an espresso to-go cup that will hold eight ounces of any espresso beverage.

Single

This is a pull of seven grams of freshly ground coffee for espresso extraction. A single (or double) can be extracted as a short pour (ristretto) or a long pour (lungo) for the desired intensity.

Sourness

A taste associated with coffees picked before ripening or with coffees that are overpoweringly acidic.

Specialty Coffees

Also known as gourmet coffees or whole bean coffees that have been freshly roasted. These coffees will be quality Arabicas that are sold as a blend from a roaster's recipe or as straight varietals.

Steam wand

A long metal tube or wand that connects to the top of the boiler to draw pressurized steam. This wand is used for heating and frothing milk as an ingredient in espresso beverages.

Steamer

A serving of foamed/steamed milk, which has been flavored with one ounce of Italian style syrup. Usually topped with whipped cream. **No espresso** (Same as hot chocolate, but using Italian style syrup for flavoring the milk).

Tall

A tall refers to a 12-ounce to-go cup, usually filled with steamed milk drinks and espresso or Americanos.

Tamper

A tool for firmly packing fresh espresso coffee into the filter basket held by your porta-filter. The best tampers are handheld and offer control of pressure and levelness of packing.

Under-extraction

This is one of the most common failures of the extraction process. Proper extraction only occurs when all of the best of the coffee has been removed and offered in the cup. When hot water passes too quickly through the coffee, or when the hot water temperature is below 192°F, some of the goodness remains in the coffee grounds. This failure in technique is called under- extracting.

Varietal coffees

These are unblended, straight coffees from a specific country or region. Examples are: Colombian, Costa Rican, Jamaican, Cuban, or Ethiopian coffees. A blend is made when these varietals are mixed.

Whole bean coffee

Refers to coffee sold in the whole bean state. Normally, Arabica beans of good quality are sold this way.

How to Say Coffee Around the World:

Country	Language	Coffee
Cambodia	Khmer	Gafé
China	Mandarin	Kafei
China, Hong Kong	Cantonese	Kia-fey
Czechoslovakia	Czech	Kava
Denmark	Danish	Kaffé
Egypt	Egyptian	Masbout
Eskimo	Eskimo	Kaufee
Europe, Israel	Yiddish	Kavé
Finland	Finnish	Kahvi
France	French	Café
Germany	German	Kaffee
Greece	Greek	Kafes
Hawaii	Hawaiian	Kopé
Hungary	Hungarian	Kavé
India	Hindi	Coffee
Indonesia	Indonesian	Kope
Iran	Iranian	Gehvé
Iraq, Jordan, Lebanon, Syria	Arabic	Qahwa
Israel	Hebrew	Kavah, Kaffee
Italy	Italian	Caffé
Japan	Japanese	Koohii
Laos	Laotian	Kafe
Malaysia	Malayan	Kawa, Koppi
Mexico, Spain	Spanish	Café
Netherlands	Dutch	Koffie
Norway	Norwegian	Kaffé
Philippines	Tagalog	Kapé
Poland	Polish	Kawa
Portugal	Portuguese	Café
Romania	Rumanian	Cafea
Rome	Latin	Coffea
Russia	Russian	Kofé
Spain	Basque	Kaffia
Swahili	Swahili	Kahawa
Thailand	Thai	Kafé
Turkey	Turkish	Kahvé

Works Cited

Armstrong, John. *VIP's All New Bar Guide.* Greenwich, CT: Fawcett Publications, Inc., 1960.

Barbieri, Heather Doran. *Seattle Emergency Espresso.* Bothell, WA: Alaska Northwest Books, 1992.

Baxter, Jacki. *The Coffee Book.* Secaucus, NJ: Chartwell Books Inc., 1985.

Bersten, Ian. *Coffee Floats—Tea Sinks.* Australia: Helian Books, 1993.

Blocker, Lynn. *Bon Appetit Cocktail Parties.* Los Angeles, CA: The Knapp Press, 1983.

Bramah, Edward & Joan. *Coffee Makers.* London: Quiller Press, 1989.

Brandt, Jane. *Drinks Without Liquor.* New York: Workman Publishing, 1983.

Burnam, Tom. *The Dictionary of Misinformation,* New York: Ballantine Books, 1980.

Castle, Timothy James. *The Perfect Cup.* New York: Addison-Wesley Publishing Company, Inc. 1991.

Conran, Terence and Caroline. *The Cook Book.* New York: Crown Publishers, Inc., 1980.

Cooper, Rosalind. *Spirits & Liqueurs.* London: HP Books, 1982.

Cox, Jill. *The Non-Alcoholic Pocket Bartender's Guide.* New York: Simon and Schuster, 1988.

Davids, Kenneth. *Coffee—A Guide to Buying, Brewing & Enjoying.* Santa Rosa, CA: 101 Productions/ The Cole Group, 1991.

Davidson, Alan. *Fruit—A Connoisseur's Guide.* New York: Simon and Schuster, 1991.

Donovan, Jane. *The Miniature Book of Coffee.* New York: Crescent Books, 1991.

Doxat, John. *The Indispensable Drinks Book.* New York: Van Nostrand Reinhold Company, 1981.

Embury, David A. *The Fine Art of Mixing Drinks.* Garden City, NY: Doubleday & Company, Inc., 1958.

Escoffier, A. *The Escoffier Cook Book.* New York: Crown Publishers, Inc., 1969.

Feller, Robyn M. *The Complete Bartender.* New York: Berkley Books, 1990.

Ferguson, William P. *How to Open Your Espresso Cart.* Seattle, WA: Peanut Butter Publishing, 1993.

Ford, Gene. *Ford's Illustrated Guide to Wines, Brews, & Spirits.* Dubuque, Iowa: Wm. C. Brown Publishers, 1983.

Foster, Carol. *Cooking with Coffee.* New York: Simon & Schuster, 1992.

The Franchise Handbook. Milwaukee, WI: Enterprise Magazines, Inc., 1993.

Grossman, Harold J. *Grossman's Guide to Wines, Spirits, and Beers.* New York: Charles Scribner's Sons, 1964.

Hattox, Ralph S. *Coffee and Coffeehouses.* Seattle, WA: University Of Washington Press, 1991.

Hoffman, Mark S. *The World Almanac and Book of Facts—1993.* New York: Pharos Books, 1992.

Illy, Francesco and Riccardo. *The Book of Coffee.* Milano: Arnoldo Mondadori Editore S.p.A., 1989.

Jones, Stan. *Jones' Complete Bar Guide.* Los Angeles: Barguide Enterprises, 1977.

Jurich, Nick. *Espresso—From Bean to Cup.* Seattle, WA: Missing Link Press, 1991.

Katona, Cristie and Thomas. *The Coffee Book.* San Leandro, CA: Bristol Publishing Enterprises, Inc., 1992.

Katsigris, Costas & Porter, Mary. *Pouring for Profit.* New York: John Wiley & Sons, 1983.

Kolpas, Norman. *A Cup of Coffee.* New York: Grove Press, 1993.

Lavazza. *Coffee: A Part of Nature's Bounty.* Team Europa.

Louis, David. *2201 Fascinating Facts. U.S.:* The Ridge Press, Inc., 1983.

Mariani, John F.. *The Dictionary of American Food and Drink.* New York: Ticknor & Fields, 1983.

Mariano, Bernard N. *Crema—The Heart and Soul of Italian Espresso.* Chicago: Trendex International, Inc., 1991.

Mario, Thomas. *Playboy's Host & Bar Book.* Secaucus, New Jersey: Castle Books, 1981.

Martin, Kymberly and Dennis. *Recipes for Espresso Magic.* Lake Forest Park, WA: Shady Lane Enterprises, 1991.

McCoy, Elin & Walker, John Frederick. *Coffee and Tea.* New York: New American Library, 1988.

Netzer, Corinne T. *The Complete Book of Food Counts.* New York: Dell Publishing, 1991.

Panati, Charles. *The Browser's Book of Beginnings.* Boston: Houghton Mifflin Company, 1984.

Perry, Sara. *The Complete Coffee Book.* San Francisco: Chronicle Books, 1991.

Poister, John J. *The New American Bartender's Guide.* New York: Penguin Group, 1989.

Regan, Gary. *The Bartender's Bible.* USA: Harper-Collins Publishers.

Roden, Claudia. *Coffee.* London: Penguin Group, 1981.

Rolnick, Harry. *The Complete Book of Coffee.* Militta, 1992.

Rosen, Marcia & Hunt, Gerry. *The Cheers Bartending Guide.* New York: Simon & Schuster, 1983.

Rothstein, Jamie. *Mr. Boston—Official Bartender's Guide.* New York: Warner Books, Inc., 1988.

Schapira, Joel, David, & Karl. *The Book of Coffee & Tea.* New York: St. Martin's Press, 1982.

Schumann, Charles. *Tropical Bar Book.* New York: Stewart, Tabori & Chang, Inc., 1989.

Simmons, Marie & Lagowski, Barbara J. *The Bartender's Guide to Alcohol-Free Drinks.* New York: The Penguin Group, 1990.

Spath, Siegfried. *Driver-Friendly Drinks.* London: W. Foulsham & Co. Ltd., 1990.

Sturdivant, Shea, & Terracin, Steve. *Espresso Drinks, Desserts and More.* Freedom, CA: The Crossing Press, 1991.

Sutton, Caroline. *How Do They Do That?* New York: A Hilltown Book, 1982.

Taylor, Sidney B. *Wine...Wisdom... & Whimsy.* Portland, OR: Winepress Publishing Co., 1969.

Tekulsky, Mathew. *Making Your Own Gourmet Coffee Drinks.* New York: Crown Publishers, Inc., 1993.

Trader Vic. *Trader Vic's Book of Food & Drink.* New York: Gramercy Publishing Company, 1981.

Walker, Michael. *The Cocktail Book.* Tucson, AZ: HP Books, 1980.

Ward, Mary. *The Top 100 Coffee Recipes.* Hollywood, FL: Lifetime Books, 1992.

Williams, Edward E. *The Concise Bar Guide.* New York: Berkley Books, 1990.

Other Industry and General Reference Works Cited

Cafe Olé, Seattle, WA.

CBI. *Coffee & Tea Handbook.* Portland, OR.

Clark, Cynthia J., coffee historian and writer.

Consumer Reports.

Espresso 101 Video. Media Productions, 1993.

Fancy Food . Chicago, IL.

Fortune. New York, NY.

Fresh Cup. Portland, OR.

Gourmet Coffee Video. Auburn, CA: Flessing & Flessing, Walters Productions, 1994.

Gourmet Retailer.

Nation's Restaurant News. New York.

The News Tribune. Tacoma, WA.

Restaurant News. Washington, DC.

Seattle Post Intelligencer. Seattle, WA.

Seattle Times. Seattle, WA.

Starbucks. *Coffee Matters.* Seattle, WA.

Tea & Coffee Trade Journal. New York, NY.

Valley Daily News. Kent, WA.

Wall Street Journal.

World Coffee & Tea. Rockville, MD.

Index of Ingredients

A

Almond Rocca® Syrup 37, 133

Almond Syrup 30, 31, 32, 35, 37, 40, 46, 57, 62, 63, 64, 77, 91, 93, 94, 99, 113, 116, 120, 124, 125, 127, 133, 138, 143, 146

Amaretto Syrup 30, 32, 33, 34, 45, 46, 47, 48, 51, 52, 53, 55, 59, 60, 64, 74, 81, 92, 95, 97, 100, 106, 109, 115, 116, 121, 126, 128, 134, 135, 136, 146, 148, 149

Anisette Syrup 38, 43, 51, 53, 74, 75, 80, 85, 87, 98, 103, 107, 109. 113, 118, 136, 146, 152

Apple Cider 34, 96, 148

Apple Juice 35, 73, 92

Apple Syrup 34, 35, 36, 38, 42, 45, 47, 49, 58, 72, 74, 75, 80, 81, 85, 86, 87, 91, 93, 95, 110, 113, 114, 116, 121, 124, 127, 131, 134, 139, 142, 145, 147, 149

B

B-52 Syrup 133

Banana Slices 40

Banana Syrup 38, 39, 40, 46, 49, 51, 55, 57, 69, 82, 85, 91, 94, 98, 104, 105, 107, 109, 110, 116, 119, 123, 124, 127, 128, 136, 138, 140, 141, 142, 148, 149, 152, 153

Black Currant Syrup 44

Blackberry Syrup 43, 44, 45, 49, 62, 134, 147 ,151

Blue Curacao Syrup 45

Blueberry Syrup 45, 86, 141

Boysenberry Syrup 58, 150

Brandy Syrup 37, 43, 46, 47, 50, 54, 67, 74, 90, 100, 107, 119, 126, 127, 139, 150

Brown Sugar 35, 36, 52, 54, 61, 67, 84, 91, 92, 94, 138, 144

Butter 77, 78, 91

Butterscotch Syrup 32, 49, 71, 91, 152

C

Caramel Syrup 40, 43, 55, 57, 58, 59, 75, 84, 110, 114, 115, 122, 137, 143, 145, 149

Cardamom 59

Cherry Syrup 38, 40, 42, 43, 44, 46, 47, 50, 52, 55, 56, 59, 60, 61, 62, 63, 74, 79, 80, 81, 84, 85, 97, 98, 103, 107, 108, 117, 118, 122, 124, 125, 127, 132, 133, 135, 145, 146, 152

Chicory 114

Chocolate Fudge 30, 89

Chocolate Fudge Syrup 106

Chocolate Mint Syrup 50, 64, 68, 77, 78, 151

Chocolate Peanut Butter Syrup 55

Lime Syrup 33, 34, 35, 36, 38,
39, 41, 42, 44, 47, 48, 56,
59, 60, 61, 62, 66, 67, 69,
73, 74, 75, 79, 81, 83, 86,
87, 88, 97, 101, 102, 103,
104, 105, 108, 109, 117,
118, 119, 120, 121, 123,
124, 125, 127, 128, 130,
132, 133, 135, 136, 139,
142, 144, 145, 146, 147,
148, 149, 152, 153

M

Macadamia Nut Syrup 81, 84,
104
Malt Powder 104
Mandarino Syrup 37, 60, 71,
73, 80, 105, 124, 144,
145, 146, 147
Mango Syrup 30, 35, 39, 41,
69, 88, 97, 104, 105, 119,
120, 146, 148
Maple Syrup 106
Maraschino Cherry 44, 133,
138
Maraschino Syrup 86, 87, 92,
117, 145, 149
Marshmallows 64, 89, 113, 133
Melon Syrup 79, 102, 108, 136
Mexican Chocolate Powder 51,
65, 66, 67, 108, 109
Mint Syrup 50, 56, 64, 67, 68,
77, 78, 79, 83, 84, 90, 95,
100, 102, 103, 111, 123,
151
Mocha Syrup 75
Molasses 55, 86

N

Napoleon Brandy Syrup 47

Nutmeg 33, 34, 35, 39, 46, 47,
48, 52, 53, 55, 57, 66, 71,
77, 78, 79, 80, 81, 86, 90,
91, 92, 93, 95, 96, 98, 99,
113, 114, 115, 134, 139,
141, 148, 151, 152

O

Orange Juice 107, 119, 126,
135, 143, 146
Orange Peel 53, 59, 80, 117
Orange Slice 50, 67
Orange Syrup 33, 34, 35, 36,
37, 38, 40, 41, 42, 45, 46,
48, 49, 51, 52, 53, 54, 55,
56, 59, 60, 67, 69, 71, 72,
73, 74, 77, 80, 81, 83, 85,
86, 88, 90, 92, 94, 97, 98,
101, 103, 104, 105, 106,
108, 110, 111, 113, 116,
117, 118, 119, 125, 126,
132, 133, 135, 136, 137,
138, 139, 140, 142, 144,
146, 147, 149, 151, 152,
153
Orgeat Syrup 62
Ovaltine 118

P

Passion Fruit Syrup 37, 42, 46,
55, 71, 72, 77, 88, 90, 96,
97, 106, 116, 119, 120,
125, 148
Peach Syrup 30, 42, 44, 65, 66,
83, 100, 111, 116, 118,
120, 121, 132, 140, 144,
149, 153
Peanut Butter 55, 103, 121,
122
Pear 130
Pecan Syrup 49, 65, 122, 138

Vanilla Syrup 31, 34, 36, 40,
    41, 44, 45, 46, 47, 48, 53,
    55, 58, 61, 62, 63, 68, 69,
    72, 73, 75, 77, 78, 82, 83,
    86, 90, 93, 95, 96, 101,
    102, 106, 107, 111, 113,
    116, 118, 119, 123, 125,
    126, 130, 131, 137, 138,
    141, 142, 143, 147, 150,
    151, 152, 153

W

Watermelon Syrup 83, 152
Whipped Cream 30, 31, 32,
    33, 34, 35, 39, 40, 41, 43,
    44, 46, 47, 49, 50, 51, 52,
    53, 54, 55, 56, 58, 59, 60,
    61, 62, 63, 64, 65, 67, 68,
    69, 70, 71, 73, 74, 75, 76,
    77, 78, 79, 80, 81, 82, 83,
    84, 85, 86, 88, 89, 90, 91,
    92, 93, 94, 95, 96, 97, 98,
    99, 100, 101, 102, 103,
    104, 106, 107, 108, 109,
    110, 111, 112, 113, 114,
    115, 116, 117, 118, 121,
    122, 123, 126, 127, 129,
    130, 131, 133, 134, 135,
    137, 138, 139, 140, 141,
    142, 143, 144, 145, 146,
    147, 148, 149, 150, 151,
    152, 153
White Chocolate 123
White Chocolate Powder 137
White Chocolate Syrup 152
White Crème de Menthe 48

Index

D

Dallas, TX 21
Dark Unsweetened Cocoa 118
Decaffeinated coffee 167, 176,
 208, 209, 227, 245, 295,
 307
Demitasse 307
Desserts 208, 232, 322
Desserts:
 tiramisu 243
Doctor's Book of Home Remedies,
 The 175
Doppio 25, 75
Doser 261, 263, 298, 308
Double shot 8, 14, 15, 16, 222,
 271, 307
Double-blind taste test 295
Dr. Pepper 228
Dresden, Germany 247
Drive-up/thru espresso 178
Drupes 193
Dry season 23, 193
Drying process 198, 308
Dutch 160, 198, 317

E

Earthiness, taste 308
East Coast 208
Egypt *157*, 317
Electric, electricity 167, 174,
 249, 253, 256, 257, 258,
 259, 261, 262
Electric filter coffee 173
England 160, 170
Enomoto, Mr. 183
Enterprise Manufacturing Co.
 165
Equipment leases 182
Espresso 1, 26
Espresso bars 2, 170

Espresso business 178, 284
Espresso cart 21
Espresso con Panna 26, 79
Espresso machines
 commercial 5, 183, 250,
 251, 252, 300
 comparisons of 183, 264,
 265
 home 183, 249, 259, 260,
 267, 287, 297, 300
Espresso Romano 26, 80
Estate coffee 197, 309
Ethiopia 155, 156, 193, 296,
 304, 316
Europe 1, 156, 158, 159, 163,
 164, 170, 173, 179, 208,
 255, 276, 296, 308, 312,
 317
Extraction, espresso 305, 306,
 307, 308, 311, 313, 314,
 315, 316

F

Fat 155, 208
Filter 222, 263
Filtering coffee 163, 174, 247,
 279, 298, 301, 306, 313
Finland 179, 317
Flavor 1, 5, 7, 8, 9, 10, 13, 14,
 16, 17, 18, 23, 191, 193,
 201, 202, 203, 205, 208,
 210, 211, 223, 225, 228,
 231, 233, 234, 235, 236,
 238, 243, 247, 249, 252,
 262, 263, 272, 277, 278,
 279, 280, 284, 289, 290,
 291, 294
Flavored coffee beans 175, 208

Foaming, milk 259, 260, 264, 265, 267, 272, 273, 274, 284, 285, 286, 287, 288. *See also Steaming milk*
Fort Laramie 164
France 5, 168, 317, 321
Franchising 182
French Vanilla Syrup 138
Frosted Mint 123
"Full City" roast 206

G

Gaggia, Achilles 248
Gahwa 156
Garnishes 23, 312
Germany 172, 247, 317
Glossary 303, 304
Gourmet Retailer 197
Grandé 303, 309
Granita 20, 302, 303
Grapes 193
Greece 158, 175, 317
Green Banana 148
Green coffee 156, 157, 192, 193, 201, 304, 310
Grinders, coffee 165, 167, 183, 251, 252, 261, 262, 263, 277, 280, 297, 299, 308, 310
Group, brewing chamber 252, 272, 298, 301, 310

H

Hard bean 310
Harvest 197
Harvesting (picking coffee) 191, 192, 193, 196, 197, 202
Hawaii 196, 197, 317
Health departments/regulations 183

Hemp 201
Hersey, Milton 6
Hersey, PA 6
High grown coffee 294, 310
Hills Brothers Coffee 167
Hulling machines 198
Human nose 294
Humidity 198, 263

I

Ice 7, 16, 17, 20, 160, 302, 310
Ice cube 20, 21
Iced coffee 19, 20
Illy Caffe 174
Illy, Dr. Ernesto 174
Illy, Dr. Francisco 174, 248
India 158, 317
Indonesia 196, 317
Indonesian Islands:
    Java 195, 196, 317
    Sulawesi (Celebes) 196
    Sumatra 196
Instant coffee 173, 191
Irish coffee 172
Italian Cream Soda (Cremosa) 27
Italian Soda 26
Italian style syrups 278
Italy 4, 5, 157, 160, 166, 167, 168, 173, 174, 179, 203, 206, 248, 249, 250, 252, 312, 317

J

Jabez Burns 165
Jackson, Andrew 167
Jamaica 177, 195, 316
Japan 19, 176, 177, 179, 183, 195, 317
Jones, Dorothy 161
Jordan, Phyllis 19

U

United States 2, 164, 165, 167,
    176, 180, 181, 195, 196,
    206, 210, 234, 243, *252*
USDA, milk calorie report 237

V

Vacuum pack 167, *249*
Valente, Ernesto *249*
Valves 210
Varietal coffees 316
Venice, Italy 157, 160, 162,
    163
Vibrating pump *249*
Voltaire 175

W

Walgreen's 168
Warranty *259, 267*
Washington State 21, 237
Water,
    chlorination 277, 278
    hard *251*, 277, 284, 300
    pressure *249*, 272
    quality 277, 299
    soft 277, 284, 300
    temperature *255*, 272, 278,
        300, 305, 316
Wattage *251*, 259, 314
West Coast 208
Wet season 193
Whipping cream 7, 244, 245
Whole bean coffee 316
Whole bean coffee 5, 307, 310,
    315
Wholesale stores 182
WIB processing method 198

Y

Yemen 156

...and finally, special thanks to Brent Bouldin of Eightball Books, who for the past five years has supervised and diligently coordinated the last two expanded and revised editions of *Espresso Quick Reference Guide*. Each new recipe was kitchen-tested, and each new piece of information or statistical data was meticulously researched and thought out—all under his careful direction. Brent spearheaded this project, and was responsible for the rewrites and the final editing. His publishing expertise was also invaluable. He literally varnished the finished product with his artist's touch. Thanks again to you, Brent.

"I was living in a town that was corrupted by a bean, where there was no place to hide from its influence."

from *The Addict*
New York Film Festival entry

Look for more exciting new titles
from Phil Janssen.